MORAL PHILOSOPHY *after* 9/11

MORAL PHILOSOPHY *after* 9/11

JOSEPH MARGOLIS

THE PENNSYLVANIA STATE UNIVERSITY PRESS
UNIVERSITY PARK, PENNSYLVANIA

Chapter 1, "A Reasonable Morality for Partisans and Ideologues," will appear, in a slightly altered form, in *The Journal of Value Inquiry* 38, no. 1 (2004).

Library of Congress Cataloging-in-Publication Data

Margolis, Joseph, 1924–
   Moral philosophy after 9/11 / Joseph Margolis.
      p.   cm.
   Includes bibliographical references and index.
   ISBN 0-271-02447-X (alk. paper)
    1. Ethics—United States.   2. September 11 Terrorist Attacks,
2001—Influence.   I. Title: Moral philosophy after nine-eleven.
II. Title: Moral philosophy after September 11th.   III. Title.
BJ352 .M365 2004
170—dc22   2003023953

The Pennsylvania State University Press is a member of the Association of American University Presses.

It is the policy of The Pennsylvania State University Press to use acid-free paper. Publications on uncoated stock satisfy the minimum requirements of American National Standard for Information Sciences—Permanence of Paper for Printed Library Material, ANSI Z39.48-1992.

contents

Preface   vii

Introduction   xi

1 A Reasonable Morality for Partisans
and Ideologues   1

2 Second-Best Moralities   27

3 The Moral and the Legal   49

4 Human Selves and Moral Agents   77

5 Humanity and Moral Diversity   101

Notes   129

Index   147

for the children of the children of the children of us all,

whose possibilities are being decided now

preface

When I was young in the profession, I took it for granted that philosophy had an essential role to play in resolving the deepest problems of human life—in science and morality and more. Professional philosophy, I discovered, tends to defeat all such enthusiasms. It favors a certain deflationary zeal that threatens to become its own adequate reason for being. Nevertheless, when 9/11 struck, well after my having spent fifty years in the academic lists, I was pleased to find that the fuse of my original conviction was constant enough to accept the surge of the new demand to be as clear as possible about the full challenge of that historic event. I had actually, in some fragments of speculation in the 1990s, already isolated the abstract theme of the present essay. But although those formulations were not completely bland, they lacked—in the way bookish philosophy tends to lack (and not to notice that it lacks)—the commanding presence of the great crises of one's own age. The essay before you is a response to 9/11—a professional philosopher's response, it's true, but a genuine response that, as I realized, instantly rekindled a welcome spark from my original naiveté. I saw in it a sign of just how difficult it really is to hold on to the humane function of one's professional calling while yielding (as one learns we all do) the fledgling assurances of first discovery that almost never survive the critical skills one gradually acquires.

I drafted the essay in one continuous writing during no more than a month—during the break between the two semesters of 2001–2002—and then let the essay lie untouched for rather a long time. I worked to round out the first draft before any extended pause, because the essay seemed to speak for itself and I was afraid I would lose its voice if I did not allow it to complete its message. What I could see at once—in a way detached from the task of actually writing—was the indisputable importance of what had happened: not merely its political importance but its philosophical and moral importance, too, and the bearing of all that on the political and historical questions that absorb us. Without belaboring the point, I may say that I saw from the very start just how 9/11 exposed the profound inadequacies of a large

part of Western conceptions of the right norms of moral and political life as
well as the unearned confidence of canonical philosophy, its frequent irrelevance for the resolution of serious conflicts, and its enormous appetite for
ideological hegemony.

The clue that I drew from my first reflections, just after 9/11, was simply
this: that American philosophy, like American politics, would probably
never yield to the idea that the attack was more than a simple attack and that
the same act might be validly viewed, from the vantage of utterly opposed
(but entirely sincere, hardly misguided) moral convictions, as open both to
being vindicated and condemned, at least *prima facie*—that is, as an act of
unprovoked violence *and* as a deliberate strike against the colonizing penetration of the Middle East by a growing American empire, whether infidel
or merely evil. To see that possibility is to turn a corner in the history of moral
reflection.

That was my opening intuition, which caught up the blander themes I've
already hinted at—those having to do with the analysis of historicism and relativism that I've been attracted to for a good many years. It struck me, therefore, that it might be worth a labor to see whether I could produce a philosophical account of the salient moral/political questions of our time under
the following constraints. First, we must resolve our moral questions without
actually being able to demonstrate that anyone *can come to know*—apart from
affirming that we obviously do know—just what the right rules of moral judgment and commitment really are, and why. Second, the sources of moral conviction drawn from the life of different societies cannot be shown to converge
toward any uniquely valid moral vision. Third, there may be diverse, conflicting, and even incommensurable moral visions that may be responsibly developed from the initial run of societal sources here acknowledged. And yet,
fourth, we can still construct different reasonable ways of resolving conflicts
as serious as 9/11 that would be at least as convincing as any that insist they
already possess the right rules and principles, while making no such assumptions in the results here tendered. Professional philosophy seems never
to have sustained any inquiry of this sort. It strikes me now as impossible to
avoid.

That was the challenge I took up and that is the challenge I lay before you.
I think we are living in a new world that requires concessions along the lines
just sketched. Indeed, 9/11 suggests the need for a new paradigm of moral/
political life that rests on a clear sense of the ineliminable diversity of moral
conviction among the peoples of the earth. I try to track its implications here,

without reneging on its deliberate charge. I see it also as an exercise that has permitted me to recover my first convictions without the embarrassment of the inept arguments by which they first took flight.

The question I raise is an "external" question: how to proceed to answer the question of how to proceed in moral reflection. The answer, I try to show, is that we must proceed by way of a critique of our "internal" resources. It's for this reason, I believe, that my examples are the examples they are—colored by my moral and political experiences. I think we cannot escape such beginnings. That is, in fact, an essential part of my thesis. We begin—and we end—as partisans. But in acknowledging the diverse, even opposed voices of other societies, we begin to see how our own habitual practice and habituated judgment are effectively leavened by the confrontations of similarly generated conceptions that oppose our own, that cannot be toppled in any obvious way, and that are unable to defeat our own convictions any more effectively.

That is another way of approaching the meaning of 9/11. What it teaches us is the extraordinary lesson of how the dialectical play of opposed societies begins to yield a constructive (or constructed) sense of how to answer the "external" question convincingly. At any rate, that is the question I have drawn out of the events of 9/11. The external answer is a projection from our pooled internal inquiries. We cannot ever rightly discover or invent any uniquely true or correct moral vision that the whole of humanity may be expected to confirm: universalism in morality is, I'm afraid, a will-o'-the-wisp. I add, therefore, with no hesitation at all, a fifth constraint to the four already mentioned, namely, that the profound contest that absorbs us now will assuredly be eclipsed by larger, implacable contests of very different but similarly opposed visions of political life.

I've tested the main ideas of the essay in discussions with some good friends and colleagues who have been extraordinarily generous in their responses. I hope I remember them all: Paul Crowe, Harald Thorsrud, Cathy Kemp, Mitchell Aboulafia, David Duquette, Lawrence Hatab, Thomas Magnell, Göran Hermerén, and Nils-Eric Sahlin. I list them in the approximate temporal order in which the discussions actually occurred, that is, based on a reading of parts or all of the original draft. I see that the essay has benefited very considerably from these exchanges, and I thank my friends for the gains they made possible. I must also thank Ruth Brooks for her usual skill and patience in putting the entire package into final form, and Sandy Thatcher, at Penn State Press, for his friendship and continuing support. I must mention, finally, a debt to a dear friend, Henry Hiż, who will not have been aware of how much a public lecture of his on the concept of *summum malum* impressed me. Our uses of the notion are very different. But I could not have come to mine without having had a prior sense of his.

J. M.
August 2003
Philadelphia

introduction

What follows is a thought experiment dated, as nearly as I can make out, from the events of 9/11, the destruction of the World Trade Center in New York City and the attack on the Pentagon. Those attacks were condemned at once, of course, as gratuitously evil. The whole world was stunned by their technical success. But very few paused to consider their significance philosophically — not so much in terms of what might justify bin Laden's act (if, indeed, it was his), though the question was raised and instantly dismissed, but more in terms of legitimating our own values in the face of incompatible convictions embedded in an attack that undeniably claimed an entirely different source of validity, however much we might oppose it.

I don't intend to dwell on what would make a good brief for plaintiffs or defendants either way, as if a proper moral court might spring into play with every such confrontation, small or large, seeking an authoritative finding and a redress of grievances. That is indeed the standard — even canonical — response that spontaneous outrage asks us to articulate, but if we take the challenge seriously, we must ask ourselves a deeper question. What are the ultimate grounds for preferring *our* sources of validity and legitimation to *theirs?* The answer that I give takes two steps. First, there are no ultimate or ulterior grounds on which the implied legitimative conflict can be resolved independently of the entrenched convictions of the opposing parties. But — second — it remains entirely possible to move to a resolution (or one resolution among many possible resolutions) reasonably deemed "objective," or "valid," in morally relevant terms without violating the sense of the first part of my answer.

I have no doubt that nearly anyone who thinks carefully about what I have just said will feel puzzled or cheated. But I suggest that we have reached a point in history at which the proliferation of contests of the 9/11 sort (just now identified) are so dangerous and destructive and so easy to match in a retaliatory way that the world cannot afford to neglect the chance to work out an answer that is at once coherent, pertinent, responsive, viable, reasonable, effective, practical, apt—and possibly even nonstandard in the way of tempering the pressure for further such confrontations.

I think my double question is almost never asked—and certainly almost never answered in the terms it lays down. For example, if the first step of my argument be granted (to the effect that there are no grounds independent of conflicting practices and conflicting convictions by which to resolve such differences in normative terms), then it is futile to suppose that an appeal to universalistic principles could possibly be counted on successfully. And yet Western models of moral objectivity are in large part based on the validity of universal, universalizable, or universalistic norms. Nevertheless, it is my conviction that no departure from my first step's simple constraint can satisfy us now. Furthermore, it comes as a surprise that such a spare postulate could possibly yield as rich a run of theorems as I mean to demonstrate. That would indeed be a useful showing, for otherwise, moral philosophy can hardly fail to be transparently self-serving. In fact, 9/11 clearly challenges the usual frame of reference of moral/political thinking in an interesting and important way. Legal provisions are already in place for its condemnation, of course, but if we view 9/11 at all sympathetically as a political act initially justified (by its champions) in an idiom opposed to the competence and adequacy of American, Western, or even UN-oriented categories, it cannot fail to draw attention to the culturally restrictive classifications of every historically evolved system of normative appraisal. We begin to see something of the reasonableness of viewing all such categories as exclusionary in intent. Not that that can be avoided—but every such system may be politically vulnerable (and brittle) in ways that we cannot always anticipate. In fact, in the opinion of many, the American "response" to 9/11—in Afghanistan, Iraq, the entire Middle East, western Europe, Asia, even in the United States—has actually strengthened the initial plausibility of admitting the original event as, at least in some measure, a form of political resistance against perceived aggression.

I offer two provisional bits of clarification here. First, if, as I am suggesting, moral justification begins with the historically entrenched practices and convictions of reasonably well-demarcated peoples (without ever being settled there), then it is effectively impossible to suppose that legitimation must take a universalistic form or that it can actually do so in most seriously contested cases. *That,* according to my postulate, is just what 9/11 signifies. The second draws attention to the present danger of ignoring the small truth just mentioned, which is not itself a moral finding but the upshot of a philosophical assessment of different ways of going at the matter of moral justification. Quite a lot of time has elapsed since 9/11. The principal aggrieved party, the United

States, which, on the evidence available, was and is still charged with being a source of grievance and great harm to the peoples championed by the perpetrators of the original attack, has now "retaliated" — justifiably, by its own lights — both in Afghanistan and Iraq. Yet it has made no public effort to identify or appraise the possible grievances of the Muslim world that prompted the attack, and it admits to anticipating even more destructive attacks from the same or related sources. I leave the question of the actual validity of the American campaign against Afghanistan and Iraq to one side here, except to note that both must count as innovations in the theory of a valid or just war and that the attacking parties have produced a new form of effective international conflict and validative presumption, the characteristics of which are not yet entirely clear. We do see how close we are to chaos, however, just at the point of current worries about "terrorism" and "rogue states" and the accessibility of "weapons of mass destruction."

What follows, then, is a fairly ramified sketch of how best to construe moral or moral/political questions and how to answer such questions within the constraints indicated. The idea is a provocative one: I argue that there are no "independent" sources for resolving moral disputes or conflicts, but also that, nevertheless, the ordinary conceptual resources of the opposed partisans in such a conflict can be made to yield a reasonably "objective" resolution of that conflict. That is, admitting the actual practices and ideologies of such disputants and whatever their disagreement about normative matters may be, there will always be enough that they share — *enough that is not already freighted in normative terms* — that would enable us to improvise various pertinent resolutions that could be fairly judged to be objective under the circumstances!

I know of no sustained inquiry of this sort. Usually, engaged philosophical disputants retreat to some form of normative privilege or, by a skeptic's reaction to *that* extreme, deny that moral disputes are capable of being resolved in any way at all — in the sense of being demonstrably valid or objective in the privileged way. So the possibility I shall tender is meant to be a third way between two completely unacceptable alternatives: that is, simply to take 9/11, as perceived, as a new paradigm of sorts. I say that it would be too dangerous to give up the effort to characterize the moral world (in which such conflicts arise) as quite capable intrinsically of supporting "objective" resolutions, and it would be extravagant to abandon the prospect unless there were a demonstrably insuperable barrier against constructing one or another such rationale. Still, it would be preposterous — possibly more dangerous than abandoning the inquiry — to affirm, in the face of 9/11 and at this particular moment in history, that "we are right and they are wrong," not in the sense of mere ideological loyalties but in the sense that "right" *is* on our side, because *we* possess (and they do not) a proper grasp of the moral norms on which a proper verdict depends, *or* that it is impossible to defend, objectively, conflicting or incompatible judgments and rationales. In any case, to abandon normative privilege is to abandon the usual grounds on which exclusionary moral/political systems appear, in the eyes of their adherents, to be legitimated.

It takes a considerable wrenching of our speculative habits to call into doubt the established convictions of our world, particularly if one does not intend to deny flat out (as I do not) that there *is* a reasonable basis for treating the resolution of moral disputes as entitled to some sort of objective standing. A good case can be made, but there is a price to pay. The kind of objectivity that may be salvaged (in the spirit of the two postulates I offer) will, ineluctably, be seen to be of a logically weak or diminished sort—*not* for that reason morally negligible but very possibly insufficient for the champions of moral privilege.

What we will find, I suggest, is that any moral objectivity that falls within the space of my third option (that is, between privilege and skepticism) will be logically weak or concessive in the following ways:

(*a*) it will not be possible to defend anything like strict evidentiary parity between scientific and moral truth-claims, along (say) realist lines;

(*b*) moral claims will be of an essentially practical nature, not theoretical, so that acts and practices will be deemed objectively valid in moral matters, not truth-claims and propositions—or truth-claims and propositions primarily;

(*c*) we will have to admit that moral questions arise only under the conditions of the *sui generis* form of life that human selves exhibit and that there, objectivity chiefly concerns the defensibility of supporting or reforming our *sittlich* practices;

(*d*) accordingly, we will be obliged to concede, in conceding the diversity of the *Sitten* of different historical societies, that moral objectivity cannot be made to yield any uniquely valid resolution of a given moral problem; hence,

(*e*) we will have to concede as well that the validity of moral claims will be unable to ensure the adequacy of a strict bivalent logic and will, in fact, be forced to admit the viability of objective norms formulated along constructivist, historicist, relativistic, and incommensurabilist lines; and

(*f*) objective resolutions will not be derivable by means of the application of universal or universalized principles, because they will require reference to local *Sitten* and particular histories and will presuppose that pertinent norms are themselves a feature, or a critical function, of such *Sitten*.[1]

Of course, my tally is much too dense a proposal to be judged on its first appearance. I collect its principal items here only for convenience of reference, and I shall return to all of my distinctions in due course.

Nevertheless, the tally identifies the main lines of how I mean to defend the force of the first part of my explanation of what we should mean by "moral objectivity." The rest of the answer provides a whole raft of reasonable strategies for recovering the familiar issues of conventional moral debate, without the advantage (or disadvantage) of falling back to privileged norms of any kind. Surprising though it may be, we learn, for instance, that our speculative resources are hardly diminished in any substantive or logical way by adopting anything close to the tally just given. Still, admitting the nature of practical judgment and commitment, what may then count as morally objective is bound to be much more concessive toward opposed and incompatible resolutions than any standard objectivist[2] or privileged or strictly bivalent treatment would allow.

Hence, if the argument goes through, it will signify the need for a considerable change in our conceptual (and practical) expectations regarding moral resolutions in real-world terms. If so, then moral theory need not be stalemated by the deeply divisive partisan conflicts I have in mind (which, as I say, oblige us to review 9/11 in a fresh way). But there can be no presumption against opposed convictions' playing a part in the objective resolution of moral disputes. To admit their eligibility, despite remaining contraries or incompatibles, would force us to scale back the would-be prescriptive or exclusionary force of moralities that plainly rely on privilege or are ideologies simply bent on extending their hegemony.

In the briefest terms, then, my answer to the first part of the question I've posed leads to the advocacy of a "second-best" morality[3] (as opposed to privileged moralities of any sort); the answer to the second part features the idea that moral resolution is best thought of in terms of a *modus vivendi* within whose boundaries individual claims and commitments may be convincingly assessed. The result is a conceptual framework that respects (without distortion) and actually presses into service conflicting moral convictions that have undoubted *sittlich* standing. The resolutions that result possess, I claim, the objective validity of a second-best morality. The usual complaint is that, although that is indeed what is needed, it cannot be convincingly worked out. You will have to be the judge of that. But if you risk the speculation, bear in mind that our moral world has changed—or that we are on our way toward viewing it in a very different light.

I begin with some intuitions that I cannot and am unwilling to betray. One is bookish and naive: I have always admired the skill with which Plato's elenctic dialogues, including the first two books of the *Republic*, pursue the norms and virtues of the good life without pretending to know, in advance, precisely how to assess their work correctly. I mean to follow Plato's lead here. Another captures my sense of intellectual fair play: it has always seemed to me that nearly every society is persuaded that it has grasped the moral truth and that those who oppose its vision are benighted. Therefore, as it is impossible to show that every such society is right, the best conjectures under the circumstances must, somehow, tolerate moral incompatibles and must reject any fixed or merely exclusionary hierarchy of norms. I am wedded to enlarging that kind of tolerance as well. A third intuition I take to be plain common sense: I think we cannot survive in our very dangerous world without a widely accepted morality, and what we now need is a proposal, fitted to a globalized world, that tries to isolate those themes that are as close to being the least common (moral) denominators that we can imagine—completely without presumptions of cognitive privilege—and that we may fashion so as to be as tolerant of diverse, even conflicting, normative convictions as we can imagine and support. And 9/11 gives this a radical meaning.

The sixteenth century witnessed the first deliberate effort in the West, in the interests of trade and science, to supersede the doctrinal rivalries of the great religions and the intransigences of local privilege. The end of the eighteenth century witnessed the attempt to detach the powers of reason from the imprisoning horizons of habituated practice. And the new century (just begun) will, I venture to say, play host to efforts to abandon any universalized theory of normative practice, however locally entrenched, in order to find whatever viable forms of practical tolerance may help us avoid the worst imaginable disasters our technologies may otherwise inflict on us.

We hardly dare suppose we can succeed. Who can possibly say what the "world" will be willing to accept as a "reasonable" proposal for revising all the diverse moral visions that we live with—in the interests of "humanity"? Certainly, we cannot pretend to rely on any privileged faculty (reason, say) to discern what is common or universal in the moral way; just as certainly, we cannot simply appeal to what "every" rational, humane, neutral, objective, or morally serious voice would "surely" endorse. These are the wrong questions to pursue, just as it is wrong to suppose that our inability to ensure the adoption of whatever we might recommend as reasonable—say, by the preponderant part of the human race—is a sure sign of a merely arbitrary proposal. Under present circumstances, what we offer may be as good as we can get. What we must aim at is a frank invention (among possible inventions) that might, over time, attract sufficient adherents and, doing that, contribute to our sense of the continued relevance and viability of what we actually recommend. But what we advance as reasonable can only be shown to be such by dialectical means, within the terms of a second-best morality. It hardly requires or depends on the success with which we manage the educative or "social engineering" problem that moral intransigence forever threatens to stalemate. The replacement of the philosophical questions by the engineering question is not my primary concern—though, as you will see, I mean to reflect on the answer to the first under the cloud of the second.

A REASONABLE MORALITY FOR PARTISANS AND IDEOLOGUES

Events like the terrorism of 9/11, cushioned in the spreading efficiency of the violence and brutality and warfare of the end of the twentieth century and the fledgling beginnings of the twenty-first, lend an unexpected legitimacy to questioning whether what we call ethics or moral philosophy may not, after all, be deeply and terribly wrongheaded. I assure you that by thinking aloud in this way, I am not calling into question all the moral dogmas and political ideologies of the race. They are safe enough as far as I'm concerned. I wouldn't know what to put in their place; besides, they are bound to thrive in spite of any philosophical exposés. The question of efficient moral engineering—the question Plato and Karl Marx and the Ayatollah Khomeini share—is also very far from my concern and competence, and I have no illusions about serving as a philosopher-king. But I do have nagging misgivings about the entire assured practice of mainstream English-language and Eurocentric moral philosophy, have had them for years (even about my own early efforts along such lines), and am only now beginning to catch a glimmer (well, more than a glimmer, really) of how that practice might be promisingly redrawn without trading rigor for imagined relevance.

When, for instance, I think of the stunningly simple point of Amartya Sen's compelling criticism of John Rawls's entire vision—I mean Sen's insistence on the need for an enabling provision ("capability" or "capacitation") beyond abstract entitlement, which suggests at a stroke at least one fundamental difference between morality and law and the inappropriateness of reading morality's practical concern in terms of the theoretical modeling of the law[1] — I am acknowledging a conceptual shift akin to the kind of vision I have in mind. Sen's undertaking is not committed to the conceptual reform my own intuitions favor, though. It's the latter that I wish to lay before you — *my* intuitions regarding how to revamp moral philosophy in order to bring it into line with flesh-and-blood life. Presumptuous, no doubt, but there it is.

[I]

I start abruptly, therefore. What strikes me about the great struggles over Kashmir, Kosovo, Northern Ireland, the Palestinian/Israeli world, Afghanistan, and more is that they cannot be easily, perhaps even legibly, captured by any of the usually debated systems of philosophical ethics that we know so well. I concede at once that my charge may be turned aside by an adept professional maneuver (say, a utilitarian or liberal feint—one of the many varieties we know, possibly abetted by a brisk reminder that there's a great deal of evil in the world, don't you know)! But that would miss the point by a country mile. The evil or deviance that would have to be admitted would be so massive, so widespread, that we would surely risk, in the very pronouncement, the advantage of our principled perch. For no one can expect, nowadays, to win a moral dispute in the global setting by claiming to belong to the loyal remnant, those who have remained true.

What strikes the eye in reviewing the whole of the last century and the troubling start of the new century is simply that all the great conflicts that have made it impossible to separate moral and political objectives—in the determined way analytic ethics has insisted on so energetically—now appear, if you allow a rough-hewn summary, to take the form of one incipient religious war or another. I am struck by the obvious sincerity, conviction, zeal, ferocity, and warrior loyalty of all the pertinently paired opposing forces. The announced evil, for instance, of the attack on the World Trade Center, an attack deemed an act of war by the Americans, seems to be the very same act as the outraged, desperate, possibly misguided but heroic attempt by Muslim "freedom fighters" (against all odds, according to the story) to smash through the impenetrable blindness and evil of the Americans' own role in perpetuating the debased condition of the Arab world (as in the deepening corruption of Saudi Arabia and the continuing occupation of Palestinian lands).

I see no way to deny the *prima facie* plausibility of *both* characterizations viewed from their opposed perspectives, each of which may claim, fairly enough, to be grounded in the moral sensibilities of the populations they serve.

What I cannot see is how one such charge could win out over the other—
objectively, disjunctively, free of ideological slant, or without regard to enlisting the actual energies and memories and aspirations of the affected peoples—
by the straightforward application of *any* familiar moral principle. I don't mean
by this to be appealing for expert advice in resolving the contest between such
opposed appraisals (by recovering The Moral Truth, for instance), but rather
to suggest as gently as I can that that is no longer an obvious or reliable or
even plausible resource.

In this regard, 9/11 is a philosophically oblique, still inchoate, but politically frontal attack on the conceptual hegemony of an entire run of Western
moral and moral/political practices deemed responsible for grave injustices
and unpardonable evil visited on a people unable (before now) to begin to
right such wrongs. History is filled with the expression of such convictions,
of course. But the present situation is widely sensed to have marked a change
of deep significance, partly because the actual event is being read, metonymically, as a "first" countermove in a developing global confrontation requiring
drastic changes in the very conception of moral and political justice; because
the most pertinent competing conceptions appear to be irreconcilable and
bound to collide in more and more intransigent and unpredictable ways; because the increasingly realist bearing of global strategies is itself evolving along
unfamiliar lines; and because the technologies of war have been democra-
tized and miniaturized. Moreover, the resolution of the gathering disputes
between powers of the emerging sorts will undoubtedly require innovations
in the forms of reasoning about normative matters that are hardly being examined now and cannot be counted on to proceed by merely adjusting the
practices and conceptions that the West has traditionally favored. This is, in
fact, no more than the blandest first step in coming to terms with a radically
altered moral landscape.

To my knowledge, there is no standard theory that belongs to the philosophical lists that would ever (i) admit the *prima facie* validity of opposed
claims in a standoff of the sort just mentioned; (ii) act to resolve the impasse
without overriding the seeming force of (i), as if by appealing to higher normative considerations not themselves subject to a similar stalemate; or (iii)
admit that the valid or "objective" resolution of the impasse would (and could)
never exceed the dialectical resources of the partisans themselves (or the resources of similarly placed parties) or the advantages of moderate revisions or
extensions of such resources, which need never be deemed uniquely or exclusively valid. Nevertheless, I think that that is how we must begin.

My own charge is simplicity itself. I say that if moral questions have any point at all, the salience, if not the out-and-out priority, of disputes of the sort just mentioned cannot be ignored. Such moral questions make no compelling sense except in terms of the *prima facie* validity of the opposed interpretations and moral/political judgments of the interested parties. They cannot be objectively resolved in terms of any bivalent principle (of what is true or right). Their valid resolution is restricted to options that cannot presume to rely on moral principles, moral rules, or moral criteria alleged to be confirmed objectively by means that are neither similarly partisan nor encumbered by *prima facie* norms—say, by inspecting human nature, responding to the dictates of reason, exercising special cognitive faculties, drawing on self-evident moral truths, or the like.

If this much be granted, then, I suggest, nearly the whole of Western moral philosophy—preeminently, Anglo-American moral philosophy—will find itself in jeopardy and may, in fact, prove completely wrongheaded. The clue may be weakly glimpsed in Sophocles' *Antigone*, except that in Sophocles, the argument is not confined to the *prima facie* and is thought to be resolved in a satisfactory way. It also appears in Plato's elenctic dialogues, except that Socrates never analyzes the kind of rigor possible (or required, more likely) in examining matters akin to the question of justice in the "second-best" state posed in the *Statesman*. And, to leap to our own time, it appears in the terrible, intractable territorial claims of the Palestinians and the Israelis regarding the same small piece of land—the implications of which, we begin to see, are not merely local.

You will, of course, need to have firmer premises in hand to vindicate my brief at all.

Broadly speaking, I construe moral or moral/political disagreement as a dispute between ideologues or partisans who seek, as their best option under the circumstances, a form of objective resolution that, they suppose, both sides may view as reasonable—as manifesting as much rigor as moral matters permit—and that, above all, never invokes normative principles or criteria that claim to be validated beyond, or essentially independent of, the actual confrontations and shared capacities and distinctive moral habits of those same partisans. I take it to be a postulate, *faute de mieux*, that we cannot rely on any objectivist ground of the kind just mentioned (and set aside) and that an alternative form of reasonable resolution must be possible. But what would it be like?

We do need to warn ourselves that moral philosophy cannot be autonomous, cannot be completely separated from the results of good work regarding the analysis of knowledge and reality in general. The argued differences in moral vision are bound to reflect deeper realist, cognitive, and normative differences that will be judged inadequate or untenable by the partisans of an opposed conviction. Think, for instance, of Kantians and Aristotelians who cannot approach the question of moral virtue without prior attention to the proper mode of reasoning about moral matters as such. I see no difference, here, between such contests and those, say, between Iranian mullahs and Thomistic theologians. (I realize that you may protest.)

This hardly means, say, that the representatives of sovereign states could never agree, *as partisans*, to anything as ambitious or explicit as occasional resolutions like the United Nations Universal Declaration of Human Rights. Of course they could—and have. It means only that the rationale for their agreement affords an important example of the kind of "objective reasonableness" that I am presuming is possible (indeed, is necessary) among ideologues arguing from the vantage of what they regard as their own interests and norms of conduct, which (like the UN Declaration), we may suppose, are not always compatible with the *sittlich* norms they themselves favor and would neither wish (nor be willing) to abandon. The Iranians, for instance, have made it perfectly clear that the severity of the Koranic code of punishment bearing on thieves and adulterers and other evildoers cannot be expected to yield to the terms of the UN Declaration! And, of course, they don't regard themselves as inconsistent.

If philosophical ethics is to succeed, it must be able to propose specimen forms of moral advice that *need never congeal in the way of canonical claims of normative privilege*—running, say, from Aristotle and Immanuel Kant to figures like Alasdair MacIntyre and John Rawls (late followers of Aristotle and Kant, respectively)—although advice of the new sort will have to be able to be fashioned *and* favored in exchanges between "reasonable" ideologues. To come to the point: I cannot see that adherence to the conditions I've collected as items (i)–(iii), which motivate my brief against familiar societal canons, could not—or would not—be supported by alert partisans in a wide range of specific disputes. In effect, items (i)–(iii) define (at a first pass) and instantiate what, in a minimal way, it *is* to be reasonable in a philosophical review of legitimating moral claims. Hence, conditionally, they define what it means to behave reasonably *as* a moral partisan. Nevertheless, "reasonable," here, cannot be already captive to any well-entrenched normative vision championed by the partisan forces of any of our familiar contests.

If even this small advantage cannot be counted on to gain a significant measure of acceptance in serious disputes (and perhaps in the most serious disputes), then the whole idea of a philosophical ethics will prove to be nonsense. For it is part of the sense of (i)–(iii) that there is no facultative or objectivist or privileged or universalized or revealed source of normative objectivity to fall back on in either theoretical or practical affairs. In fact, I would argue that objectivity regarding what is true or right can never be more than a reasoned or critical *construction* regarding questions of fact or questions of how we should live and behave. I deem it "unreasonable," almost by definition, that moral partisans would perseverate in a prolonged dispute—one that would put their own concerns of life and death at increased and irreversible risk—by falling back onto privilege or revelation when debating dangerous opponents who, as they surely know, do not share their privileged or revealed norms.

Think, for instance, of the dispute between Israelis and Palestinians regarding the right to control Jerusalem, their competing claims marked by privileged reference to divine authority. Of course, I don't deny that it is entirely rational to promote such claims in order to muster the latent militancy of one or the other of the affected peoples. The fact is that negotiations between the Israelis and the Palestinians have, by and large, distinguished very clearly between what would be viable in the opinion of the world community and what is needed to maintain the internal discipline and solidarity of the warring parties themselves. I also admit that it is entirely reasonable that a religiously committed people, convinced of the overriding worth of their strict adherence to revealed obligations, might be willing to be annihilated rather than betray those obligations. But even the Jonestown massacre shows its unlikelihood— and surely the great powers associated with the United Nations are unlikely to be willing to permit such a slaughter.

A constructivist reading[2] of objectivity is, I submit, an important—even a decisive—finding, but it is *not* a specifically moral finding. It also rests on no more than *faute de mieux* considerations. I mean, by "*faute de mieux*," literally to endorse forms of reasoning that we cannot escape inasmuch as a "better" (or "best") discipline is simply lacking and would be impossible to legitimate anyway. Here, we find ourselves obliged to follow Socrates' example in Plato's early (elenctic) dialogues: we may, Socrates confirms, analyze piety or courage or justice if we wish, but we lack any assured method of discovering what such virtues essentially entail. Plato, I would argue, never exceeds this preliminary finding. Certainly, the *Republic* supports the idea that he was well aware of the limitation. I shall venture only a hint, therefore, about the defense of a "constructive realism"—in science or morality. But I say at once that constructivism (or constructive realism) signifies at least that the philosophical analysis of science and morality cannot be disjoined and that, as a result, disagreements about objective norms in matters of practical life need not be entirely confined to the convinced ideologies of opposed partisans.

To pin matters down a little more securely, let me introduce the term "reasonably" (as in "acting reasonably") as a term of art. Perhaps "*rationaliter*" is more apt than "*rationabilis*," so as not to suggest *any* determinate facultative capacity having normative competence or any virtue construed as an essential excellence of human nature, but only to designate what accords with my first tally, (i)–(iii)—or what the tally may be made to yield (possibly something like the UN Declaration or ordinary treaties and agreements that convinced opponents show some willingness to accept). There can be no doubt that the Kashmir dispute is deeply colored on both sides by considerations *rationaliter*. What the concerned world worries about is that such constraints may not be capable of keeping Pakistan and India from some nuclear adventure.

I admit the tally has some normative (that is, some moral) import, but only derivatively or consequentially, and only *prima facie*, which means in accord with, within the tolerance of, the avowed practices of contending factions (with their *Sitten*, as I say, borrowing G. W. F. Hegel's term for a deliberately thin use) regardless of whether the disputes to which they are applied are intra- or inter-societal. The qualification must already be part of the *sittlich* competence of opposed partisans faced with the potentially disastrous consequences of adhering—implacably, under real-world conditions—to their own disjunctively valid and apparently entirely adequate norms. Also, defining "*rationaliter*" is not a specifically moral affair, although, when applied to the *sittlich* world, it does yield constructive (or constructivist) moral proposals.

This is a somewhat tortured way of saying that it is a plain fact that societies *are* generally able to resolve practical or moral disputes involving norms and values in ways that converge on items (i)–(iii), even where, frankly, they are embedded in other ideological, doctrinal values that are thought to be privileged one way or another, are intransigent there, and often stalemate the resolution of an actual dispute. (My suggestion here has distant affinities with Thomas Hobbes's doctrine, in his *Leviathan*, in the sense of favoring prudence—but, contrary to Hobbes, not with the notion of a faculty of reason that may be said to yield invariant laws of practical life.) Such values may be affirmed in a dispute without being called into play as a privileged normative factor in reaching a resolution. On the contrary, whatever holds *rationaliter* plays its best part just where privileged norms seem inadequate to their task under real-world conditions.

I should like to think, for instance, that the abortion dispute in the United

States could be resolved, in part, step by step, *rationaliter*, even though many among the "pro-life" cohort embed the entire question in church doctrines that claim (but can never actually validate, *rationaliter*) the authority to define, in morally pertinent terms, just what it is to be a person. I note as well that, when all is said and done, Protestants and Catholics in Northern Ireland — and even Indians and Pakistanis in Kashmir — hold rather well, however problematically, to items (i)–(iii) in their political deliberations and disputes.

In any case, *"rationaliter"* signifies a minimal procedure (or, perhaps better, a meta-procedure) for managing *practical* matters of normative importance, however doctrinally entangled, within the pale of (i)–(iii), as in matters in which a contest between partisans threatens to be stalemated though it is seen to be unacceptably destructive. Moreover, this minimal procedure provides in an open-ended way for possible changes in *sittlich* practices, still in accord with partisan interests, that can provide no compelling grounds for claims to independent normative validity.

My general assumption is that something of this sort is almost always in play in the life of complex societies and has only to be regularized where it is wanted. Here, practical reasoning seeks a *modus vivendi*, rather than a theoretically valid finding, where the doctrinal defense of stalemated *Sitten* and the entrenched norms of opposed partisans threaten to be futile, dangerous, and used up within their shared world. I admit that some contests may never be resolved. But it is really quite difficult to mention bona fide cases — where, that is, sustained disputes are already in play. (As you may guess, I don't see why war must be outside the pale of moral resolutions produced *rationaliter*.)

Even this small part of my brief depends on the decisive lesson[3] bequeathed us by the philosophical tradition that runs from René Descartes to Hegel respecting realism: namely, that the Cartesian model is hopelessly aporetic because of its fixed disjunction between cognizer and cognized world and its representationalism; that Kant realized (however problematically) that the *aporiai* of pre-Kantian thought had to, and could only, be overcome by a constructivist alternative; and that, against Kant, Hegel rejected all reference to the noumenal, confined valid judgment to the data of socially shared *Erscheinungen* (the various ways in which "the-world-appears-to-us," especially uncritically), rejected any facultative division between the theoretical and the practical, claimed no privileged or transcendental powers, and realized in some measure that experience was itself subject to historicized change. The upshot of the entire lesson is that we cannot claim that inquiry is ordained to lead to any final form of human freedom or similar excellence or any perfect knowledge of the world. Reason and objectivity are contingent constructs.

They take different forms in the lives of different societies, all within the evolving space of historical inquiry.

All I need add, at the moment, is that items (i)–(iii) are meant to be in complete accord with this much of the Hegelian resolution, and they count, accordingly, as a methodological constraint, not a moral one. Put more narrowly, there is no viable ground on which the would-be norms of practical life could be legitimated in *theoretical* terms akin to whatever may be thought to be true about the world, or (failing that) in terms subject to the authoritative directives of some specific facultative competence (reason, let us suppose, in the Kantian sense, or moral intuition in one form or another). Therefore, objectivity in practical affairs, and in moral/political affairs in particular, is, at bottom, constructivist in a deeper sense than (or in as deep a sense as) truth is in scientific inquiry. You see why, in practical matters, we must work with the initial "data" of what may be deemed valid *prima facie* in practical life (in our *Sitten*), just as we must rely, in theoretical matters, on what is "given" (as Hegel says, presuppositionlessly, in the *Phenomenology*) in the way of *Erscheinungen*.

This is as close as I can come to endorsing what Hegel identifies as the *Sitten* of practical life, the customs and practices of viable societies that clearly exert some normative force on the members of those societies in a *prima facie* sense, one that accords with what anthropologists describe (but do not independently confirm) as rightly binding on a given society's behavior. If, in reviewing the *sittlich*, Hegel's account of first-order norms invests them with a deeper sort of legitimation—possibly objectivist, in some historical sense—then Hegel and I part company.

I appeal to Hegel chiefly to facilitate my own account of moral constructivism,[4] my account of the methodological conditions on which a second-best morality may be validated in a second-order sense. It's for this reason that I favor Plato's pronouncement in the *Statesman* to the effect that we are confined to conjectures about the second-best state. Though we cannot grasp the Good, we must still construct our laws in spite of our ignorance of the best state! Hence, I advance the idea that our *prima facie* norms are essential to our normative reflections *rationaliter*. By "*prima facie*," then, I mean the familiar, habituated, first-order aspect of the normative functioning of our *Sitten*, which themselves need not (and normally do not) conform to any preferred second-order norms constructed *rationaliter*. In particular, if reasoning must be second-best—if we cannot claim to know the Good, or any comparable surrogate—then moral partisans *cannot* justifiably rely on *their* privileged norms vis-à-vis one another.

[II]

I turn to the philosophical record primarily as an economy—to remind you, first of all, that twentieth-century Anglo-American philosophy is, in analyzing theoretical and practical questions, largely pre-Kantian (that is, Cartesian) or Kantian in the sense in which Kant was himself Cartesian, and second, that there is a very clear alternative, initiated about two hundred years ago, that runs subversively, possibly ahead of its original mentors, from Hegel through Marx, through Friedrich Nietzsche, through John Dewey, through Martin Heidegger, and through Michel Foucault at least. This alternative conception views the human world in constructivist and historicized terms—abandoning transcendentalism, cognitive privilege, teleologism, essentialism, invariant norms—and concedes the diversity, even incompatibility, among the executive values of different societies. In short, as I read it, the Hegelian tradition suggests (perhaps only in a desultory manner) the notably strong idea that objectivity in normative matters is best captured by the model of partisans acting and disputing *rationaliter*. Partisans, of course, may not and need not agree among themselves about the weight and decisiveness of particular arguments or norms or competing methodologies. This still does not violate the spirit of my original tally. You see, therefore, how spare—and yet coherent—the idea is. Endorse it, and a huge library of humane longings that masquerade as undoubted moral truths collapses at a stroke!

In short, in the interval spanning the contributions of Kant and Hegel, early modern philosophy reaches its most decisive finding in coming to realize that the recovery of any defensible realist reading of the work of the natural sciences (as well as of the human studies, or human sciences) must yield in the direction of a constructivist and historicized account of our cognitive competence. We cannot justify the idea Descartes "originated" (as we conventionally say), namely, the idea that we confront the independent world directly and adequately in the realist sense. Rather, we must "construct" what we take to be the world we know—which is *not* to invent the world itself but to admit the limitations of what we may conceivably defend as true. That, philosophy finds, is the price of escaping the Cartesian paradoxes and pretensions of privilege. We can hardly claim to have improved on this part of the academy's splendid discovery; on the contrary, it would not be unreasonable to say that we have been battling the same "Cartesian" demons down through the whole of the twentieth century. The point of mentioning this larger history is to flag the fact that, if all *that* is conceded, then it follows instantly that moral theory must yield as well in the direction of a constructivist and historicized account of the objectivity and legitimation of moral norms.

That is indeed the nerve of my reflection on 9/11—and, I hasten to add, my limited use of the work of the tradition that spans Hegel and Foucault. Put another way, moral philosophy is not autonomous. It is, in fact, hostage to larger philosophical inquiries regarding the competence and conditions of human knowledge anywhere. Because I judge the best prospects of philosophy to depend on Hegel's critique of Kant and on Kant's critique of Descartes, I see a powerful advantage in construing the import of 9/11 as touching in a coherent way on the lesson of that essential conceptual episode. But I do not pretend to resolve any substantive moral issues by doctrinal privilege.

In my view, the pivotal discovery lies with realizing that there *are* no moral/political (or normative) concerns apart from the reflexive inquiries of human selves, *and* that there are no selves (or persons) apart from the transformative processes of enculturation.[5] Human selves are not natural-kind entities. They are not the mere members of *Homo sapiens*. If biology were thought to be explanatorily adequate, there would be no morality at all: there would be no conception of what to count as morally significant, except on some expressly privileged ("best") ground. Persons—selves, agents, "subjects"—cannot be defined apart from language and culture. They cannot exist, though, save as biologically "embodied," indissolubly emergent through enculturing processes (internalizing linguistic abilities, say, in a manner comparable to the adult competence of the already apt members of their home society).

That is the decisive complication that sets the human being apart from the rest of the animal world—however close, biologically, its life is to the life of the sublinguistic primates. It's the *sine qua non* of our reflective powers: of our sense of responsibility, of judgment, of deliberation and choice and commitment. On my reading, it is also the ineluctable lesson of the philosophical inquiry that spans Descartes and Hegel. I insist on the point, because it confirms the constructive nature of morality itself, confirms the impossibility of making progress in our understanding of moral matters without a modest grasp of philosophy's contribution, and confirms the deep importance of reflecting on the meaning of 9/11 within the historicized constraints of how our moral concerns arise at all. Discussants often suppose that we have only to return to the moral verities to secure our bearings in the practical world, but that, I say, goes contrary to the initial intuitions offered at the very start of this essay. I regard that as a Darwinian lesson, though not a lesson contemporary neo-Darwinians usually draw. Apart from the perfectly understandable courtesies extended to prelinguistic infants, fetuses, the permanently comatose, those who cannot function beyond (or much beyond) an essentially vegetative life, and so on, selves remain the encultured transforms of *Homo sapiens*, uniquely competent in terms of their mastery of a first language and whatever abilities such mastery makes possible (notably, in terms of thought and action, on which moral agency depends).

Selves are, literally, artifactual hybrids, *sui generis* emergents somehow generated by submitting to the enculturing process. They may be said to be "distinct" from *Homo sapiens* but surely not separable. They are, I suggest, culturally emergent but inseparably embodied in one or another of the individuated members of *Homo sapiens*, in the plain sense that they exhibit competences that cannot be adequately described or explained in biological terms alone but (once again) cannot exist if not indissolubly incarnated biologically or, conceivably, by other technological means.

Paradigmatically, selves are moral *agents*, in the joint sense of judging themselves and others and of being the distinctive kind of creature about whom such judgments are rightly rendered—creatures who can judge and make commitments. If, of course, the way in which selves function *could* be described and explained in terms of the biology of *Homo sapiens* alone, then, to be sure, "moral" norms would be reduced to natural or Darwinian functions. Hence, the irreducibility of the specifically cultural world, which applies to the emergence of selves preeminently, *is* the single "metaphysical" condition on which the analysis of moral objectivity depends. It is this encumbering condition that I emphasize rather than any *obiter dictum* of the moral sort. (I shall treat rather lightly the metaphysical complexities I've just noted. But there can be no question that, in a suitably ramified analysis, I would have to acknowledge and give an account of the philosophical complications I've broached.)

What's needed here seems to be comparatively straightforward, in accord with my initial intuitions about moral theories and my attraction to the least controversial innovations of Hegel's thought. You begin to see, therefore, why we cannot presume to answer our own moral questions without considering what we take to be a philosophically adequate account of ourselves! Indeed, 9/11 forces us back to a question that the assurance of our own moral/political visions—in effect, our dreams of moral hegemony—would rather ignore. I need only mention that neither Aristotle nor Kant provides an instructive clue about the decisive difference between biological nature and human culture: that, I believe, accounts for Aristotle's essentialist leanings and Kant's transcendentalism. Neither could otherwise have supposed his theory of science and morality to be objective at all. The admission of the cultural "construction" of the fully human (*a fortiori*, the moral) makes possible an entirely different conception of validity and objectivity. That is precisely what Hegel's innovation affords.

The "ontology" by which I choose to advance my thesis may of course be challenged. But the empirical facts about selves and the conceptual irreducibility of cultural attributes remain indisputable—and, with all that, the uniqueness of the human *and* the moral. I would be unwilling to allow the nerve of the argument to be lost in the quarrelsome subtleties of metaphysics. We need only affirm that selves, in acquiring language, acquire the ability to query their own behavior, to ask how they should behave—aware, as they are, that they will be able to act in accord with what they judge to be fitting. In this sense, they acquire a "second nature" (name it as you please). Only in this context do questions of objective norms and morally valid behavior make any sense at all. Yet as soon as we ask ourselves what we should understand by "true" and "right," we grasp the import of the profound asymmetry between the two questions. If, indeed, *we are selves*, then surely the cultural world is entitled to realist standing—every bit as much as the physical world. But it remains a hybrid and emergent world, and the physical world is not. In fact, according to the picture I've been sketching, our conception of the physical world or of independent nature—not the world itself—cannot fail to be an artifact of our own history, our encultured second nature. There's the entire lesson of the philosophical interval that spans Kant and Hegel. I believe that there can be no valid account of science or morality apart from that concession. That is why I read 9/11 in the way I do.

Grant all that, and *there are, then, no grounds for correspondentist or coherentist—or, simply, objectivist—presumptions regarding the norms of practical life and conduct* (that is, regarding what is right). The analogous presumption remains in play (that is, must be met or properly displaced) in determining the sense of "true." I don't deny that presumptions of the latter sort may fail. But those presumptions will fail (if they must—and I think they must) for a broadly Cartesian reason: because objectivism must fail. Yet, when they fail, they fail in the process of attempting to answer the perfectly answerable question of how, finally, our beliefs and assertions relate to what can be known of the world. Presumptions of the former sort fail for altogether different reasons. *They* fail because, to succeed in cognitivist terms, we would first have to pretend to have discovered that the world actually harbored (in some factually pertinent way) the independent practical norms we wished to consult, so that we might then consult them! There cannot be any "independent" norms that govern what exists only in the way of socially constituted (or constructed) artifacts. But that's to say that there cannot be any natural-kind norms governing the judgments and practical commitments of human selves. This extremely radical idea—contested, to be sure, on all sides—fits rather nicely with the facts regarding the constructed nature of moral norms and the "second-natured" nature of moral agents. It offers the best "metaphysics" for construing the significance of 9/11 in the way I do.

The most favored option regarding the true—in effect, the Cartesian vision of the true—confuses an acknowledged paradox for a viable strategy; another, regarding the right, construes its own fictions as discernible features of the actual world, though it errs in different ways in Kantian and Aristotelian accounts. In the work of recent Kantians (John Rawls and Jürgen Habermas, for instance), the normative competence of reason is *found* in the human world.[6] Kant is more careful: he holds only that we may "think" of ourselves as capable of following the dictates of autonomous reason, though we cannot possibly know it to be so. Furthermore, in the sense in which a good part of twentieth-century analytic philosophy favors the first mistake, nearly the whole of Western moral philosophy favors the second—or, if it abandons cognitivism but still craves a version of objectivity beyond the resources of disputing partisans, it tends to fall back, as with Kant or Rawls or Habermas, on some sort of inviolate reason capable of vouchsafing the objective standing of the directives we need. Nevertheless, if "reason" *is* a hybrid artifact of human history and cultural formation, as I believe, then this last alternative will be as feeble as the cognitivist option it would replace.

Once we give up appealing to supernatural, revealed, fictional, utterly utopian, indubitable, unrealizable moral resources, as well as obviously false and unconfirmable beliefs, preferring to proceed *rationaliter* (as among those who do not share our norms and values), there cannot be any compelling account of human interests that would ignore our hopes and fears regarding life and death in all its forms. These worries define the principal part of the content of our *prima facie* norms. They concern ourselves and all those we are likely to hold especially dear. There cannot be a fixed list of them, for they will vary from group to group, from one age to another, from the sensibilities and technological resources of one society to another. And, of course, they will depend in good part on our organizing ideologies. Yet it is well-nigh impossible that some run of such interests will not play a decisive role in the moral vision of whatever society we choose to examine.

I call such interests prudential (*prudentiae*), though I do not mean, by that, to designate any determinate virtue essential to human nature itself. They are bound to include familiar worries about security of life and limb and property and family and community and reputation, as well as enabling arrangements of health and education and economic opportunity and food and shelter and care; worries about natural disasters and war and violence and opportunistic forays against our interests; and more attenuated worries about equality and freedom and respect of person and the gratification of desires. The point is that these are *not* intrinsically legitimating norms but only the salient data that, cast prudentially, are collected in our *Sitten* and serve as the ground on which our corrective moral visions build — in accord, say, with items (i)–(iii) of my original tally. Normally, our *prudentiae* are defended in a coherent and holistic *sittlich* vision. They are never initially collected as discrete values that may be found to be, as anthropologists often suppose they are, "universally" acknowledged within the human species. That sort of universalizing, not atypical among recent Aristotelians, is completely opposed to admitting the distinction of the cultural, historical, constructed, and partisan nature of the moral world itself.

To reason *rationaliter* is to intend to address prudential concerns effectively — more or less in accord with worries like those just mentioned and as well as possible within the range of our *sittlich* constraints. It would not violate the spirit of items (i)–(iii), therefore, to add, as item (iv), that persons, functioning as the partisans they are, may be expected to be prudent — or, better, to make provision for their *prudentiae* by what they judge to be reliable means, their *providentiae* — where the sense of that accommodation is not meant to define an objective or essential virtue apart from our *prima facie* norms but, rather, to spell out the going concerns of particular societies, the determinate details of a determinable *modus vivendi*. By such means, societies form a more flexible, more informal policy of how to modify their practices and norms responsibly along lines that cannot easily be judged to be merely arbitrary or question-begging. Moral reflection, you realize, is insuperably informal and improvisational.

It may be the principal business of moral reflection to resolve conflicts between different prudential interests or between such interests and what (presumably) history and social custom have already entrenched as valid practices. Conflicts are bound to be common here, as with slaves affirmed and denied as property in antebellum America; unequal property holdings that make it impossible for sizable populations to gain a viable share of whatever is judged to meet their prudential needs, whether confined to a single society or not (as in the impoverishment of the whole of black Africa); or unequal entitlements deemed valid by custom or law when viewed through some local tradition or revealed doctrine (as in the recent treatment of women in Afghanistan, under the rule of the Taliban).

Nothing that arises here shows that proceeding *rationaliter* must be less resourceful or less stable or less balanced than what may be yielded by treating any of our *prima facie* norms as if it were already independently legitimated. It may also be prudent (in the sense supplied) to respect the *sittlich* practices of the society we inhabit. But the plain truth is that, whatever their *prima facie* standing, prevailing customs and even our determinate *providentiae* (slaves as property, for instance) are likely to be the principal sources of conflict within our evolving concerns.

Here, I offer three small lessons. Two of them bear on the sort of social engineering that moral/political concerns inevitably entail; the third, the radical cast of the conceptual reform I have in mind. The first conveys a bit of malice, though I admit I find it entirely convincing: viz., that there is, in general, a greater danger of producing deep, widespread suffering and destruction through social changes confidently pressed into service on grounds said to be independent of our *Sitten* than there is from conformity with whatever is historically entrenched in the *prima facie* way, almost without regard to its specific content. I am thinking of the crusades and recent uses of the *jihad*, the policies of Pol Pot and the Bosnian Serbs, and, supremely, Hitler's vision of greater Germany. I say, quite frankly: beware of men of principle! (This applies to Hobbes as much as to those he feared—and to ourselves as well.)

The second lesson concerns a timing problem. It often requires no more than a glance to see a reasonable resolution of a deeply felt injustice or a conflict that threatens the entire fabric of a society, but it may well require an age or more—and discipline enough to match the patience needed—to set in motion all the *sittlich* changes that would produce the workable reform intended. In the process, patience and correction stumble; opposing factions find that they cannot, over lengthening time, keep their agreements with one another; small breaches often prove to threaten much more than was ever in place before. Think of the Indians and the Pakistanis in Kashmir. The sense of justice tends to be focused on verbal agreements, as if in a court proceeding, but the resolution of practical disputes is a matter of *altered practices*.

In this regard, there can be no determinate principle of justice read in the moral way. To say that justice requires "giving everyone his due" (beyond *prima facie* considerations), for instance, signifies that potentially *any* of a range of practical resolutions congruent with our entrenched practices *and* their adjustment *rationaliter* (in accord with our partisan *providentiae*) may function as one or another tolerable resolution under the circumstances given. So *justitia*, as we may call the moral sense of justice—a care for the well-being of all relevant parties, according to our lights—is intrinsically never more than improvisational under historical conditions. (We may refer to *justitia* to distinguish the moral sense from any strictly legal alternative [*jus*], that is, the sense of a determinate jurisdictional space and its rules of competence and authority.)

Its effective defense, however, cannot be determinate, simply because *justitia* applies to a *modus vivendi* as a practical resolution, which, as such, is only determinable.[7] That is, *justitia* is validated as a general "form of life" that may be acceptably instantiated, in this contingency or that, in many different ways that are not set out antecedently or in a modally obligatory way. But for all that, *justitia* must be made determinately effective by way of one or another actual commitment or resolution. Hence, for practical (not jurisdictional) reasons, when *justitia* is satisfied, it is always satisfied determinately. A great deal of Western moral philosophy falters on the confusion that lurks here: *reasoning about legal propositions and reasoning about moral commitments (or actions) are, logically and conceptually, never the same, though they are normatively inseparable.*

This same lesson inevitably colors our grasp of the social engineering issue. For, on the argument being mounted, *there is no determinate, principled solution to any moral/political dispute.* There are only tolerable or effective commitments, and alternative ones at that (that is, determinate instantiations of a determinably acceptable *modus vivendi*). This is, in fact, the heart of what it is to live as a partisan contending against other partisans for the same goods or an acceptable division of entitlements, whatever they may include. But it also means that pertinent disputes may be interminable without being irrational, or that resolutions *rationaliter* may require means that one or another putatively "higher" canon would refuse to countenance — war, or terrorism, or torture, perhaps, where a perceived injustice appears otherwise insoluble. Here, all seeming contracts and treaties — morally and politically construed — are qualified by *ceteris paribus* considerations that cannot be defined in any formal manner *ante*. (Officials of the U.S. government, for example, have been willing, in connection with the action against the Taliban, to air in a public way the possible defensibility of using torture against captive al Qaeda terrorists — on humanitarian grounds!)

In fact, a valid moral resolution, the resolution of a practical impasse, is hardly obliged (and may be unable) to solve, at the same time, any implicated theoretical or ideological claims thought to be inseparable from the practical matter. Think of the insoluble doctrinal differences that separate the very factions that would have to agree on a practical policy in order to resolve one or another part of the abortion impasse or the interminable theological disputes regarding the control of Jerusalem. The first leads to what is or would be right in the way of action; the second, to what, presumably, is or would be true or plausible in the way of belief. Both have their constructivist resources, but they normally apply in different ways. The first centers on the resolution of a practical (an actual) impasse; the second, on assessing the validity or the truth of a particular doctrinal claim. The first yields no more than an instantiated *modus vivendi*, not (or not necessarily) a judgment about the standing of a truth-claim or a proposition. One can see the need for conceptual economies in both sorts of circumstance, applied *rationaliter*. (I concede that the model I am sketching might be characterized as a form of pragmatism. But then, on my own argument, that is simply to say that pragmatism is itself an attenuated form of "Hegelian" thinking.)

Moral/political issues are practical affairs, though they often arise for doctrinal reasons. The resolution of the first is bound to implicate the relevance and fortunes of the second. But there can be no principled or independent derivation of the resolution of practical disputes on grounds drawn *from* the presumed priority of any theoretical puzzle. *There simply are no objectively discernible or determinable moral/political norms at all*, apart from what may be identified as valid *prima facie* or constructively proposed—second-order— from a review, *rationaliter*, of our actual *Sitten*.

To confuse the two is to risk confusing the moral and the legal (possibly even the moral and the factual) or to mistake what is common to both. The *legal* is never more than the result of a regularized agreement to treat what might otherwise serve as an improvisational moral or political norm as a formal rule for a theoretical dispute within a well-defined jurisdiction *(jus)*. You may, if you wish, treat this as a solution to Socrates' philosophical question in the first two books of the *Republic*—a solution possibly less offensive and more interesting than Thrasymachus's answer (that justice is the interest of the stronger) but closer to Thrasymachus's sense of the doubtful standing of independent moral norms than to Socrates' mock essentialism.

When we revise our *prima facie* norms in the direction of the supposed objective validity of the change intended, we mean the change to "take its place" (so to speak) within our then-altered *sittlich* norms, so that it itself acquires thereby a measure of *prima facie* force. But adjustments of these sorts remain forever improvisational (even where formal agreements may have been reached), simply because there is no principled way to decide, in moral/ political matters, when such new constraints are themselves rightly open to further change. By contrast, in the legal context, the courts are authorized to decide questions of relevance, *ceteris paribus* questions, and questions of jurisdiction in addition to actual findings. In short, legal matters rightly arise within an antecedently defined closed space, whereas moral matters do not arise in the same way. Nevertheless, a "closed space" need not be forever closed: history and technological change inevitably defeat the idea that the law is changeless in "normal" circumstances.

Think, however, of Osama bin Laden's charge that the presence of American troops in Saudi Arabia defiles the sacred homeland, whatever may have been the formal treaty or agreement between the consenting sovereign powers involved. To see the point is to see that there can be, finally, no principled division between the legal and the moral. But consider this, too: to construe religious revelation in terms of the legal model and to treat that same decision as rightly defining the paradigm of acting *rationaliter* (as, apparently, the Iranian mullahs do and as bin Laden opportunistically insists is true) is to disorganize the very possibility of rational dispute among opposed partisans and, of course, to fall back to moral and political privilege. Put more narrowly, the right or wrong of, say, abortion or suicide *cannot*, in a republican or, more restrictively, a democratic political order, admit the argumentative pertinence of any revealed truth about abortion's or suicide's moral standing. This is the case even where it remains morally (hence, rationally) admissible, and perhaps advisable, that local religious sensibilities be taken seriously into account in fashioning a valid *modus vivendi*. Contemporary American political debates about abortion and suicide and homosexuality, for instance, quite frequently risk being irreconcilable with proceeding *rationaliter*. (Alexis de Tocqueville, you remember, was struck by the American penchant for mingling republican, even democratic, themes with religious tenets.)

Furthermore, granting this much, you see as well that, precisely because of its practical nature, a moral/political impasse cannot preclude on principled grounds the relevance of the division of actual power (separating the contending parties) in arriving at a valid resolution of a pertinent dispute. This does not mean that "anything goes," or that "might makes right." But because moral matters are prudential matters, a would-be resolution that disregarded the actual sources of power that may be brought to bear on a matter at hand is not likely to have been arrived at *rationaliter*. Nevertheless, a moral/political commitment is not merely (really, not at all) a matter of brute force. The Polish resistance against the Nazis and the Finnish resistance against the Soviets make this abundantly clear. Both hoped to enlist the effective sanctions of important powers that were not directly involved, and both succeeded, but hardly in the way they themselves had hoped. Hence, in yielding to Thrasymachus's important theme, we need not yield to his actual thesis. Utopian thinking, we may say, is a would-be form of moral/political thinking that ignores practical or existential constraints in the here and now and, in doing that, construes valid judgment as essentially theoretical. (That, effectively, is the confusion Sen perceived in Rawls and, in a curious way, what Lenin supposed he saw in Trotsky's doubts about the proletarian nature of the Russian Revolution.) But of course there can be a utopian strain in would-be practical decisions, and there may be valid theoretical questions that practical policies must consider.

The fact is, if a moral resolution means to be effective in practical terms, it must take existing imbalances of power into account. The relevant circumstances are, however, not always apparent. For example, the struggle between the Israelis and the Palestinians is surely being waged, increasingly now, in the international media. Similarly, in domestic American affairs, the power of an entrepreneurial press has changed the balance of effective political power so much that moral/political concerns, managed through the reporting of the news, successfully brought down both the Nixon and Johnson administrations and hampered the prosecution of the Vietnam War so thoroughly that it could not finally be won. But the powers of the fourth estate are also changeable and fickle, as the threat of a consolidation of privately owned news media in America now makes clear.

Again, we do not need to define the true nature of a "person" in order to resolve — objectively — the abortion dispute *as a moral dispute*; similarly, we do not need to demonstrate how a valid territorial agreement between the Israelis and the Palestinians *derives* from the supposed determinate entitlements and rights of either party. To reverse the order of resolution is to prefer the legal or the theoretical to the moral/political or the practical. Otherwise, in the moral order, a political resolution of a dispute may itself impose (though it need not) a further legal encumbrance on the opposing parties. This is an extremely useful distinction, constructively advanced as being entirely in accord with reasoning *rationaliter*. The division of actual power is almost always morally relevant in the cases in question. Stalin did not see matters altogether clearly when he asked how many divisions the Pope had at his disposal. Political power is drawn from collective sources, and no one can confidently anticipate how power will actually form. Think of 9/11, for instance, as the transformation of political weakness into a weapon of incalculable power.

Beyond that, among responsible peoples, to be committed in a moral way is, in some sustainable measure, *to bear witness to* — to preserve the memory and record of — all *prima facie* claims of great injustice and wrong that have not yet been adequately reviewed or righted, approximating to what I shall call *summum malum.* Ultimately, it is to inform the entire world, to enlist the power of every society willing to function as a living archive of shared opinion or a spontaneous tribunal of a remembered wrong—or, possibly, an ally. In part, the formation of these effective memories constitutes a source of morally informed power, however partisan it may be; in part, too, these memories constitute and give direction to the moral world itself. It is not so much a question of ensuring *justitia* as ensuring the continual conversation of justice. Tiananmen Square is an excellent example of what I mean.

There may be a reason to be sanguine about would-be moral sympathies, sanctions, consensus, and influence, no matter how informal: they may, over time, produce effective centers of concern or outrage or serious assessment (self-appointed monitors, for instance, like Amnesty International, or even governments moved by such tribunals to inform the world about global warming, nuclear waste, environmental hazards, drought and famine, and incipient holocausts). There is no reason to suppose that such activities will not be the work of convinced partisans. But what does that matter? There is no alternative. And if we remain consistent with the analysis being offered, we may suppose that, where *summum malum* is least in doubt, consensus will be of wider scope and more in accord with our intuitions of a humane life than otherwise. You must think of the reciprocating horrors of the Tutsis and the Hutus in Rwanda, for example, or of something of even greater influence (though not necessarily of greater harm), like the Nazi or Cambodian holocausts.

[III]
You will have noticed that I have made no reference to disputes about norms or virtues of personal life: that is, matters of life and death in which the moral import of what we do is confined to how we live our lives, without reference to the bearing of one's acts on the lives of others—as in, with pertinent constraints, suicide, physician-assisted death, homosexuality, self-development or self-realization, possibly prostitution as a profession, the exercise of personal choice, and the like. The reason is plain. There are bound to be different codes of conduct in the various societies that spell out their different *sittlich* constraints defining admissible and inadmissible ways of conducting one's life. For Jews, Christians, and Muslims, for instance, suicide is forbidden on grounds that include, at least, doing harm or wrong to oneself *(noxae, peccati).* But the Stoics recognized suicide as an honorable act.

Suicide cannot rightly be forbidden on theoretical grounds, unless we construe ideologies or legal rationales against "self-harm" as morally valid in second-order terms. I see no possible argument there, *rationaliter.* But that is not to disallow protecting selves against the dangers of their own irrational behavior, calling selves to bear responsibility regarding the lives of others (children, for instance) who may be adversely affected, or respecting the *sittlich* practices of a society as well as possible. If persons *are* indeed cultural artifacts (as I believe they are), then there simply can be no independent basis for forbidding suicide as such. It cannot be more than a prudential or practical decision—or a moral decision constructed on prudential grounds—but, if it is, then it must be held hostage to the changing tolerances of a society's evolving history. To admit that much is not yet to address suicide's moral standing, but it points to a surprisingly powerful strategy.

Here, I suggest a normative policy going beyond the *prima facie* but congruent with the sense of reasoning *rationaliter,* which I call *nullum malum.* By that I mean that there is, and can be, no changeless rule or principle applied to human nature or human reason that could possibly justify any moral injunction against living one's own life *rationaliter*—on the grounds of violating human nature or intrinsic reason or cognitively privileged norms. For we can find nothing but *nullum malum* at any legitimative level beyond the *prima facie*—even where our *Sitten* claim otherwise. You cannot fail to see the radical possibilities that begin to loom.

The point of *nullum malum* is to justify relieving a society of any of its former codes—or supporting its resistance to instituting new ones—that impose normative constraints on one's personal life, in the sense supplied. The upshot is to reconcile a society's *sittlich* vision with reviewing (in a distinctly stronger sense) its validity *rationaliter.* Any policy favoring *nullum malum* may be construed as morally generous *because* it applies a conceptually generous distinction morally. This makes vulnerable targets of all would-be norms regarding the choice of personal lifestyle, norms that speak of harming or wronging oneself. Moral generosity based entirely on conceptual generosity, as with *nullum malum,* I call *liberalitas.* Thus, it would be entirely appropriate, *rationaliter,* to hold that all societies should eliminate as far as possible the most egregious *sittlich* constraints they impose on personal life (female circumcision, for instance). Doubtless, it would be well to pursue such matters with patience, in accord with developing resources, in ways that preserve as well as possible the remaining *Sitten* of the affected societies—that is, with due consideration. But you have here a strong example of precisely how a substantive moral change may be made compelling in terms that make no objectivist moral claims at all! You begin to see how such a strategy works even in restricted contexts, such as the American experiment to admit gays in the military, or, more problematically, in the post-Taliban Afghan effort to restore the rights of women. Of course, you also realize that the argument works just as well in the opposite direction. Think, for instance, of converting, *ratio-naliter*, security at airports into a central system for deciding who may fly and who may not—and more. I think analogously of the My Lai massacre construed as a condition for saving the village.

Critics may be distressed to find that my proposal greatly diminishes the sense in which resolutions of moral/political disputes are capable of being objectively confirmed as theoretical claims. I concede the initial relevance of the charge *only where* moral objectivity (beyond the *prima facie*) is construed in constructivist terms. There, a seemingly propositional claim is no more than a heuristic surrogate for the practical commitment that is being directly appraised. Think, for example, of the slowly gathering support for the institutionalization of homosexual marriage.

Those same critics may be further distressed to find that, whether theoretically or practically construed, moral resolutions are not likely to conform with the supposed requirements of a bivalent logic applied to propositions. For what I am urging is (i) that validity regarding moral matters is primarily practical, not theoretical—a question of action or commitment rather than of affirmed propositions; (ii) that it concerns a *modus vivendi* (and the particular acts by which that may be *made* determinate) rather than judgments of what *is* determinately true or right in a moral sense (for instance, regarding the virtues); (iii) that valid resolutions are arrived at in a practical way, *rationaliter*, *liberaliter*, with due consideration, but not by consulting objective norms independent of our *Sitten*; (iv) that the resolution of moral/political conflicts cannot be more than determinable, never strictly determinate, as in providing a *modus vivendi*, which may be realized in various determinate ways; hence (v) that the logic of moral claims is bound to be relativistic rather than bivalent or merely pluralistic; and (vi) that the would-be rationale for such claims must be ideological and cannot be defended more rigorously than resolutions defended *rationaliter*. Propositional claims simply lack the practical and objective import they require, *if* they are not already tethered to the resolution of a practical dispute about how we should live in the face of actual opposition. (Ideological dispute is entirely arbitrary if separated from a practical dispute, itself already grounded in *sittlich* practices that, arguably, should be preserved or changed.)

The point of *nullum malum*, then, is this. If we cannot legitimate a code of personal life on the grounds of independent norms that we claim to discern but not construct—*which, indeed, we cannot do*—then *nullum malum* is likely to be as good as any other moral policy that can be defended *ratio-naliter*, for it seeks no more than a second-best morality liberated as far as possible from whatever in practice and ideology (bearing on the choice of a life) cannot be reconciled *rationaliter*. If you allow the argument, then every catalogue of "human virtues" can be no more than an abstraction from the *sittlich* practices of one historical society or another. No such catalogue can ever be universalized as normatively objective. (This goes entirely against the Aristotelian tradition, whether ancient, medieval, or contemporary.)

In matters of personal and political conduct, I take morality to be an improvisational art of practical reasoning that issues primarily in the resolution of actual disputes and conflicts—*never* independently in claims about what is true or right in any merely doctrinal or ideological sense. It cannot favor the latter, because there is no theoretical inquiry that *can* yield independently true normative claims and because there is no essentially fixed faculty of practical reason (whether natural or transcendental) that could possibly issue neutral or universally binding directives about how one should live. This is why thought-experiments and hypothetical cases are so dubious in moral matters as opposed to legal and factual ones.

Faute de mieux, moral reasoning begins with the initial data of our *sittlich* norms and the contingent *prudentiae* and *providentiae* that our society favors—in effect, favors *rationaliter*. It is bound, therefore, to challenge its own *prima facie* values wherever they conflict with evolving prudential concerns or with items (i)–(iii) of my original tally, now amplified in the direction of prudence—item (iv). As a consequence, moral reasoning proves to be inherently improvisational, logically informal, and more likely to be defended in accord with a relativistic logic than a bivalent one.

I have attempted here to construct an argument that deliberately abandons any and all forms of cognitive and rational privilege regarding would-be moral norms and to demonstrate that—without any conceptual trickery or arbitrariness—we can still (i) defend a viable conception of objectivity in moral matters, (ii) begin with a thoroughly conservative view protective of the *sittlich* norms of our own society, and yet (iii) draw out of such slim provisions a perfectly reasonable sense in which those same *sittlich* norms may be radically and responsibly transformed, without seriously weakening the objective standing originally accorded their validity. That is surely an important gain.

But if my argument stands, if any one moral vision of the sort I've sketched is attractive or viable at all, there must be many different, even conflicting, visions *that are as "good" as any other, on theoretical grounds* (second-order and constructivist), and certainly "better" than any of the "best" moral visions. (The "best" could never demonstrate the legitimacy of their own cognitive or rational principles.) Yet, in saying all this, in suggesting the advantages of relativism, I am emphatically *not* saying that I construe relativism to hold that "anything goes" or that it is impossible to show that one judgment or commitment is better than another. (I shall take up the question later.) In a way, my demonstration is meant to explain the good sense and force of Socrates' intuition in the elenctic dialogues (including the first two books of the *Republic*) and the important joke in the *Statesman* about the second-best state: that is, to explain the sense in which we *can* reason objectively about moral matters without ever calling on the prescriptive resources of a faculty of pure reason or a cognitive competence to discern in nature the true norms by which we should live (invented whole cloth for the purpose).

This is exactly what I do believe to be true about moral/political matters. But if the argument holds, it would show, hands down, that Western moral philosophy has a hopelessly inflated view of what it can achieve. It cannot, for instance, legitimate any account of what is normatively necessary or essential to the moral life, or binding in any strictly exceptionless way, or categorically obligatory or forbidden, or morally objective in any way free of partisan or ideological preference, or morally right or good in a sense so strict that it cannot be made to yield in the direction of a relativistic tolerance for incompatible alternatives.

This means that in the real world—this world more fraught with peril than it has ever been—we cannot take for granted the optimistic hope that reasonably responsible antagonists are bound to converge on what *we* take to be the assured normative lessons of our own reflections. Not on your life! But if that is so, then what it is to *be* reasonable in moral/political matters will have to be defined in a way that almost no one is prepared to admit. Certainly, what it means at least is that speculating about moral matters *rationaliter* is *not* aiming at the recovery of a uniquely valid moral norm. Rather—and at second best—such speculation hopes to achieve no more than a prototype of a reasonable paradigm of normative construction (among alternatives) on the expectation that prudent agents will keep in mind the ineliminability of such diversity and its import on legitimation.

SECOND-BEST MORALITIES

[I]

The gathering assurance that we can indeed arrive at an objective moral vision (possibly many such visions, including incompatible ones), one that admits without hesitation the seamless unity of its normative convictions and *sittlich* practices as well as its having no knowledge of any ultimate Good beyond its habitual routines, must pause somewhere to review its legitimating credentials. Otherwise, it could hardly persuade us that its most heartfelt convictions and commitments are capable of supporting its seeming fluency. Furthermore, there is a perfectly plain sense in which, in all candor, we realize that we have no compelling reason to trust the practices and doctrines and normative intuitions of societies very different from our own. We also realize that the reverse of our reaction to any alien *Geist* is likely to confront our own convictions in a hostile way and that, nevertheless, a society of any complexity cannot rightly function without the habituated morality its members rightly believe they can count on among themselves—without yet knowing how to mount a compelling defense of *their* norms or a refutation of *ours*. Yet, in morality, there is surely always in play something analogous to the ubiquity of bilingualism.

There is also something quite breathtaking about the discovery of a viable contemporary society that has woven into its *ethos* utterly different customs and convictions from our own—and has done so with no more difficulty or self-doubt than we have. One senses, there, in the blink of an eye, the abyss—the deep contingency of all our ways—and, at the same time, the alien possibility that *we* could have lived among *them* as their kin. In recent experience, we owe to the Taliban, especially, the undeniable evidence of repugnant forms of life that could have been our own. We also know, as Nazism made burningly clear, that *any sittlich* order, any *ethos* of the most humdrum or routine sort—Weimar Germany, to mention an interesting case—must be quite capable of morphing into a radical descendant of itself, one that, judged by its own lights *ante*, might have been thought to be utterly evil. Every society senses in itself incipient possibilities that it fears and despises.

This is very close, in fact, to the blander political worry implicit in Socrates' puzzle in the early dialogues, except for the absence (in those dialogues) of our distinctly modern insistence on the challenging diversity of the *Sitten* of different cultures. The theme was certainly not unfamiliar to the Greeks, as Euripides' *Medea* and *The Bacchae* make clear in a shocking way. But the Greeks never seem to have doubted (as we do) the assured superiority of their own moral and cultural visions. Not even Alexander, that marvelous adventurer—more barbarian than Greek, more Greek than the Greeks themselves—ever doubted the validity of the classic norms. On the contrary, Alexander was a visionary (a kind of moral/political engineer, if you like) of a sublimely intractable sort, a soldier who dreamed of uniting the Hellenic and Persian worlds under an improbable transformation of the *polis*. Aristotle seems never to have explicitly examined this idea, though he must have had an inkling that the experiment was in the offing, that the days of the classic *polis* were surely numbered, and thus that the rambling assurances of his own deliberations in ethical and political matters (including the comparative study of the constitutions of different states) were already outmoded at the very moment of his lectures. That is, *if* he knew he could never guarantee the changeless norms on which he would have had to depend—which are mercifully vague in the *Nicomachean* and *Eudemian Ethics*.

There you have what may be the first truly "modern" threat to the fixed moral/political vision of our intellectual ancestors, a change that might have led the most advanced thinkers to wonder whether and how their own *prima facie* norms could possibly be validated in a rapidly changing, somewhat alien world. Not even the Peloponnesian War ever probed so threateningly, as Aristotle's collection of Greek constitutions confirms—or, for that matter, Pericles' oration, or the undertaking of the *Republic* itself, which is something of an answer to the oration. Even without a theory of history in the modern sense, societies cannot fail to glimpse, in the deviance and diversity and seeming arbitrariness of rival cultures, the stigma of their own contingent norms and local loyalties.

The speculation of the *Republic*—perhaps more a statement of a felt need and a response to the cultural flux that surrounds us than a resolution of our underlying worry—gives way to a franker admission, in the *Statesman*, to the effect that we are fated to build our moral world as best we can. For, as the dialogue concedes, we know that we lack the conceptual resources the *Republic* tempts us to believe may be sufficient for inventing a model of an enlightened state—if only such resources were actually accessible! (They are not, and Plato knew it.)

To advance in political matters (as well as in the sciences) without ever knowing the ideal Forms—which are never actually worked out in the *Republic*, except through the eyes of those who admit they "do not know"—is, we may suppose, the Greek equivalent of the Hebrew account of Adam's eating of the fruit of the tree. Adam had no need, in Eden, *to know* how, in the philosopher's sense, to legitimate his beliefs and behavior until he first reflected on the human condition. But Socrates, who makes everyone address the philosophical question at the start of every day, reports that *he* knows he does not "know" at all. Know what, you ask? Well, for one thing, what it would take to validate the world the *Republic* imagines might exist somewhere, perhaps in greater Greece: in effect, the paradigm instance of a would-be ideal rule for the reasoned replacement, under any circumstances, of any ordinary norms or practices of societal life. We are all minor Alexanders in this respect. Something of the sort appears to be a naive part of the public rationale for the American attack on Saddam Hussein's Iraq.

The history of moral and political life is, I suggest, the history of "second-best" societies. Such societies are "better," perhaps, than the "best" such societies (utopias, of course), in the plain sense that we usually offer a legitimating defense only within the terms of our own *ethos*—even if in "ignorance," as when, ignorantly, we insist that there must be a "best" way. (In the other, utopian case, there is no legitimating ground to invoke at all.) In this sense, *everything* humans touch is second-best: science, politics, art. There is no assured disclosure of the changeless truths by which we ought to live and act. I read Plato as struggling, through a good number of his dialogues, with the implication of rejecting the Eleatic models[1] of scientific and moral knowledge (in effect, the progeny of the Parmenidean vision). He realizes, I believe, that we cannot possibly recover those models, but he is not entirely ready to replace them, either.

That is, in fact, the condition under which Plato composes the *Republic*, the *Statesman*, and the *Laws*. It provides the implicit stalking-horse of his mature philosophy. In a sense, therefore, in pursuing what I regard as a successor to the elenctic method of the *Statesman*, I am attempting to respond to Plato's deeper worry by advancing a moral theory that benefits from the more than two thousand years that have brought into view an account of the historicity of human life that was never accessible to the Greeks.

That is also the lesson of the classic phase of early modern philosophy that runs from Descartes to Hegel and goes on, from the beginning of the nineteenth century, to radicalize Hegel's own finding against Hegel himself,[2] against all the forms of pre-Kantian fixity and Kantian relapse down to the beginning of the twenty-first century. The point of grasping this entire progression is the numbingly audacious realization that *we humans have no assured idea of how best to govern ourselves*. At the risk of chaos, however, we must act, and we must draw on whatever conceptual resources we find we have.

Provocatively, in our own time, the rejection of the recuperative lesson has been called "postmodernism"[3]—that is, the flawed conviction that science, politics, and art (and religion and education and the very calling of philosophy) must rest, if they have any validity at all, on something close to the sources of certainty or changeless truth or rational necessity already glimpsed in the ancient world and still pursued in a sanguine way within the pale of the Cartesian and Kantian *ethos* of the modern world, down at least to the fateful turn in Hegel. That turn qualifies our trust in the continuity of Kant and Hegel, the historicizing of the Kantian vision, and the discovery of the fluxive clue that threatens to subvert the entire tradition of philosophy. Postmodernism thus conceived—and, in American philosophy, associated most particularly with the recent career of Richard Rorty—holds that the true model of knowledge in science and morality requires cognitive or rational powers of the sorts just mentioned, in spite of the unhappy truth that such powers cannot possibly be vindicated and that, as a consequence, the cognitive pretensions of Western philosophy, of science and morality, are now at an end.

If the argument I am tendering succeeds, then postmodernism in Rorty's sense would be little more than an extravagance. Otherwise, postmodernism may be the keeper of that most modern of philosophical conjectures, namely, that human thought, understanding, knowledge, and intelligent and responsible commitment are inherently historicized, incapable of any sort of privilege deemed apt for collecting necessary, universal, objectivist, changeless truths or dictates of reason read as the *sine qua non* of scientific and moral validity.

You may see in this the radical challenge 9/11 poses in a sense opposed to the postmodernist verdict Rorty has advanced. It catches up the Hegelian (and post-Hegelian) lesson of historicity and constructivism in the direction of opposed, even incommensurable, modes of *sittlich* life. Treat that as an inescapable theme of the globalizing forces that now draw us in their wake. Rorty, I remind you, after dismissing all the classic presumptions of pre-Kantian and Kantian cognitive assurance, turns on his own doctrine and urges, in effect, (i) that we abandon altogether every second-best inquiry *if* (as we must) we abandon the prospect of ever invoking the "best," that is, cognitively privileged resources, or (ii) that we construe our loyalty to local practices of science and morality (in effect, our adherence to our own *sittlich* world—what Rorty calls "ethnocentric solidarity") as itself the only prospect that can be defended. The first option amounts to a kind of skepticism. The second may be a kind of second-best policy itself. The first is trumped by composing a "better" alternative that does not rely on the privileged fixities Rorty rightly condemns; the second is hardly an option at all. What, for instance, would Rorty's reading be of the import of 9/11 with respect to the normative standing of ethnocentric solidarity? All of the leading philosophers Rorty considers his immediate mentors—W. V. Quine, Wilfrid Sellars, Donald Davidson, Dewey, Heidegger, Ludwig Wittgenstein—had already embraced the constraint against privilege without any sense of philosophical disadvantage. In effect, they have all abstracted the robust possibilities of "postmodernism" without the slack theme Rorty favors.

The lesson to draw is hardly more than the codification of an elementary intuition: societies are human aggregates that have somehow fashioned *sittlich* (or collective) habits of thought and action congenial to themselves and to which they are themselves loyal. That is the *sine qua non* of practical life and judgment, a first constraint (but no more than a first) on the validity of any would-be reform that we expect is viable without being arbitrary. Famously, Nietzsche transforms this small truth into a large banner that honors the sheer drive of subterranean life itself—a vein of Darwinian thought that captures the profound contingency of every *ethos*. You may see in this the liberating power of what, in the post-Hegelian world, becomes postmodernism. But if it is, it is the very opposite of Rorty's doctrine. The nerve of responsible theories of moral judgment and commitment lies between these two extremes, but neither Rorty nor Nietzsche favors the near banality of what is minimally needed. Every humane moral vision is dialectically poised against its rivals. Each admits and accepts without privilege an uncertain union in which the conditions of species survival and the devices of culturally informed intelligence are held in a perilous balance. Moral philosophy is profoundly comparative within the terms of its changing history. We cannot dismiss or go beyond the validity of all our visions. That would be a form of suicide, the denial of the culturally shaped conative impulse that affirms, effectively, that "life has meaning"—or a constructed meaning potent enough to keep us from losing heart as a viable people.

We cannot validate every viable form of life that humans have ever favored, though Dewey seems to have been tempted in his generous optimism by such a possibility—perhaps by a pragmatist recovery of something akin to Nietzsche's Darwinian dictum.[4] In any case, the salient visions of actual history tend to include doctrines that are incompatible with one another, and the defense of any one against the others, or against significantly many others, subverts its own attempt to fix its own rightful standing. The very idea of moral validity presupposes the play of a *sittlich* and second-order opposition. We are drawn to view our moral and political opponents as routinizing something akin to the impulse to live that Nietzsche celebrates. But in doing that, we go beyond Nietzsche's marvelously crazy preference for the impulse over the routine. Morality has its self-herding aspect, which Nietzsche and the Plato of the *Statesman* read in opposing ways. Plato is surely closer to good sense. Still, if you take the lesson seriously, then you can hardly fail to consider that 9/11 fits both visions in just the way I have taken as my opening intuition.

Being practical rather than theoretical, moral comparison arises only in the context of some entrenched sense of what makes life routinely meaningful. There, we cannot fail to be struck by the elementary fact that one or another human society has found some version of nearly every conceivable condition of life we find repugnant to be not only tolerable but actually exalted. Recall the sacrificial practices of the Incas and the Aztecs, the headhunters of the South Pacific, and the cannibals of the Amazon. Then remember the murderous extremes of the most pious zealots among the Jews, the Christians, the Muslims, the Hindus, the Buddhists (if the Khmer Rouge may be originally so counted)—just about every grand doctrine you've ever encountered.

Put this way, there is no alternative to a poor choice between paradox and arbitrariness, except by falling back to the culturally entrenched but hardly invented *Sitten* of our home society—*whatever they may be!* (That is, *if* we agree to forgo the pretensions of cognitive or rational or revelatory privilege.)

Perhaps you already see that if persons are second-natured artifactual *agents* distinguished by their culturally internalized powers, then the same socially constructed conditions that generate selves generate the diversity of the norms by which such agents are first formed, live out their lives as apt selves, and find such lives meaningful. In other words, the explanation of the "meaning of life" and the explanation of the "nature" of selves and the *prima facie* validity of their *sittlich* norms are really one and the same. This is because (i) there is no ulterior legitimation of the *sittlich qua sittlich* that is not itself formed, in some measure, by the same forces; (ii) the cultural world and what it makes possible in its "second-natured" and "second-naturing" way is emergent without end, *sui generis*, irreducible to the merely physical or biological, not dualistic for that reason, real only in socially constructed milieux, and therefore inexplicable, except reflexively, in one or another culturally habituated idiom; and (iii) any effort, *rationaliter*, to validate, confirm, legitimate, or demonstrate, as "true" or "right," the *prima facie* norms by which we live in the *sittlich* way (or by any reform, extension, modification, abandonment, or restriction of such norms) cannot be more than a constructed rationale advanced by selves who are themselves similarly constituted *ante*. Otherwise, we would be driven to something like the utopian vision of the *Republic* or Rortyan despair or "Whiggish" solidarity or the Nietzschean sort of madness.

If we agree that selves are partisans, agents committed *prima facie* to the norms and values of their home society or to whatever modification they favor in accord with their *prudentiae*—or, indeed, by way of any departure from their *Sitten* by cognitive or "rational" privilege or revelation—then every would-be *legitimation* of their norms counts for no more than an *ideology*, that is, an effectively enabling, second-order, normative construction of practical life adopted as rightly governing the moral/political interests of the members of the society affected, yet (withal) incapable of being objectively validated on grounds independent of those same *Sitten*. An ideology, therefore, is, let us say, either a first-order rationale of the *prima facie* force of our *sittlich* values or a constructed second-order attempt to legitimate "objective" changes in those *Sitten* in ways that would permit such changes to become as entrenched as the initial practices they modified or displaced. Nietzsche makes the same point, perversely, in order to burst any pretense at a revealed or exclusively correct moral vision. His is, in a way, the most apt voice for our age, if we are willing to recover the good sense he casts as shameful.

What is important here is the fact that *if* legitimation cannot be "constructive" or "constructivist" (critical in that reflexive way that distinguishes cultural life), then there remains no sense at all in which there is any legitimation of theoretical or practical claims. That would, of course, be a conceptual scandal. To draw only the negative conclusion would be utterly to confuse (as Rorty does, and as Socrates threatens to do—though ironically) the mere rejection of epistemic privilege and whatever might otherwise be recovered by an elenctic or dialectical or *sittlich* analysis of the constructive and emergent conditions under which selves exist and thrive at all. Wherever our cognitive or rational powers are in play, whether privileged or constructivist, we may say (mimicking Kant) that first-order claims are "blind" without second-order legitimation, that second-order legitimation is "empty" unless applied to first-order claims, and that the distinction between the two is itself a second-order claim.

If you concede the argument, you must concede as well that (i) moral or moral/political disputes are disputes among ideologues; (ii) they cannot claim any independent cognitive standing through any reliable facultative powers; hence, (iii) any *objectivity* accorded the resolution of moral matters is itself constructivist, plural, and even open to conflicting alternatives—if any resolution be admitted at all; (iv) our options are weighed and pursued *rationaliter*; and (v) they are valid in a determinable sense only, in that they seek a *modus vivendi* rather than a particular propositional truth or comparably right directive.

The rationale for this entire argument cannot be more than a *faute de mieux* bet that begins and ends with the lesson of the *Statesman*. We cannot know the ideal Good of all "there is" or what, finally, *is* good or right for human nature and human existence. *Faute de mieux*, we must decide as best we can. The result is that, in practical matters, objectivity can be no more than dialectically constructed on grounds that claim no independent privilege.

I am gambling, therefore, that no one will be able to propose a firmer norm than one that begins in the *sittlich* way, *in medias res*. There are no norms or normative questions or normative attributes apart from second-natured human concerns. But *there*, in whatever sense we admit selves to be real entities, moral/political questions do *have* realist standing. That is the underlying theme of Nietzsche's anti-Hegelian way of ridiculing conventional morality. There is no morality but conventional morality—which Nietzsche certainly knew. ("Conventional morality," of course, is not "morality by convention.") But then, also, there is no way of validating any morality, or the reform of any existing morality, that is not itself subject to the same self-congratulatory function. What I seek here are second-best proposals about what to regard as yielding reasonably objective judgments and commitments in the face of moral and moral/political disputes, disputes for which 9/11 begins to serve as a new paradigm.

This, then, resolves the paradox of the elenctic dialogues. There is no legitimative answer that does not begin and end with our entrenched practices— and hence does not begin and end with our partisan engagements. The objectivity of moral/political matters is an issue among ideologues. In this uncomplicated sense, there *is* no original question of what life "means," normatively: it "means" whatever accords with the fluency of actual *sittlich* practices!⁵ In the same sense, there is no original question of how the norms of human life arise or are legitimated. Our home practices provide the original setting in which validity and legitimation *first* make sense—because, of course, they provide the conditions in which we ourselves are first formed *as* selves, are made capable of raising the moral question in the first place. Any other resolution yields mere dogma or an interminable regress or the sham of escaping both—or, frankly, utter despair and a sense of meaninglessness. But if you bring the lesson to bear on the horror of 9/11, you see at once the permanently nagging truth that societies in conflict with one another are perfectly aware of the arbitrariness each will discern in the other's norms and may begin to suspect in their own.

[II]

All this seems sensible enough until we acknowledge the radical postulates on which the argument depends. To admit them threatens the objectivism or rationalism of the entire tradition of Western moral philosophy. Those postulates include the following, at least: (i) that, relative to resolving a moral impasse, we can indeed define and defend a *modus vivendi* that accords with what, in second-order terms, will be objectively good or right, and (ii) that we can construct, *rationaliter*, a moral vision based on resources consistent with (i) that can match the appeal of any "best" alternative it might compete with, while being, at the same time, epistemically less arbitrary, conceptually more economical, and methodologically more scrupulous in legitimative terms.

In short, we can arrive at an *objective* morality, but we can do so only according to the kind of rigor the inquiry can support. Any such inquiry will proceed deliberately, with due patience, *rationaliter*, *liberaliter*, in a way committed to guarding our *prudentiae*, venturing changes in accord (as nearly as possible) with our *sittlich* values. Responsible moral dispute is, as I see matters, inherently conserving rather than merely conservative. Temperament may rebel, therefore. Impatience here tends to view human nature as more malleable than it may actually be: it tends to minimize the gap between the utopian and what is possible, in practical terms, here and now. For the same reason, a "responsible" impatience is drawn to privileged principles and hence to one or another form of self-deception. Any "objective" strategy I call "second-best," meaning by that that it is usually "better," argumentatively, than any would-be "best" morality. Of course, the would-be comparison can never be carried out, except virtually (as in the *Republic* or in Khomeini's Iran), for there are no legitimating grounds for confirming the "best" morality! We may, therefore, add another postulate to those just offered, viz., (iii) that if there is any one defensible second-best morality, there are bound to be many, possibly incompatible or incommensurable with one another from time to time — and certainly incompatible with our own. Why not?

The argument depends on acknowledging the following points. Admitting the usual enculturing transformations by which the members of *Homo sapiens* issue as an aggregate of second-natured selves, we ourselves discern the *Sitten* by which we judge ourselves to have been first formed. Moreover, given our animal natures, without pretending to discern any intrinsic *telos* there or any normative criterion governing the proper "functioning" of selves, we cannot (in fashioning a second-best morality) ignore the saliency of our *prudentiae* and *providentiae*. Acting *rationaliter* with respect to these, then, we find that we can modify, attenuate, restrict, or purge any *sittlich* norms that violate or exceed the limits of our cognitive and rational powers—for example, those that are open to validation only in a life hereafter or, if confined within nature, only by reducing moral norms to evolutionary functions or something of the sort. The same constraints, you realize, defeat the authority of revelation and the fashion of reductionism.

The history of moral philosophy is dominated by a succession of normative theories that privilege the independent validity of one or another particular source or criterion or principle of what is right or good. I reject all such resources unconditionally as impossible to defend. The reason rests with the convergent force of a whole series of considerations, *none* of which discounts the possibility of "arriving" at valid moral norms. On the contrary, there are a great many moral norms that are entirely reasonable. Too many, of course; no one can possibly live by all of them at once. Yet none is demonstrably independent of our first-order practices. (There is no moral analogue, say, to Marcus Aurelius's canny piety.)

Qua sittlich, the standing of our *prima facie* norms *cannot*, as such, claim second-order validity. For to be able to legitimate what is normative in the limited sense I have been calling "first-order" would imply that moral norms, admittedly irreducible in physical terms (and thus never rightly described as paraphrases of what obtains in physical or biological nature), would signify some sort of normative grounds apart from, or prior to, whatever are conceded to be the *sui generis* complexities of the cultural world. That is the route of the *Republic*.

Seen in this way, the answer to the question of the objective standing of moral (or moral/political) norms depends on the outcome of the analysis of what *is* culturally real. By "cultural realism," I mean no more than that cultural phenomena — including selves and what selves "utter" (that is, do, produce, make, create) — *are* real, as real as any physical or biological phenomena, emergent in their *sui generis* mode from the physical and biological world. These phenomena are second-natured, constructed or constituted by second-naturing processes, indissolubly embodied or incarnate in the physical and biological, irreducible nevertheless,[6] and hybrid, uniting, by emergence, the physical and what distinguishes the cultural as such: the linguistic, the semiotic, the symbolic, the significative, the expressive, the representational, the historical, the institutional, the rule-like, the agental, *and the normative*, all of which I name, by a term of art, the *Intentional*. That is the sense in which norms, whether first- or second-order, arise in and only in Intentional contexts — the sense in which I proceed entirely *faute de mieux*.

If all this holds, then, because moral objectivity is of interest primarily in the sense in which norms can be validated (or legitimated) *in second-order terms*, and because the normative cannot be independent of the constructed world of human culture, the legitimation of moral norms as objectively valid (rather than merely reported in the anthropologist's way as the first-order "data" of our cultural life) *cannot fail to be a cultural construct itself.* The point of this insistence is to afford a sense in which the objectivity of our moral norms does not depend on any circular or question-begging maneuver. Moral norms (beyond what is "given" *prima facie*) cannot fail to be constructed from our *sittlich* roots.

But if so, we see at once: (i) that morality and its legitimation are confined to second-best conjectures; (ii) that (i) is not itself a moral finding of any sort; (iii) that nearly the whole of Western moral philosophy is, as a result, definitely wrongheaded; (iv) that the objectivity of moral norms — *a fortiori*, the objectivity of moral judgments and commitments — cannot be exclusively restricted to the terms of a bivalent logic; and (v) that there can be no disjunction between the practical and the theoretical or between the ethical and the metaphysical, as respectively favored, for instance, by Kant and by Emmanuel Levinas.[7] Moral matters arise because (and only because) of the second-natured nature of human agents. Moral matters, then, can be resolved only in accord with the Intentional features of the cultural world.

You may flinch a little at my use of the term "metaphysical." But I mean no more than that moral matters are rightly said to have realist standing (in a sense confined to "cultural realism") and may therefore be judged to be valid and objective in a sense that admits the constructivist standing of the entire cultural world. There may be other conceptual devices by which to ensure these last two theorems, but these theorems *are*, finally, decisive. (That is the point of contrasting the strange dualisms advanced by Kant and Levinas.)

A strategic lesson beckons—and a potential dilemma looms. *If* moral objectivity is grounded in the *sittlich*, and if the *sittlich* is contingent and historically diverse (as it obviously is), then to admit that we cannot exceed the resources of a second-best morality is to question the moral (or practical or theoretical) relevance of any would-be paradigm that cannot be fitted to our *sittlich* history! What, for instance, is the *moral* relevance of the table of virtues in Aristotle's *Nicomachean Ethics* or the table of exemplary obligations in Kant's *Metaphysics of Morals?* If Aristotle's *Ethics* draws its virtues from essential human nature, it will have yielded to epistemic and ontological (or metaphysical) privilege; if, in the context of practical life, it draws its virtues, rather, from the actual *Sitten* of the Greek *polis*, then the account it offers will have been already outmoded by the time of Alexander's campaigns. In our own time, Alasdair MacIntyre attempts, heroically, to apply Aristotle (along Thomistic lines) in the essentialist way. Martha Nussbaum counters in the way of favoring the salient contingencies of *sittlich* history (as in reading Henry James as matching the *Ethics* by way of James's novelistic studies of the *ethos* of early-twentieth-century American society abroad). So the dilemma is actually played out in contemporary attempts to recover the point of Aristotle's great contribution. *But what was it?*

Both MacIntyre and Nussbaum fail us at the philosophically critical point, though they do not fail in their own imagined milieux.[8] They nowhere explain how they draw from the historical contingencies of "human nature" the normative force of their own examples (beyond the merely *prima facie*). Kant himself never quite explains whether the "heteronomous" features of the Pietist values he draws on have any universalistic force as a result of testing their congruity with the formalism of the Categorical Imperative. If they have such force, then Kant has omitted the decisive argument; if they do not, then his rationalism is entirely vulnerable to Hegel's well-known *reductio*.[9]

For his part, Aristotle never explains, when he sketches the specifically moral or moral/political virtues he takes notice of (apart from his idiosyncratic account of would-be intellectual virtues), whether, in effect, he intends his theory to have objective validity only *prima facie* (which, of course, he does not) or in terms of second-order legitimation, the details of which are unmanageably uncertain. If he means the first, then, surely, he has not yet launched his philosophical inquiry. If he means the second, then, equally surely, we are at a loss to understand exactly how he means to proceed.

It is extraordinary to think that the two greatest systematic philosophers of

SECOND-BEST MORALITIES   39

the Western world (and I concede they are the greatest in influence) should have been so lax in addressing the puzzles of constructing an objective morality. On the argument being advanced, the Categorical Imperative has nothing, finally, to do with the actual validity of the proposed values it means to test, and Aristotle's constitutions and related data have nothing to do with the second-order validation of how the Greeks *and we* should live!

I do see how easily Kant's and Aristotle's moral specimens *could* be caught up in a second-best morality, but I have no doubt that they would condemn any such theory. Still, I have never seen a convincing explication of the actual philosophical arguments by which their own would-be second-order proposals might be effectively legitimated. The argument Kant needs—not yet supplied in the *Foundations of the Metaphysics of Morals*—would require containing in one account the privileged tests of transcendental reason *and* the normative validity of at least some part of heteronomous human nature. But, as matters stand in Kant's text, the two elements are irreconcilable. Aristotle's argument, in turn, if it yields any second-order validity at all, must rest on an essentialist alternative to any merely *sittlich* account of the virtues. If you allow the complaint, you must concede the need for a radically new defense of Aristotle's doctrine.

Kant's transcendentalism is entirely vacuous, as Rawls's and Habermas's failed supplements confirm; Aristotle's alternative is demonstrably insufficient to bridge the gap between first- and second-order validity, as MacIntyre's and Nussbaum's defective explications similarly attest. There is no way to validate a second-best morality except by some straightforward treatment of our *sittlich* norms. But what that maneuver could possibly be, neither Kant nor Aristotle explains convincingly. Bear in mind that you cannot simply condemn 9/11 if you cannot validate the second-order strategies of Aristotle and Kant— or the strategies of any more up-to-date rationale you may happen to prefer. That is also the Achilles' heel of the American response to 9/11.

Hegel saw the point, of course, under the conditions of history. But, as in *The Philosophy of Right*, if he may be said to have advanced a pertinent solution, he is open to the charge of having confused or deliberately conflated the larger moral scope he assigns actual political states—in contrast to the assigned scope of individual, familial, market, and civil interests—*and* the specifically legitimative function of his own concocted mythical state. Hegel exposes the admittedly partial, even provisional, horizon of this or that historical appraisal of the human condition; then, suddenly, he confronts us with an inclusive, allegedly objective, holistic vision of that same condition viewed from the vantage of "absolute *Geist*" (or from the vantage of approximating to the vanishing limit of absolute *Geist*). I don't deny the brilliance and plausibility of Hegel's partisan rationale. But how is such closure possible on Hegel's own assumptions? How can we correctly grasp the exclusive normative thread (the *Geist* or *geistlich* rationale) of our contingent *Sitten?* Or, if we cannot achieve closure, how can we claim to approach closure? It's precisely at this point that we realize that Hegel is either adopting the Kantian conception in some "regulative" way or else exposing its own impossibility by rhetorical approximations that yield one attractive narrative or another — which, Hegel must realize, will be superseded, contested, or denied in accord with the vagaries of historical (or Intentional) interpretation.

We cannot be certain, in Hegel's case, whether he advances his account as an objectivist form of second-order legitimation or as an exemplar of the improvisational appeal of a second-best legitimative strategy. I take him to favor the second; the first is the "right-wing" reading that speaks quite literally of God's march through world history. The choice depends on how we construe Hegel's own transcendental longings. But, read as a second-best strategy, it is very good indeed — *and* a worthy successor to the "method" of the Socratic elenchus, now informed by a modern grasp of human culture.

Hegel never surpasses the *sittlich* in the anthropologist's sense. Rather, he infuses a deeper second-order significance into the *sittlich* itself, which greatly complicates our account of what he's up to. He is indeed aware that "ought" cannot be disjoined from the "is" of actual historical life, but he fudges the adequacy of drawing out of that connection a deeper, *second-order*, still (allegedly) *sittlich* validity of how our norms evolve. Here, Hegel exposes the deepest sense in which Kant's moral vision fails — but *he* "succeeds," because he implicitly exposes a similar fault in himself. (Otherwise, he deliberately dramatizes every such fault by constructing rhetorically attractive specimens that betray their transcendental inadequacy. He can, of course, do no better.) But he equivocates on the first- and second-order meaning of the *sittlich*.

[III]
There's no gainsaying moral philosophers' admiration of Aristotle's and Kant's paradigmatic texts. I admire them as well. But I defy you to say precisely what it was they accomplished! You may, of course, counter, "What would you replace their visions with?" (The one had featured "the good" and "the virtuous," and the other, the "right" and the "obligatory." What must be added?)

Kant, I would say, is stronger than Aristotle in at least one regard: he never actually states what *is* substantively right or obligatory in the way of how we should act in specific practical circumstances. He does not attempt to demonstrate *any determinate* (categorical) *obligation* as objectively binding in these or those circumstances. He insists only that if we are to act morally, *we must act as "rational agents."* (We *may* act, as well, in ways that are morally attractive for other reasons—as with an eye to happiness.) We do so, he thinks, only if we can construct a pertinent maxim for our actions that at least meets the severe constraints of the Categorical Imperative. In this way, Kant preserves the rational freedom of morally autonomous agents. He does not speak of our being obliged to act, here and now, in this or that determinate way—as, say, in the way of the good Samaritan. We are not even obliged to tell the truth. We may remain silent rather than speak, but *if* we speak, we cannot justify lying. Also, we cannot preclude the possibility that if someone offers a maxim for acting one way in given circumstances, another may offer a different maxim—one that conflicts with the first—without violating the Categorical Imperative. (That was the point of Hegel's subversive example regarding the management of property.)

Furthermore, apart from formal consistency ("similar things must be judged similarly in similar circumstances"), Kant never demonstrated (and could not demonstrate, except as an internal requirement of his own conceptual system) that we must, as moral agents, consult that to which every "rational" being would agree. For one thing, no one is actually capable of considering what would accord with the rational interests of *every* actual human being (or every "rational being"!). For another, it cannot be shown that every human or rational being actually *has* a pertinent interest in every (or any particular) concrete moral issue. For a third, the very idea of what is "rational" is itself an artifact of contingent cultural history. And, for a fourth, Kant never quite explains (beyond considerations of consistency) just why this or that would-be commitment must be appraised in universalistic terms. For example, if I act to benefit my own son exclusively, does that automatically require a utilitarian finding of what is "good for all" (admitting, of course, that Kant is not a utilitarian)? Or does it require that its maxim should be "rationally" acceptable to all who are competent to judge? Suppose I offer the following defense: "I favor my son because he is my son and everyone should do the same." (The formula is sufficiently general that it would allow both a formal and a consequential reading.) Might that be sufficient? Well, if it is, then it surely trivializes Kant's own thesis by making it much too easy to satisfy; if it is not, it is hard to see how else to delimit responsible replies so that the easy answers can be harmlessly set aside.

I'm afraid Kant's formalism cannot be made convincing, because every interpretation of a particular case can elude Kant's intended strictures (as Hegel has shown) and, what is more important, because Kant's moral subject is not really a human subject at all but a "Transcendental Ego" (pure rationality, say) invited to judge what are sketched as human problems seen from that ego's point of view. Universalism—beyond coherence and consistency—is little more than a formula for elevating local ideologies to privileged standing. There's the fatal weakness in Kant's moral theory and in the theories of the lesser Kantians (Rawls and Habermas, for instance).

What we do, in morally pertinent respects, we do "here and now," confronting what is already admitted to have *sittlich* standing. But it seems that in Kant's view, we are never actually obliged *to act* in any given circumstances. That is, we are never "categorically obliged" to act: we are only obliged to act rationally *if* we choose to act! We are never (as I've already remarked) obliged to act as a good Samaritan, as current French law apparently requires. In that sense, neither Rawls nor Habermas is a true Kantian, for in their firmest statements, both formulate what appear to be substantive categorical obligations or universalized constraints in given circumstances. Rawls retreats[10] in *Political Liberalism*; Habermas, in his "Discourse Ethics," implicitly admits the utopian nature of universalism in the press of the here and now.

It seems that Kant invented—brilliantly, no doubt—an entirely new sort of obligation (a "categorical" obligation) capable of enlisting the entrenched severities of Lutheran *Sitten*, which successfully infected the *ethos* of the entire Western world. The formal side of Kant's moral methodology is woefully inadequate, and the substantive side, if it were filled out in the clever way that Habermas or Rawls attempts, would surely prove more partisan and ad hoc than Kant would ever have allowed. In fact, Rawls has now reinterpreted his own notion of "justice as fairness" as a partisan ideology rather than a determinate rational principle, though his final account still slips between the two notions. Habermas wavers between a purely formal version of universality and allegedly substantive deductions drawn from the "categorical" formula when applied in contingent contexts. Rawls's account, then, abandons its Kantian pretensions, and Habermas "completes" the moral "unity" Kant had always aspired to—but only formulaically.

There is nothing in Aristotle to compare with Kant's precision. Yet, as we have seen, Kant's strength is also his principal weakness. By parity of reasoning, we may conjecture, therefore, that Aristotle's weakness is probably also his principal strength—which, of course, is true. No candidate specimen of a "virtuous act," in Aristotle's sense, must submit to the test of the "mean" with respect to any determinate system of virtues. Indeed, the "mean between the extremes" is never more than an informal and purely rhetorical way of featuring the favored "moderation" of any would-be Aristotelian virtue. It cannot confirm the right inclusion or exclusion of any candidate virtue in any coherent system of virtues, and every would-be such system must reflect our *prima facie Sitten* or an ideology imposed on them.

What, for instance, is the "moderate virtue" of a bin Laden "terrorist"? Can we actually demonstrate that so-called terrorism cannot but be an unacceptable "extreme" with respect to the true virtues? To confirm such a finding would require higher-order virtues or higher principles beyond the virtues themselves. Here, Aristotle is noticeably and necessarily vague. "Virtue," as we see in David Hume and John Locke and even Hobbes, is no more than an unguarded formulation of our *sittlich* values, which are hardly self-validating. Marx was particularly clear about this matter, as in his refusal (in his best moments) to condemn the values of bourgeois life. Bourgeois morality (or rationality), he thought, was essentially different from, and even opposed to, proletarian virtues.[11] Moreover, Marx believed that historical objectivity could never justify, as such, conflating class opposition with the pretensions of neutral or universalistic moral judgment. (He obviously believed, though, that proletarian morality finally did speak for the whole of humanity.)

You see the problem of choosing between, or reconciling, essentialist and historicized considerations. Aristotle never resolves the problem, though he is aware of it in his own terms. I believe that *it cannot be resolved*—or it cannot be resolved by invoking the "essential" human virtues. There is nothing in the sheer generality of a *sittlich* virtue that supports *its* second-order validity. Anthropologists are very fond of drawing up alternative lists of "universal virtues" that are reasonably common to most (or even "all") societies— provided, of course, we read them as instantiations of the partisan virtues we ourselves favor. Still, in matters regarding plural systems of virtue, there remains an insurmountable difficulty: there *are* no virtues, except as nominalized abstractions drawn from the collective life of specific societies. The coherence of any set of virtues is nothing but the functional viability of an actual society read in terms of its *sittlich* interests. But that is a matter of *prima facie* description—the anthropologist's way of reporting the virtues of different societies. An Aristotelian account would require a second-order, specifically universalized argument. But what could it be, if it were not essentialist?

Aristotle is praised for invoking the virtues or, as in his *Politics*, for criticizing practices that fail to do justice to the true virtues. But in the *Nicomachean Ethics*, he does not provide (as one might suppose he would) a compelling account of how to determine the validity of the virtues he actually advances, or, indeed, their proper mode of application to diverse (non-Greek) histories apart from his own paradigm. In fact, if you compare the idealized norm of Aristotle's *Poetics* with the norm of his *Ethics,* you cannot fail to see that another commentator might easily have preferred Euripidean to Sophoclean tragedy and, say, Spartan or Ephesian politics to the Athenian *polis.* Aristotle clearly constructs a rationale for a personal preference, but he nowhere shows that his own preference (with regard to tragedy or politics) is distinctly favored, in comparative or criterial terms, by any objective essentialism we may attribute to him.

MacIntyre offers a clever suggestion, it's true, though it is also seriously flawed. Every functional social practice, he explains, may be assigned its intrinsic ("proper," internal) virtue by some reasonably direct first-order inspection of our actual practices. Any pertinent would-be practice that lacks an assignable (congruent) virtue is, MacIntyre claims, objectively disordered. Very neat. But if you admit the multifunctional institutions of modern societies—the market, the family, the state, for instance—you soon realize that it is just *there* that the deepest second-order disputes are bound to arise. We are hardly confident about what "the" function of the family or the state really is (*pace* Hegel). MacIntyre presses his own point precisely in order to condemn modern society! But why should we follow him in this? And why should we conflate our first- and second-order descriptions? The elenctic Socrates would surely have demurred.

MacIntyre's picture of a "practice" is too pat to be convincing. The best *we* can hope for—whether in Aristotle's time or Alexander's or Aquinas's or our own—is no more than this: that whatever first-order virtues we impute to the *sittlich* practices of any age can, *if we choose,* be said, trivially, to be viably supported by those same practices. But their second-order validity cannot rightly be deduced from their mere *prima facie* fit. For example, MacIntyre's account cannot make plausible sense of systematic attempts like those of present-day Iran to reconcile an up-to-date market economy with Islamic *Sitten* recovered in Khomeini's revolution (however adjusted *rationaliter* to the pressures of real-world forces). There cannot be a unique or exclusive fit between virtues and practices in any evolving history or across different societies, whether, say, in Aristotle's time, verging on Alexander's campaigns; in Hume's time, just prior to the American and French Revolutions; or in Henry James's time, ignorant of the changes leading to World War I.

In fact, once historical diversity and viability relative to the Intentional life of particular societies are introduced, the very idea of any underlying, single, unique, transcultural, universal, or essential scheme of virtues will be seen as deeply problematic, if for no other reason than that its validity will depend on interpretations tendentiously imposed on the practices of other societies (as in Nussbaum's Aristotelian accounts) or on mere *obiter dicta* (as in MacIntyre's condemnation of modern market societies).

To appreciate the first complication, you have only to ponder Dewey's famous pronouncement: "The worse or evil is a rejected good." And to appreciate the second, you have only to reflect on the actual crazy-quilt formation of modern societies and modern states, as reported, for instance, in Michael Oakeshott's *On Human Conduct*.[12] As Oakeshott painstakingly explains, there are no reliable rational functions that follow closely the historical careers of any of the important structural parts of complex European states moving from medieval sources to early modern times. The accounts we have are, on the whole, ingenious piecemeal rationalizations for connecting all sorts of contingent changes. This bears directly on the credibility of Hegel's dialectical rationales, of course, as well as on the misguided "Darwinian" functionalism that ignores the difference between species and communities and between biological and cultural "objectives." Needless to say, it also disallows the arguments of MacIntyre and Nussbaum. It is worth remarking that, in their *sittlich* setting, virtues are functionally distinguished in a holistic way, that is, as the abstracted subfunctions of a viable societal practice. But if so, then the very idea of universal virtues (Nussbaum's theme) cannot fail to be self-serving. I have no doubt that such considerations will drive us in the direction of moral relativism—but that is not my primary purpose, though it *is* a consequence.

The objectivity of moral matters is hardly jeopardized by the data of moral relativity. After all, every society has its own sense of accurate and admissible description, interpretation, explanation, and appreciation close to one or another reflexive (or Intentionally apt) reading of its own *ethos*. That fact alone draws attention to the importance of the *sittlich*, though it hardly ensures a uniquely correct characterization of *any* episodes within its usual ken— episodes important enough to oblige a society's members to ask themselves what is right or wrong about what they collect, even in *prima facie* terms, as moral. That, again, is part of the meaning of 9/11.

Sophocles' *Antigone* makes this perfectly clear. One and the same act may be spontaneously construed—validly, in *sittlich* terms—in opposed ways. Why not? Such opposed interpretations will be confirmed, objectively, *prima facie*. More instructively, they may also, as Sophocles apparently believes, be found to be valid in second-order terms, in spite of being incompatible with one another in particular circumstances.

Every complex society must acknowledge opposed but well-entrenched interpretations and appraisals of whatever has taken place in its own world. The partisans of the abortion dispute, for instance, are almost always nonplussed by the suggestion that their opponents *may* be deemed to have made a plausible and responsible first pass at a disjunctive judgment favoring their own conviction *and* that, given reasonably amended versions of each position (both of which strain for exclusive validity), each may still prove as valid as the other, though still opposed. I know of no compelling reason why this should be impossible—or less plausible than its denial. We would only need to admit that moral/political judgment is not necessarily (cannot always be and is often not at all) bivalent, because, of course, objectivity of the second-order sort *is* a constructive matter, must be favorably traced to its *sittlich* sources, and can always favor forms of cultural relativity that may prove hospitable to relativism itself. Every modern society, acknowledging the *sittlich* sources of its normative commitments, is already poised to collect every strong objection to such commitments drawn from its own sources *or* those of other societies. Such candor cannot fail to affect our reading of the events of 9/11.

You begin to see, therefore, how the advocacy of a second-best morality is strongly inclined to favor some form of relativism. It could hardly be otherwise, once we grant the facts of cultural relativity, the absence of any assured privilege regarding objective moral norms, the ineluctability of construing objective norms in constructivist terms, the historicity of human life, and the defensibility of revising our *sittlich* norms *rationaliter*. Under real-world circumstances, bivalence pretty well requires some form of moral privilege! In fact, in our increasingly globalized world, there can be no principled difference between intra-societal and inter-societal considerations. (I hasten to add that I shall return to the question of relativism and its relationship to bivalence.)

One last qualification suggests itself as a way of bringing these remarks to a close and hinting at a further issue of a very different sort. It is a notorious fact that in the description and interpretation of acts open to moral/political appraisal—think, for instance, of the Indian/Pakistani skirmishes in Kashmir, or Microsoft's efforts to expand its control of the markets it must use, or Arab/Israeli negotiations over the cessation of violence and terrorism—there is no neutral rule for introducing normatively freighted descriptions or interpretations of given events that opposing parties can always (or usually) be expected to share *and* apply uncontroversially. (That, I may say, is a complication Habermas never considers. It separates him at once from consistent pragmatists.)

I view this lack of descriptive closure as a natural consequence of the initial inapplicability of any model of merely legal sanctions and legal authority to specifically moral and political disputes. It follows that moral/political disputes *are*, ineluctably, the disputes of partisans *and* that predicative uniformity in moral description is, in good part, evidence of some ideological hegemony.

If there is no way to secure an objective vocabulary—a descriptive or interpretive or appraisive vocabulary—on independent grounds, then there is no way to avoid construing normative objectivity in constructivist terms tethered to opposing partisan convictions. But, of course, if moral questions arise only within the historical contingencies of cultural life, then it is simply true that moral disputes are disputes between committed ideologues. A *fortiori*, moral objectivity is the work of dialectically plausible strategies of what would make such disputes more "reasonable." Whatever the answer, we are bound to nothing firmer than second-best moralities. In the present political climate, let it be noted, none of the principal contending parties involved in the most dangerous confrontations of our time has the least inclination to concede the point in principle—not the Americans, not al Qaeda. Moral description is already moral ideology.

THE MORAL AND THE LEGAL

[I]

There is a very telling difference between legal and moral/political disputes. On most accounts, legal proceedings are inquiries duly authorized within a jurisdiction to reach a verdict as to whether a proposed characterization of an act or acts, a charge advanced by plaintiffs admitted to such proceedings, is valid or may be rightly imputed to agents not yet charged. There is nothing in any "merely" moral or political dispute that compares with this kind of formality, although it is of course more than merely possible that moral, political, religious, and related matters will be treated as "legal" proceedings. The banning of books in accord with what was once the Catholic Index, for instance, was a kind of legal proceeding, as was the excommunication of Baruch Spinoza from his Amsterdam congregation. The inquiry as to whether President Bill Clinton's sexual behavior while in office constituted an impeachable offense—apart from his statements before a grand jury—was indeed a legal matter.

Broadly speaking, legal questions concern formal findings of responsibility or liability or guilt with regard to normatively freighted charges drawn up in advance (or findings of sufficient cause for initiating such charges drawn from an authorized table of possible charges already at hand). The sense of the legal rests with the sense in which defendants, when charged and found to have acted as charged, are automatically subject to authorized penalties and punishments matching such charges. By comparison, whatever in moral and related "inquiries" are deemed fair analogues of such charges and penalties are likely to be completely informal and informally applied, improvisational, idiosyncratic, possibly even ad hoc as to "charges," and expressive of personal conviction and public sentiment in matters of disapproval and sanctions. Legal deliberations take the form of seeking to reach (and of reaching) determinate findings, propositions demonstrably true or valid according to an antecedent canon; moral/political reflections are primarily centered on reaching informed and deliberate commitments in the form of actions responsibly undertaken or policies directing such commitments. Both have their *sittlich* sources, but the first judges what is right according to the law *(jus)*, whereas the second weighs alternative actions *rationaliter* in an attempt to realize, as best we can, some pertinent *modus vivendi* by advancing the care and concern of all parties rightly affected *(justitia)*.

It is only when we can speak of a "moral law" (effectively, a revealed law) that the distinction between the moral and the legal can be erased without jeopardizing the rigor of legal proceedings. Normally, the legal rests informally (but not, as a consequence of that, unreasonably) on a consensual sense of a society's *Sitten*. That, of course, is precisely the source of the strength and weakness of legal positivism. At the present time, it is primarily in countries like Iran, where a strongly Islamicized government and constitution are effectively installed, that the law itself can be said to be directly informed by a revealed moral law (as in instituting the so-called *shari'a* courts). At the present time, American foreign policy unquestionably lends credence to the perception, worldwide, that the United States views its own role in global matters as assuredly benign, *a priori*, so that (as in its role in UN peacekeeping efforts in Bosnia, for instance) it ought not be subject at all to UN-sponsored war crimes tribunals. One sees the danger on both sides of the argument, of course. But one also sees the embarrassment of linking the moral (and political) and legal too closely in defining the conceptual space known as international law.

We may surmise just how severe and effective moral and related judgments and sanctions can be by recalling the Ayatollah Khomeini's putting a price on Salman Rushdie's head for having published his *Satanic Verses* — or, for another example, the rather impressive practice of shunning among the Amish. But the principal conceptual difference between legal and moral matters lies with a plain fact. Among the first, the pertinent normative categories are formally specified in advance of any particular charge, and the work of a duly empowered court is directed toward reaching a finding as to whether an actual charge is valid or confirmed; characteristically, among the second, there is (and need be) no formal or prior constraint at all on what to count as a pertinent complaint, no provisionally closed or finite table of possible complaints or charges, no specific procedures for adjudication, and no rule of entailment linking complaints and formal sanctions. Moral complaints are drawn im-⟩ provisationally from our evolving *Sitten*, without the need for antecedent definition. Legal charges normally presuppose a table of antecedently fixed categories.

One may believe, reasonably enough, that the entire system of legal pro-ceedings will be informed by one moral/political ideology or another but that such proceedings are, in fact, normally hemmed in by their own (internal) proprieties. It is difficult to avoid the conclusion, though, that however valid a moral complaint may be, it is itself the very expression of a doctrinal or ide-ological interpretation of actual *sittlich* practices—an expression made pub-lic partly to become known and partly to influence and affect the consensual support of others in shaping our future *Sitten*. Confrontations between a re-vealed "moral law" and a secular system of law tend to be noticeably unsta-ble, even dangerous. The presumption of a revealed moral law is, of course, formally incompatible with the presumption of a second-best morality or, indeed, with its legitimation of an intact legal system sustained *rationaliter*. Nevertheless, a commitment to the latter (a second-best morality and its sys-tem of law) need not—and cannot rightly—conclude that a *modus vivendi* involving the partisans of the former is inherently impossible or unreason-able. In an important sense, a rational morality *intends* to overcome in prac-tice the theoretical opposition between the two sorts of doctrine. This is the very purpose *of* a second-best morality applied within its entire *sittlich* space— the conserving theme, if you like, of global justice, the decisive *agon* of moral evolution.

Viewed dynamically, moral disputes (of whatever complexity or danger) seek, *rationaliter*, a steady level of provisional public tolerance amid all chang-ing saliencies. Legal disputes under the aegis of a second-best morality expect to be able to subsume progressively every emergent novelty bearing on charges and evidence within the processes of a relatively closed system of ad-equate procedures. Our willingness to rely on routine such practices is at its most vulnerable wherever the *Sitten* on which normative appraisal depends are themselves undergoing considerable change or challenge from "revealed" moral sources. The truth is that *Sitten* are inherently fluxive—more fragile, more radically penetrable in our increasingly globalized world than they ever were in a piecemeal colonial world. That is surely part of the meaning of 9/11.

On the canonical view of moral philosophy, merely to characterize moral/political judgments as ideological is to exclude them utterly from any possible objective standing. That is indeed the mate of C. L. Stevenson's conclusion, for instance, cast in his well-known emotive theory of moral judgment.[1] But it is hardly an ineluctable finding. On the contrary, on the argument advanced here, once we grant that moral and political norms arise within the boundaries of the reflexive life of human societies—where selves are emergent artifacts of enculturation—there cannot be any source of moral norms independent of the *Sitten* of one or another contingent *ethos*. Yet that is already enough to secure the objectivity of the moral world. That, at least, is my brief. Stevenson's account of moral judgment is deliberately designed to yield as crude a model as possible in order to satisfy his positivist taste in philosophy. But he's missed two essential factors: pertinent disputes are practical, not theoretical, and partisan commitment is the rule rather than the exception. It's not partisanship that threatens the prospects of moral objectivity; it's the collision between revealed and second-best moral intuitions. For, of course, the two approaches yield incommensurable processes regarding objectivity, even if they happen to agree. Partisan opposition means one thing in second-best terms and quite another in terms of privileged revelation.

Prima facie normative convictions cannot fail to be expressions of *sittlich* values. For that same reason, they and whatever second-order reforms may be advanced *rationaliter* cannot fail to be *ideological:* that is, partisan, contingent, problematic, centered in the here and now, horizoned, historicized, Intentional, prescriptive, potentially hegemonic—not otherwise objectively or independently confirmed. *If* moral/political objectivity cannot be validated on grounds other than what can be elicited from our *sittlich* sources, and *if* we are prepared to invest our energies in determining what kind of second-order rigor is still possible in such circumstances, then, short of outright self-contradiction, there can be no bar against constructing a kind of objectivity in moral matters that is inevitably confined to disputes between ideologically opposed agents. I trust you see in this the charm of a moral philosophy that abandons every prospect of normative privilege but means to draw its sense of objectivity solely from the very play of partisan interests.

In a plain sense, we *know* when a legal charge is valid or not. The courts are authorized and empowered to reach a finding and to decide the matter. The puzzle in moral matters, by contrast, is precisely *to* decide (and to decide how to decide) whether a *prima facie* charge or complaint, open to dispute within our *Sitten*, is demonstrably valid. Legal proceedings are managed as first-order affairs precisely because they tend to be defined procedurally, though they are always open to second-order challenge, piecemeal as well as in the large. Characteristically, moral/political disputes about *prima facie* (first-order) matters at once pose second-order questions about the objective standing of the very *Sitten* on which their resolution depends. Think of America's preemptive war against Iraq, for instance. Was its defense a matter of law or not?

This helps us see why a kind of legal positivism *could* appear (misleadingly) to account for the existence of a viable body of law.[2] It cannot do so, however, because the "explanation" (that is, the validation or legitimation) of actual legal authority must exceed any merely causal account of the *sittlich* processes by which a given practice may actually have been generated. The very existence of legal authority poses the question of its second-order normative validity. Hence, would-be legal processes (which cannot be self-validating) are inherently open to validative challenge. In this sense, there can be no principled difference between the problematic application of "international law"[3] to the contingencies of so-called wars against terrorism and the disputed changes in the very source of legal authority within existing states, as in recent attempts in Nigeria and elsewhere to replace secular law with Koranic law. The very difference between the legal and the moral is more a matter of a stable and honored division of labor than a matter of principle, for the legal is, everywhere, the respected deputy (when it *is* so respected) *of* the moral and the political. If so, then moral positivism makes no sense at all. And if the legal and the moral cannot ultimately be disjoined, then legal positivism makes no sense either. To acknowledge the *sittlich* source of the legal (as well as the moral) is hardly tantamount to positivism. The difference between the causal and the normative is not a matter of degrees of explanatory formality; it is, rather, a genuine conceptual distinction.

Obviously, the most troublesome challenge to legal positivism rests with the notion of the legitimation or right promulgation of law *(lex)* viewed in terms of its normative force *(jus)*: if it is not rightly promulgated, a statute cannot claim legitimacy, but if it is validly uttered, its legitimating sources should be demonstrably valid as well *(justitia)*, however we divide or conflate the legal and the moral. On the strength of such arguments, there can be no principled disjunction between the legal and the moral, and there seems to be no convincing alternative strategy if we are to avoid arbitrariness or privilege. That is the insuperable *pons* of positivism—in effect, the consequence of admitting the irreducibility and ineliminability of the normative. Nevertheless, to admit these commonplace difficulties is *not* to seek the "relief" of a revealed moral law (that of Moses or Hammurabi or Muhammad, say), although it is to acknowledge the *sittlich* relevance of any such pronouncement. There cannot be an argument *rationaliter* that directly unites such a "law" and the policies addressed to our *prudentiae*, though practical reasoning is bound to weigh what is worth conceding to the champions of such a law. I see no conceptual difficulty there—but I do see inevitable conflict. If I may speak in a laxer way: we must render unto theory what is theory's due, and unto practice, what belongs to practice. The idea of a revealed moral law pretends to gain a theoretical advantage by means that preclude theoretical dispute at the very start. Alternatively put, a second-best morality makes no pretensions at neutrality, but it does afford a constructed picture of objectivity among opposed partisans and ideologues.

If I may also invoke Thomas Kuhn's principal distinction regarding the work of the physical sciences, I would say that legal proceedings tend to be "normal" with respect to our *Sitten*, whereas moral disputes threaten our *Sitten* with "revolutionary" possibilities at every turn.[4] The trouble is this: unlike what occurs in the sciences, first-order moral impasses tend to acquire the interpretive language of our second-order disputes regarding the validity of the *prima facie* practices that they instantiate. In the sciences, by contrast, explanatory impasses that depend on partisan disagreements about the way the world is tend to be uncontroversially acknowledged by all parties disputing what the final explanation should be (as in the Joseph Priestley/Antoine Lavoisier dispute over the combustion of mercury). We think of reaching "objectivity" in these circumstances as hardly open to any single mode of legitimation. ("Ideology" is not entirely eliminable in the physical sciences, however.)

In any case, there can be no radical discontinuity between the legal and the moral, because the very sense of the legitimacy of legal proceedings ultimately rests on the same kind of practical or consensual tolerance that serves in moral matters. In the United States, for instance, the practice of abortion may be violently condemned by a militant public in spite of its falling within the pale of actual current law. (Would-be moral sanctions may prove far more extreme than anything the law would ever authorize. "Moral" opposition to abortion may, as we have come to realize, endorse the killing of a practicing physician as a valid homicide.)

The difference between the legal and the moral is not a difference in degree of importance or severity of any kind but a difference, rather, of methodological approach and conceptual linkage—a difference that affects the manageable control of certain kinds of complaints relative to public interests and in accord with the perception of the resources, limitations, and intent of enacted law. Behavior that would be actionable in public places may, in the privacy of one's bedroom, be ignored by the law as a matter of course, being too difficult to prove or probe or control. Other forms of public behavior, though severely condemned—for instance, the betrayal of a friend's trust—may not be legally actionable at all.

Generally, the law is guided by minimizing departures from a legible and convenient policy of controlling what falls squarely *in foro externo* with regard to our *Sitten*. Hence, not only subversive thought but effective privacy as well are usually tolerated by the law. When a new technology, say, makes the surveillance of the interior of an unentered private house as accessible to the police as direct observation, however—contrary to the laws—we grasp the importance of admitting the continuity of the moral and the legal, the contingency of the distinction between the two, and the continual need to survey the impact of our enabling technologies. Think, for instance, of the control of news media and the monitoring of cell phones, e-mail, credit cards, computers. The argument clearly affects the deputizing of the legal. But covetousness and adultery "committed in the heart" cannot be legal matters at all—yet. The distinction rests on the changing concept of a public world.

Still, these are tangential matters. The main lesson is this: there is no general rule or decision-making procedure governing the right moral description or interpretation of acts and conditions of life touching on discerning evil, wrong, *malum*, injustice (*injuria* or *injustitia*, in the moral sense). Nor is there an algorithm for what to regard as rational in terms of the normative aspects of practical decision making.[5] Such pretensions inevitably betray a need for the same kinds of distinctions between first- and second-order thinking that we have already met in the moral context. The concept of "economic man," for instance, was premised on the doubtful assumption that economics was a science that might compare favorably with the rigor of physics and might (ideally) have no need for ideological models of human wants and interests and moral/political reasoning. There is no compelling argument to show that we could ever demonstrate that the mode of decision making favored, say, by al Qaeda violates an invariant model of objective rationality. There is, in fact, no way, even in general logical theory, to separate in principle the formal syntax of valid reasoning from our (debatable) decisions about how to treat the would-be paradigm cases that our logics are meant to follow. No purely formal analysis of truth itself exists, for instance. Language and reasoning are in no way closed or autonomous systems; theoretical inquiries of every kind are contingently and changeably embedded in our shifting understanding of historicized experience. Moral and political thinking (ideology, let us say) is inseparable from practical life, and thus inseparable from logic and science themselves. There is, in short, a *sittlich* aspect to every inquiry.

There are two very different issues here—easily elided, ultimately inseparable, but different nevertheless—regarding the possible objectivity of moral judgment. One addresses the validation of what to take as the right categories of second-order normative judgment beyond whatever is merely *sittlich* in the *prima facie* sense. The other concerns the determinacy and precision with which our normative predicates (once entrenched) are actually applied in concrete circumstances, whether in first- or second-order terms.

Consider, for example, that many who are opposed to abortion on the grounds of abortion's being the murder of innocent persons (or human beings—in effect, human fetuses) are prepared to allow the abortion of fetuses produced by incestuous union or rape or in cases where the mother's life would otherwise be lost. But this, of course, would be blatantly self-contradictory, unless abortion in the cases mentioned was *not* construed as murder. Yet, if the permitted cases are deemed murders, the defenders of the generic ban would need to explain consistently just why a more generous public policy (say, honoring in the first trimester a mother's unwillingness to bear an unwanted child) *was* a case of murder.

There is an obvious difficulty here, where a policy of *liberalitas* might seem dialectically strengthened wherever the argument is made to proceed *rationaliter*, that is, without appeal to revelatory assurances or *obiter dicta* regarding the sanctity of life (or "innocence"). I remind you that this sort of reasoning may have very little to do with effective social or moral sanctions or "engineering." Yet, as in chess, a stalemate here need not signify that the opposing arguments are of equal strength. *Liberalitas* would recommend that we favor the conceptually more generous public policy, even where the ideological convictions of its opponents are just as sincere and just as compelling (to their own advocates) as they are to the partisans on the other side. I am not arguing here in a bivalent or exclusionary way; bivalence can hardly be exceptionlessly guaranteed, if one proceeds *rationaliter*. The matter is more complicated.

Generally, if the issue invites considerations of what I call *nullum malum*— abortion is such an issue, as the "interests" of the fetus cannot actually be consulted—it will appear unreasonable, proceeding *rationaliter*, not to favor *liberalitas*, precisely because of the profound impasse between pro- and anti-abortion convictions taken together with the logical standing of substantive moral norms. Of course, it is always possible that the parents-to-be or other interested parties may fall out among themselves. But, then, the issue would no longer be confined to abortion. It would begin to center on the implications of the marriage bond itself, and it would go beyond the terms of *nullum malum*. You see, of course, that we cannot tamper with *sittlich* disputes *ra-*

tionaliter without offending partisan convictions in some way. But such disputes are themselves already part of the *sittlich* data in question! It's their very existence, or the threat that they will surely take form, that justifies our moving to a second-best morality.

In fact, it is notable that theories of the normative standing of abortion tend to resist introducing subcategories regarding the killing of fetuses, as if to avoid imitating the subcategories (in terms of deliberate intent) of killing fully formed persons. The reason is not difficult to guess: the fetus cannot have any intentions of its own vis-à-vis the agents responsible for its abortion. Hence, though we obviously are concerned with an agent's intentions with respect to abortion, there are no familiar gradations there that compare with the grades of murder, homicide, manslaughter, *crime de passion*, self-defense, suicide, and the like. Some distinctions regarding intent are obviously needed, but these are normally linked to further categories that obviate defining abortion itself as a kind of murder.

On the strategy I propose, it cannot be compellingly shown that abortion as such is wrong. Moreover, it can be shown that the resolution proposed is reasonable, viable, and even respectful of opposed convictions that are not likely to be reconciled conceptually. If the abortion impasse leads, say, to the murder or severe harassment of opponents or facilitators who mean to press their case in an honorable way, then proceeding *liberaliter* is likely to be as objectively valid as any resolution could be. But, if so, then bivalence will have been outflanked. For if, as I say, the legal must confine itself pretty well to what is effectively sanctionable in a public way, then the acknowledgment of irreconcilable *sittlich* positions (say, pro- and anti-abortion views), just where a legal (inevitably disjunctive) provision is obviously needed, does not count, as such, as morally irresponsible or inconsistent or less than objective! That is the saving feature of viewing the legal as limited to certain forms of manageable control within the more informal and improvisational space of the moral. Those who cannot count on legal satisfaction may yet have another day to press their moral convictions. (They may not be satisfied, however, with less than unconditional victory.)

It would not be unreasonable, therefore, to suggest that a stalemate regarding second-order norms should, particularly under conditions of urgency involving contested *prudentiae*, yield in the direction of *liberalitas* viewed as an extension of a society's behaving *rationaliter*. If we abandon all forms of cognitive and rational privilege regarding second-order norms, if we construe moral objectivity as inherently constructivist, if we admit that *prima facie* norms are subject to second-order review, then there will be no viable alternative but the bluff refusal to weigh competing reasons at all. Under the circumstances, it seems (to me at least) that there is a very good reason to refuse, *as a matter of public policy*, to construe abortion *tout court* as murder. (The private convictions of its opponents may remain as firm as you please, though, *and* a charge—even a legal charge—of "wrongful killing" may be brought against certain acts that, in effect, entail or would otherwise entail abortion.) As a consequence, abortion may not, in most Western countries, be rightly deemed a crime.

In any case, what we have just considered chiefly addresses the first of the two issues originally raised. That part of the argument concerns the right way to construe the category of abortion as a moral charge—and also, perhaps, as rightly informing a legal policy where wanted. Viewing abortion as an exemplary case, we see how we may act to change a *sittlich* category for second-order reasons without relying on grounds beyond those that fall within the competence of a second-best morality. The predicative question is an altogether different matter.

There are really two distinct issues posed by normative predication. One is indistinguishable from the most general question raised by predication itself. The other concerns the peculiar bearing of the predicative question on the moral treatment of persons or human agents, and this latter issue yields a lesson of the greatest importance. The point about the first may be put in a single line: viz., predication is inherently and insuperably informal.

It is conceptually impossible to formulate a rule or criterion or principle by which all true instantiations of a general predicate, abstracted or projected from the natural world, can ensure that *any* further extension of that predicate—beyond the specimens we first admit, of course, as fixing its sense—can be derived from any such rule. That is the *pons* of every form of nominalism and conceptualism. Every such extension, however spontaneous, automatic, unchallenged, or consensually tolerated, relies on the *sittlich* solidarity of the society whose language admits such terms. Predicative extension, in other words, is inherently artifactual—constructed, historicized, subject to *sittlich* tolerance. If you concede that the moral and the legal (all forms of normative discourse) concern the valid use of general predicates, you cannot fail to grasp the radical implications of such a modest point. (It bears decisively, for instance, on the entire Platonist undertaking that I have been tracking from the start, and it is obviously a cornerstone in the relativist reading of both factual and normative distinctions.)

To admit this much is *not yet* (or not at all) to admit that *sittlich* validity is a criterial affair. The problem is intrinsic to speech itself, unless, *per impos-*

THE MORAL AND THE LEGAL

sibile, humans can know the fixed Forms that earthly predicates somehow represent. (I regard my own demurrer as a Wittgensteinian argument, though what Wittgenstein himself says, in speaking of "family resemblances" and "strands of similarity," is not entirely perspicuous.[6]) Again, in moral terms, this insuperable laxity suggests a policy of *liberalitas* wherever small predicative distinctions may gradually or even suddenly mount — for instance, over time or through historical accident or because of an unexpected interpretation of a term in such a way as to put someone in undeserved peril or greater jeopardy than circumstances would otherwise require or allow. Think, for instance, of how a careless but innocent remark that one might make, when publicly denounced by someone of importance and influence as an unpardonable insult, might thereby come to count *as* an unpardonable insult. The drift of the meaning of the law through accumulating precedents affords a suggestive analogy.

Yet, as I say, the more important matter concerns the conceptual conditions under which, interpretively or improvisationally, we judge the acts of human agents, actually applying one or another predicate to our own acts or those of others. In the Kashmir skirmishes, for instance, the same agents and the same problematic acts are often quite sincerely described in normatively opposed ways by opposed partisans who speak, say, of the work of "terrorists" or of "freedom fighters," where most informed discussants construe these terms as mutually exclusive and as signifying, respectively, the clear indefensibility or the assured defensibility of the very same acts. What is decisive is that these and, in general, all moral/political predicates are drawn from the unrestricted improvisational resources of our *sittlich* practices — intra-societal or inter-societal as they may be — which are actually often meant to fix passably objective "verdicts" applied to opposing commitments in a given quarrel.

The important point, almost never featured, is that *in* a moral/political dispute, we cannot rightly draw on a formally prepared array of categories procedurally fitted for determinate moral findings (as we do with their legal counterparts). A legal charge begins with a carefully circumscribed inquiry, but a moral "charge" institutes a partisan dispute *de novo* and shapes the very sense in which the involved partisans believe the dispute ought to proceed — precisely *by* attempting to muster the ideological inclinations of an interested population, no matter how small or large, that may be drawn to contribute its moral weight to the "finding" wanted. In the legal case, we carpenter our (partisan) briefs *to* the verdictive options permitted in advance. In the moral case, we try, as partisans, to carpenter the public perception of the case itself, the very description and interpretation of the acts in question, *in order to lead, in medias res*, a potentially interested public to a consensual charge or finding here and now.

In both cases, we rely on our *sittlich* practices and normative vocabularies; in both, we also invoke a community's sense of its own precedents. But in the legal case, we are always guided by the actual prior formal findings of the courts whenever we claim a precedent in our own favor; in the moral case, there is no strict formality at all to rely on, only the shifting contingencies of effective and ineffective interpretations of our *sittlich* practice, which, in modern societies, almost always harbors a *prima facie* opposition on every important question. That is precisely what, applied to our own world and shorn of its original fixities, the *Antigone* now conveys. And, if I may suggest a more problematic case, it is what Marx perceived everywhere in political and economic history.

I hasten to add that the *Antigone* rests on a contingent conflict or contingent incompatibility, not a principled opposition (although, of course, prioritizing loyalty to crown or family is indeed a principled matter, often a conflict between the legal and the moral). By contrast, pro- and anti-abortion policies are inherently opposed. I have already suggested that *nullum malum* applies to the second case but not in any obvious way to the first. Class opposition in the Marxist sense affords a third sort of case, one that is based on a contested theory of historically formed interests. The case of *Antigone* begins in *sittlich* circumstances and invites a resolution *rationaliter*. The Marxist case seeks to entrench a second-order opposition *as itself* a *sittlich* conflict, thus shoring up the effective power of one ideology over others. In resolving disputes of all these sorts, however, we tend to seek a *modus vivendi*, not a verdict.

In the terms I have been favoring, the moral narrative tends to be historicized, labile, open to divergent lines of extension and choice of exemplars, subject always to being informally altered and reconfigured as a result of the interpretation of evolving cases, supported in a *sittlich* way but resisting all categorical fixity. For its part, legal thinking always prefers closure and a settled classification.

In a sense, therefore, the distinctive rigor of moral dispute never gets matters quite right *if* it is to hew only to confirming propositions in a disjunctive way. At its best, it leads to something of a stalemate between opposed convictions and practices. We aim, in the moral case, to avoid unquestionably arbitrary norms and commitments as well as to maintain a measure of respect for entrenched practices that we nevertheless intend to change. Any resolution, therefore, tends to favor reform that proceeds with due regard for what the affected society is prepared to accept. You may, for instance, take the events of the American Civil War (with respect to the slavery question) and the deposing of the Iranian Shah (with respect to the Islamic *ethos*) to begin to mark the sense of what counts as moral objectivity in the search for a *modus vivendi* rather than the validity of one doctrinal claim over another.

There is something essentially conservative about morality and legality, but there is also no prospect of progress in the reforms morality or legality can license as objective that does not stand the test of time. Time, too, requires patience regarding stubborn or opposed convictions that may not be equally defensible here and now when cast in terms of *prudentiae* or when viewed *rationaliter* or *liberaliter*. Nor can moral convictions be defended as determinate propositions that may be shown to be objectively true, regardless of consensual support. The prospect of the latter sort of confirmation is surely a complete illusion, though to say so is not the last word about morality. The fluency of legal resolutions among secular states presupposes the stability of the second-best morality on which their systems of law depend. A pious people committed to a revealed law will undoubtedly manifest a similar tolerance. But the practice of revealed law cannot provide, in principle, for the incommensurabilities of revealed and second-best procedures.

Moral progress—what may be judged to count as moral progress, if we favor a second-best morality—takes the form of weaning a society in the direction of construing its *sittlich* practices in terms of *prudentiae* pursued *rationaliter*, so that successful reform may be tolerated in the same *sittlich* manner as before. Legal matters, I have suggested, are laid out from the start in a conserving way. We see, therefore, that the risk of consensual instability in the law lies chiefly with the drift of legislation itself, for the making of law is, at its most disputatious, the *institutionalizing of second-order moralities as systems of first-order legalities*. That, of course, is part of what I mean by the problem of "moral engineering." Nevertheless, legal positivism characteristically avoids acknowledging the continuity of the moral and the legal: admitting the connection effectively undermines the positivist thesis itself. Yet to admit the need to avoid utter arbitrariness in the promulgation of laws in the first place is, ineluctably, to make the same admission.

Restricting ourselves to the question of what to count as moral objectivity, we now see—assuming that there is no viable alternative to a second-best morality—that objectivity belongs to *any modus vivendi* that resolves important *sittlich* impasses and opposed ideologies that threaten, internally or externally, the important *prudentiae* or *providentiae* of a society prepared to proceed *rationaliter*. That answer, however, cannot be admitted without abandoning the fixities of a bivalent logic imposed on the constructive resolution of our moral contests.

I put it to you that such a finding runs entirely contrary to the canonical theories of Eurocentric philosophy—and very probably to the moral doctrines and philosophies of most of the world. But that is indeed a decisive part of the radical import of distinguishing between the practical and the theoretical—that is, always within the terms of a second-best morality. Or, as I have already said, insistence on a policy of exceptionless bivalence is, in moral/political as in scientific matters, very probably part and parcel of a commitment to cognitive or rational privilege.

[II]

I don't deny that the answer I've given regarding the nature of moral objectivity will be a disappointment to zealots and visionaries. But normative reforms must stand the test of time as well as of the flexibility of the practices they would replace; if they are meant seriously at all, they are meant to gather a *sittlich* force comparable to that of the practices they challenge. (Think of the final dismal failure of Akhenaton's instant success in installing the worship of the *aton*—or, more interestingly, of Marxist worries about the success of the Bolshevik Revolution in a country that had to enlist the long-term sympathies of the bourgeoisie to ensure the hegemony of an almost nonexistent proletariat.) Responsible reform seeks a *modus vivendi* for a troubled world— one that can be defended *rationaliter* and survive in the *sittlich* way.

This is, at least, close to the example set by the great religions of the world— except that, by and large, the religions have hardly proceeded *rationaliter!* Perhaps human societies cannot make profound or rapid changes of normative conviction solely within the conceptual confines of a naturalistic vision (or even sustain their *ethos* by such means). That was Freud's sobering assessment, of course. You have only to consider the extraordinary conversion of entire populations (Magyar, Armenian, Afghan) to either Christianity or Islam during their early history and the significance of such a possibility. If you grant all this, then a second-best morality must judge moral progress by *la longue durée*.

In any event, moral objectivity cannot be (i) centered in the appraisal of propositional claims alone or propositions apart from practices; (ii) centered in the appraisal of isolated acts alone or acts apart from their *sittlich* contexts; or (iii) confirmed in any exclusionary way (as, say, valid resolutions of one or another impasse threatening acknowledged *prudentiae*) or in any way that would, in principle, preclude the validity of ideologically opposed or incompatible options viewed as possible instantiations of the same *modus vivendi*. In short, although the historical record confirms that a good part of Western philosophy has been strongly disposed to treat moral judgments as entitled to systematic primacy over acts and practices—as, say, being logically atomic, or contextless, or propositional, or best represented by propositional claims modeled in accord with a bivalent logic, or demonstrably true or right in a way convergent and consistent across all informed societies, or at least potentially or progressively universalizable, or not to be construed in the *sittlich* way at all, or not relativized or confined in *sittlich* histories, or confirmed by cognitive or rational powers that are not themselves confined to partisan interests or tethered to our *Sitten* or even bound by naturalistic limitations— the fact remains that the issues already broached provide sufficient reasons for supposing that all such proposals are completely unconvincing. In the West, utilitarianism in all its forms may have been the most ambitious offender, but it is certainly not the only one.

You see, of course, that to grant this much is, effectively, to place in jeopardy nearly the entire tradition of Western moral philosophy. At a first pass, I would say that the accounts of theorists such as Nietzsche and Foucault may be among the very few that share a good number of the objections I've just laid out, though they hardly attempt to recover a valid morality themselves. Certainly, all criterion-driven conceptions—utilitarianisms, egoisms, liberalisms, libertarianisms, game-theoretic ethics, policies of rational universalizability, and policies of self-realization—will be rendered doubtful at a stroke. Once we abandon cognitive or rational privilege in practical matters, it is difficult to be convinced that we should hobble our accounts with inflexible rules of any sort. That is not what "objectivity" requires.

The most plausible view of moral dispute is that it is a contest between opposed partisans who seek consensual support or possible hegemony and who muster their arguments—drawn in a mixed way from inventive interpretations of their *sittlich* history and conformable ideologies of every stripe—to gain their objective, which is a measure of moral/political power in whatever protean form may be possible.

Whatever one supposes their exclusive validity to be, Christianity and Islam, for instance, are surely sources of great power cast in normative terms that often produce instant opposition and sudden forms of opposing power, which secular readings of economic and political struggle may not easily fathom or control. To this extent, Thrasymachus—though utterly benighted— was surely right to some degree. He nowhere considers that there *is* a kind of objective validity that can be claimed and applied to disputes and impasses that threaten those *prudentiae* that we are committed to preserving—practices abstracted from the problematic doctrines that surround our *sittlich* life, impasses to be resolved even among opposed partisans, all in accord with the slimmed-down idiom of one or another second-best morality (that is, *rationaliter, liberaliter*, with due consideration).

Thrasymachus makes no provision for a *practical, constructive* (or constructivist) *objectivity*. And Habermas, who rises to meet the question of objectivity, concedes (in Kantian fashion) that though we may propose moral changes and reforms that are *not* confirmable on independent normative grounds, once admitted, they *become* testable by way of the normative "rules" of rational discourse, which, Habermas believes, obtain universally. Our moral "norms" thus become pragmatically "necessary"—rational, neutral, binding on us all.

Habermas's rather daring but unconvincing assumption holds that there *is* a fully determinate rule of "practical discourse" that, "dialogically," satisfies (uniquely, it seems) the rational and argumentative needs of every possible participant in any such discourse. He then argues that only those would-be moral norms suited to resolving practical disputes that can "meet" the constraints of practical discourse (in the sense intended) could possibly be valid in the moral way. This is clearly a Kantian proposal. But, for one thing, Habermas's generic rules of practical discourse are already substantive in the liberal way, not merely formal at all. For another, they appear to be morally, even politically, biased prior to any specifically moral disputes. And, for a third, their apparent "violation" is said to constitute a form of "performative [or pragmatic] contradiction," which appears to be circularly supported. I believe Habermas's proposal fails decisively and goes well beyond Kant's own conception of rational constraints.

Thrasymachus intends no legitimative argument at all. He is no more than a spoiler. But Habermas does intend a heroic recovery of practical objectivity among admitted partisans. Nevertheless, his use of the term "universalizable" reduces to nothing more than consistency of usage (which is not what he requires), or else the "contradiction" he uncovers proves to be unacceptably slack, uncompelling, and very probably question-begging. Habermas begins with ideological disputes, but he claims a Kantian-like criterion of moral/political objectivity. He never shows that universalizability *is* operative in any discernible way (apart from consistency of usage). He nowhere considers the analogue of Hegel's critique of Kant's Categorical Imperative, or, for that matter, Kant's own insistence on *thinking of* (conceiving, *not actually discerning*) our noumenal identity.

You may test the force of the legitimative strategy I am recommending by recalling the proposal of *nullum malum*, which applies as persuasively to legal as to moral matters. Of course, it would have to apply at the legislative level if, as I say, legislation is at times a bridge between *justitia* and *jus*. The decisive point is that *nullum malum* proceeds only by removing, however gradually and respectfully, would-be substantive norms that impose unconfirmable *sittlich* restrictions on one's use of oneself, insofar as one's acts do not affect in any pertinent way relationships with others (that is, in a sense opposed, say, to the acts of a mother that adversely affect the child she is bearing). I count *nullum malum* as a compelling instance of how substantive moral reforms can be proposed, defended, and shown to be objectively valid—assuming all the while the culturally constructed nature of moral norms as well as selves— but without assuming any independently confirmable norms. (In effect, by-passing Habermas.)

If you grant the argument in favor of *nullum malum*, you are bound to see that there must be a large, entirely open-ended run of similar proposals that would make perfectly good sense without broaching privileged norms of any kind. For example, once you concede that reviewing *sittlich* practices *rationaliter* cannot fail to feature selected *prudentiae*, it is easy to see that if there are such concerns (preeminently, *nullum malum*), there is a place as well for other such concerns (for instance, what I call *summum malum* and *minimum bonum*).

By *summum malum*, I mean massive suffering, deprivation, or the like that marks the misfortune of a substantial population, where the grading of what will count as such is likely to be qualified *liberaliter*—that is, in conceptual terms, more generously than not, proportioned to our technological capacity and resources and expectations. I mean matters like the dire lack of food and water and shelter on a large scale; torture; natural disasters; the spread of AIDS and other terrible diseases; the dissolution of families; wholesale slavery; genocide; the loss of basic resources and the means of subsistence; war; constant unemployment; and the large-scale disorganization of ordinary life. You get the idea. Certainly, extending relief *liberaliter*, to smaller groups and lesser forms of disadvantage, pain, and the like, cannot be less valid, objectively, than relieving *summum malum*—cannot be flatly impermissible, for instance. (To my way of thinking, it involves and implicates *humanitas*. I return to the latter notion in the final chapter.)

Conventional claims regarding what is *right* and *obligatory* accommodate such a spread. That is, whatever we do to offset *summum malum* and its effects is more likely to be judged obligatory if anything is thought to be obligatory at all, apart from what is internal to any function or role or office assumed or entailed in some *sittlich* process *(officium)*, whether by contract or convention or in some similar way. (*Not*, you realize, by any moral teleology or moral functionalism imposed on human nature.) *Summum malum* is only a constructive proposal, one that is almost impossible to avoid within the terms of a second-best morality. The *malum* featured is *not*, originally, a moral matter. It gains its standing *rationaliter*, once we note the prominence of prudential concerns within our standard moralities as, also, among our first-order *Sitten*. It gains its moral standing *faute de mieux*.

I am not claiming that we are obliged (categorically, say) to aid one another where *summum malum* strikes. But I cannot see any point to urging or disputing what to take to be morally right or obligatory, whether *prima facie* or in second-order terms, *if* obligation does not extend to something close to *summum malum*. Conformably, I see no point to featuring what to count as right or permissible conduct if it does not reach up to some significant share of relief from *summum malum* or its lesser manifestations. (Think of black slavery in the Sudan!) But I put it to you that this is a much more plausible, much more easily defended, much more pertinent analysis of the possibility of "categorical" obligations than, say, Kant (or any of the lesser Kantians) provides. It is also, I may add, a substantively responsive answer to the challenge of 9/11. There is nothing in either Kant's or Aristotle's official accounts to compare.

Conceptual niceties do arise here. What do we owe, say, to the flood-prone Bangladeshis, to the genocidal Rwandans, to the starving Somalis, all of whom are far away? The more we insist on globalization, the more plausible it will be to speak of objective obligations that may encompass all the peoples of the earth. To admit the moral relevance of a global context, as in environmental matters such as global warming, is not at all the same as invoking universalizability as a moral criterion or as morally advocating a globalized market (which is, more often than not, a form of economic hegemony). You see by this that policies that seek to fix the determinate rightness of what to do in given circumstances—by invoking universalizability or the consequences of universalizing—are likely to exceed the *sittlich* gauge of a second-best morality.

Nothing hangs on the informality noted, as far as objectivity is concerned. In its deepest meaning, morality is the formation of our sense of responsibility in these and related cases. We bear witness to the entrenched conduct of others and ourselves—and understand, at least prudentially, what may be expected from our own and other societies. In this sense, moral judgment is ho-

listic, and benignly so: alternative parsings of what is right and good and obligatory may be defended as valid, even where such parsings are incompatible
with one another—that is, within the terms of the supposed validity of some
general *ethos* or *modus vivendi*.

Moral "inquiry" proceeds as if it were analogous to legal inquiry. But the
analogy is a very thin one—*a fortiori*, one that affects the second-order pretensions of both law and morality. Perhaps, even more, it is a reckoning and
a public record of what a people holds itself responsible for, comparing its
past history and anticipated prospects with those of other peoples similarly
placed. In that reflexive space, there *is* room enough for dialectical dispute
and thus for the kind of practical objectivity that favors one *modus vivendi*
over another, within second-best terms, as well as divergent instantiations of
the *modus* favored. But though we tend to feature the appraisal of such
disputes—they have their obvious role—our worries about the objective
standing of this or that would-be resolution contribute, in the larger span of
human affairs, to a sense of a society's disciplined conviction as to what may
be thought to fortify its habits of life, otherwise captured in its ideological
pronouncements.

Moral objectivity is, in this respect, logically quite weak, because without
invoking privilege, it cannot be made more determinate than I have shown
it to be. *But the argument as to what to count as objectively valid in the moral
way is not logically weak at all!* It is, as Aristotle says, as rigorous as the subject allows. My complaint against the standard theories is that they have confused two distinct matters. Believing (correctly) that an adequate philosophy
must be able to explain in a determinate way what should properly count as
right or obligatory, these theories wrongly suppose that what *is* objectively valid
morally must be determinate in a way that compares favorably with the acknowledged determinacy of ordinary matters of fact. But we have seen that
moral inquiry cannot support such a finding. (It seeks no more than a *modus
vivendi*.)

Should we, then, fall back to views like Thrasymachus's or Stevenson's or,
possibly, Foucault's? I see no need for that.

Toward the end of his career, Michel Foucault seems to have realized that
he never collected his thoughts on what we should mean by the effective
agency of human persons in a way that would be pointedly adequate for answering direct questions about the objective appraisal of moral judgment and
moral commitment.[7] It would not be unfair to say that Foucault came to see
the issue as inadequately aired in his own work. It remains true, nevertheless,
that *an* answer of sorts—possibly, a satisfactory answer—lies sprawling, not

yet formulated, in what Foucault has actually written. Foucault may be thought to have favored a doubtful form of relativism in which, say, we can rightly supply no sense at all in favor of normative comparisons across *epistemes*. On that view, Foucault may be judged to be committed, *faute de mieux*, to a policy of "anything goes." There is that sort of anarchy in much that he has written. (By comparison, Nietzsche's use of genealogy as a critique of morality is always focused on the illicit presumption of being able to discern and vindicate one or another privileged morality.)

Foucault does not quite see that the idea of moral agency, or the self, implicates the propriety of moral comparisons across historical and cultural lines — for instance, in repudiating the arbitrary authority of the Roman *paterfamilias* or, of course, the radically unequal distribution of the world's goods relative to *summum malum*. Foucault and Nietzsche hardly mean the same thing, therefore, by "the genealogy of morals" or "power" relative to the generated *Sitten* of one society or another. What is missing in Foucault's sense of the genealogy of diverse *epistemes* is precisely what is *not* missing in Nietzsche's "genealogical" reflections on morality itself. The truth is, Foucault's work is inherently fragmentary, capable of being reconciled with an adequate moral theory but never tempted, itself, to formulate an adequate account. (I take this to be a characteristic feature of poststructuralist French philosophy.) Nietzsche's work is, by contrast, abbreviated but hardly unsystematic! It goes to the very nerve of moral and cognitive privilege.

Returning to the underlying issue, then: if you admit the constructed, second-order objectivity of *nullum malum* and *summum malum*, you will not be able to disallow *minimum bonum* either. I mean, by *minimum bonum*, a selection of *providentiae* scaled to the *sittlich* history of a particular society, relative to its technological resources and its own avowed conception of the least acceptable level of goods of individual and societal life deemed adequate (*rationaliter*) for the "capacitation," in Sen's sense, of its own offspring. *Minimum bonum* addresses development from infancy to adult agency in terms of what would enable offspring to compete effectively for a fair share of success in reaching a society's acknowledged *summum bonum*, its own ideal of the good life. Thinking in such terms cannot, as we shall shortly see, fail to yield in *some* measure to the reasonableness of admitting what I shall call *adaequatio*. For it is difficult to admit one's own (or one's society's) notion of *minimum bonum*, say, and to deny *some* degree of parity affecting other societies along the same lines. It doesn't matter how strictly or opportunistically such parity is initially applied. Almost any grudging admission along these lines, regarding the children of other societies, will set us on our second-best speculations.

Minimum bonum, therefore, is not only a matter of practical consistency in prudential terms keyed to a society's *summum bonum* but also one of the clearest instances of objective moral judgment that the prudential cast of *sittlich* practices could possibly support—within the terms of a second-best morality. If it could not yield any reasonably assured sense of normative objectivity along these lines, then, as far as I can see, moral philosophy would be a complete failure. The obvious and least quarrelsome rationale features the comparative moderation with which a society measures its *minimum bonum* relative to societies of comparable history and technological resources and relative to what it is prepared to project as its own *summum bonum*.

It is worth considering, therefore, that without a sense (an ideology, frankly) of how the alleged "goods" of a society (what Cicero calls its *optimi mores*), whether cast in terms of virtue or of what is permissible, are conceptually unified in the manner of a viable *ethos* or *modus vivendi*, the entire matter of assessing particular acts piecemeal would be no more than arbitrary, privileged, incoherent, inexplicable, or, most important, *not demonstrably relevant* to the executive constraints of moral judgment itself. This helps to explain the validity of charging that insofar as Aristotle and Kant address the historical contingencies of their own worlds, *their* implicit visions of the *summum bonum* of those worlds may be irrelevant or inadequate for ours. Furthermore, if you grant the point, you see the inevitably partisan nature of every would-be objectivist form of rational decision theory.

The only possible way to redeem Aristotle's and Kant's speculations is to hold, and to *demonstrate*, that the contingencies each entertained are indeed integrated in an encompassing vision of the *summum bonum*—eudaimonia, in Aristotle's sense, and the unity of the empirically "pragmatic" and the purely "practical," in Kant's—*and* that *that* is fixed for the human condition itself. This is also, according to MacIntyre's bold line of thinking, the rationale for Aquinas's amplification of Aristotle's account of the virtues. But if, as I say, there is no viable sense in which moral norms *can* be discerned apart from our contingent *Sitten* or independently of the interests and (holistic) ideologies of second-natured selves (or their second-naturing norms and practices), then the absence of a unifying *bonum*, cast *rationaliter* in terms of some proposed reform of our *prima facie prudentiae*, is telling evidence of the probable irrelevance or inadequacy of moral ideologies formulated for other ages and other peoples. Moral merit must be relativized to history and technological capacity and ideology along second-best lines pursued *rationaliter*.

I don't deny that there is something risky in this admission, but I think it cannot be helped, and its denial is even riskier—downright dangerous, I would say—in the light of the "terrorism" of 9/11. I refer to the "terrorism" of the al Qaeda attack on the Pentagon and the World Trade Center in scare quotes, because, of course, without prejudice to the question, Pervez Musharraf, the president of Pakistan, understandably found himself obliged, in denouncing bin Laden, to characterize those whom India regards as terrorists operating in Kashmir as "freedom fighters," that is, partisans validly committed to the "self-determination" of Kashmir. I regard this as a proper political analogue of at least one aspect of the conceptual dilemma that appears in Sophocles' *Antigone*, which informs the master questions of my entire discussion. As we have seen, the conceptual puzzles about the objectivity of moral discourse (and more) rest, in part, on the matter of resolving the question of the logic of predicates in actual use. My own view is that, failing a viable Platonism, we cannot help but fall back to a constructivist solution. To be sure, that is only a piece of the argument, but it is an important piece—even a prescient one.

[III]

I venture a final specimen of second-best policies—one, however, that differs in an important way from *nullum malum, summum malum,* and *minimum bonum* but makes explicit the sense of historical relevance that informs those other proposals as well. For the purpose, I co-opt somewhat arbitrarily the term *adaequatio,* or commensuration. Wherever (i) the control of the world's natural resources (on earth or even in outer space) or the sharing of the marketable goods of the world (regardless of who has effective control of or legally recognized "rights" to such goods) or availability is so unequally distributed or unequally accessible that it threatens a society's *modus vivendi* in a direction approaching *summum malum* or, alternatively, makes it desperately difficult or impossible to secure what it views as its *minimum bonum* (where other societies are noticeably not so threatened) or, in particular, wherever (ii) such inequalities are validly judged to have been caused and/or sustained by the policies and practices of other specific societies (as by war or chance territorial advantage), any thus adversely affected society or societies may reasonably claim that *adaequatio* has been breached or not suitably respected in the "capacitating" way. Because the matter is essentially prudential, I see no reason why war itself (if feasible) might not, *in extremis,* be objectively justified as a means, *rationaliter,* by which to resolve a grievance of either sort (but, in particular, one of the second sort). Clearly, at the present time—and surely even more insistently in the future—*adaequatio,* or cognate doctrines, will be pressed into service against Western or American forms of "globalizing" markets.

Adaequatio is peculiarly relevant at the present time. Only now has globalization (regarding natural resources, marketable goods, pollution, and the reach of international law) become a fact of life; furthermore, a breach of *adaequatio* can only now be reasonably measured and quantified and the possibility of relief made feasible. *Adaequatio* applies, then, to the disproportionate control, say, of natural gas and petroleum by a handful of states as well as the disproportionate use of those same nonrenewable resources by a handful of the world's technologically advanced states (notably, Saudi Arabia in the first instance and the United States in the second).

Strict distributive equality is not the issue. *Adaequatio* comes into play where the extremes already mentioned are seen to be at noticeable risk—or more than merely risked. Its scope may be enlarged, of course, *liberaliter* (as with *summum malum* and *minimum bonum*), as a function of technological advances and the economic and political advantage of a critical core of states in just such ideological terms, relative (at least) to their own conceptions of *summum malum* and *minimum bonum*. In that way, the objective charge of breaching *adaequatio* need never presume to fix a second-order obligation or the like, except dialectically, in accord with the constraints of a second-best morality. What is particularly significant about *adaequatio* is, first, that it affords a plausible (but radical) extension of the sense in which war may be morally justified and, second, that it does so in a way that confounds the canonical disjunction between war and peace. *Adaequatio* suggests the sense in which economic hegemony may itself be taken to be a form of war—a distinct kind of territorial penetration and colonial control. Once you grant the conceptual bankruptcy of the "just war" concept and the proliferation of new forms of war and warfare,[8] you cannot easily dismiss the idea. I find it implicated in 9/11 as well as in global capitalism.

Plainly, the plight of large parts of Africa and Asia and South America cannot be deliberately or systematically relieved without some implied adherence to *adaequatio* or cognate notions. I have, however, deliberately avoided casting these distinctions in terms of dispositions such as humanity, benevolence, charity, or the like, *not* because such temperaments are irrelevant—they are not—but because there is no obvious way to invoke them in working out the terms of a pertinent morality *rationaliter*. The British empiricists (notably, Locke and Hume) were appealingly realistic in drawing on such dispositions in their own moral visions. Too much reliance on such uncertain resources, though, much like appealing to the virtues, makes a moral theory seem more utopian than is reasonable.

Dispositions are not normally manageable parts of political programs (though Nazism showed us how they might be). *Adaequatio* is, however, centered on prudential concerns and can be harnessed to any motivation that will advance its cause. Certainly, the resentment of a significant part of the Muslim world toward American hegemony and the perceived complicity of America's allies explains in good part the sense of "moral" frustration that has issued in "terrorism"—and may yet issue in more insidious, more ubiquitous, more dangerous, less manageable forms of "terrorism" worldwide that, doubtless, will then be viewed, oppositionally, in terms of "freedom" or "self-determination."

The point is this: the domestic and global policies of modern states (and their peoples) can no longer be separated from one another, and the risks to the domestic well-being of any and all states are bound to be viewed, implicitly, as the possible consequences of perceived breaches of *adaequatio* and unruly efforts to redress pertinent grievances in its name. Such risks are bound to be cast in increasingly extreme prudential terms. Witness, for instance, the repeatedly affirmed new American policy of the "preemptive strike" in the "war on terrorism," which effectively erases the line of demarcation between war and peace. I grant, of course, that North Korea's policy of marketing "weapons of mass destruction" has produced a related erasure—and there may well be other rogue states to consider. That's not the issue for the moment, unless we are asked to admit that the line has been irreparably crossed. What the example makes clear is that the one-sided condemnation of 9/11 as an act of war is itself cast in terms of an outmoded idiom.

In the nineteenth century and a good part of the twentieth, militancy regarding *adaequatio* was effectively entrenched in the Marxist perception of class warfare. Class warfare and its analogues have certainly not disappeared from the underprivileged world. But by the beginning of the twenty-first century, the disproportionate gap between advantaged and disadvantaged peoples has become very steep indeed and increasingly intractable. From the side of the latter (whether expressed in class or gender or ethnic or racial or national or religious or other terms), the miniaturization of destructive technologies, for example, and the willingness of "terrorists" (or "freedom fighters") to sacrifice their lives argue very plausibly, it seems to me, that the prudential interests of the advantaged world dictate the need for policies capable of restoring a greater measure of perceived *adaequatio* than now obtains. There is no ideologically neutral perch there.

I'll venture a final qualification. The Western world, from about the end of the seventeenth century to the present, has been fashioning a doctrine of "human rights" promulgated more and more effectively as citizen rights within well-ordered states. The doctrine, however, was never fully empowered within the jurisdiction of actual states, and its instantiation as citizen rights has always been controversial, chiefly because of the crucial difference between formally promulgated rights and what may be called "capacitating" rights (in Sen's sense). Viewed in the large, it is often (wrongly) thought to have reached its globalized form in the UN's Universal Declaration of Human Rights, that is, in a form that occupied a contested "no man's land" between the legal and the moral. But the UN Declaration has very little to do with capacitation. That is a terrible truth about the political history of liberalism.

My own sense of the matter is this. Where human rights are treated as legal rights, "capacitation" is always the focus of pertinent dispute, but it also remains an incompletely resolved concern—not unsatisfactory for that reason, but always in need of amendment in order to meet the changing circumstances in which particular rights continue to be operative at all. What, for instance, do the rights of the handicapped signify, legally, regarding the changing conditions of education, medical care, work opportunities, and the like, considered without regard to capacitation? Almost nothing.

By contrast, when human rights are viewed as moral rights, capacitation is usually completely ignored, and rights threaten to become merely formulaic. Disadvantaged minorities in the United States, for instance, are often said to have the same educational rights as those groups that are pertinently advantaged, even though they might never be able to compete effectively for, say, a restricted number of admissions to the best universities. In the United States, "equality of opportunity" among blacks and whites has, until recently, ignored the capacitation question. When it *is* raised in the context of legal rights, capacitation is often constrained by the supposed need to construe "equality" as no more than the strict "uniformity" of certain would-be enabling conditions (for instance, comparative performance on competency tests). Deviation from this rule tends to be regarded as a violation of "equality" itself! That is precisely why so-called affirmative action—which attempts to take into account the historical contingencies of actual capacitation in the United States—has been found by the American Supreme Court to be, more often than not, characteristically incompatible with the strict equality doctrine, itself construed in a formal and entirely ahistorical way that accords with a markedly narrow "liberal" ideology. In general, though, one sees easily enough that there is no straightforward way to ensure the effective equality of "human rights." Such equality cannot fail to be historically contingent and locally apt where it is apt at all. That is, it illustrates once again the fundamental difference between legal and moral reasoning.

In much the same sense, the Universal Declaration of Human Rights cannot now (rightly) be bound to the parochial themes of philosophical liberalism. It may even be forced to resist the liberal thesis in the interest of potential gains. In the eighteenth and nineteenth centuries, it's true, it *was* the serendipitous appeal of the liberal ideology that permitted the ancestral form of the Declaration to gain adherents across the world. But history has overtaken its advantage, and liberalism now plays an equivocal role, globally, in widening the divisions opposed by *adaequatio*.

The doctrine of universal human rights is, I believe, the single most successful moral/political proposal (and possibly the only such proposal) offered as a second-order normative reform of every *sittlich* morality the world has ever spawned. It is also a thesis cast entirely in terms of prudential interests viewed *rationaliter*. There's no question that its early history was intertwined with the fortunes of various versions of the liberal ideology. But it is, by now, effectively detached from liberalism itself—as it should be, both because of the doubtful metaphysical essentialism of pre-Enlightenment and Enlightenment conceptions of what it is to be a human being and because the greater part of the world's population is prepared to adhere (wherever it *is* prepared to adhere) to one or another favorable interpretation of human rights while not subscribing to the questionable individualism, rationalism, essentialism, and ahistoricism of the liberal account. (In East Asia, for instance, one such alternative to the conception of human rights in the liberal sense is associated with what is often called "Confucian democracy.")

It is extraordinary that the thesis should ever have succeeded in gaining the adherence it now commands. It is, in a way, the principal example—slim and utopian though it is—of a universalized version of what I have been calling a second-best morality. It is not important that it be more strictly regularized, now, as a universal legal doctrine beyond the shadowy sense in which it straddles the moral and the legal in the manner sketched. Its importance lies, rather, in providing a sense of direction to the mode of reform that a fully formed second-best morality must favor. It confirms its viability. It resists false fixities. It focuses on prudential generalities without challenging in any frontal way the actual *sittlich* practices of a great many nations that (we must be aware) could not, as matters now stand, easily reconcile their own form of life with the Declaration's proposed norms.

It is, in a word, the slimmest, most inclusive, *and* most likely of all utopian formulations to be at all effective in diverse ways in our actual globalized future. It may, eventually, cease to be primarily utopian, though I doubt it. It is, in short, a possible master theme for whatever second-order *modus vivendi* any particular people might construct *rationaliter* on the basis of their own contingent *ethos*.

As a utopian proposal, the universality of human rights entails (at least for formal reasons) treating all peoples equally, but the goal envisages neither capacitation nor any operative correction of actual injustices. In that sense it cannot replace *adaequatio*, which is essentially dynamic, corrective, comparative, and context-bound. The critical point is this: to invoke *adaequatio* is to imply that "we" believe we should be capacitated, proportionately at least to "their" more successful practices and enabling circumstances, and thus, consistently, that others may make similar claims of "us" in similar circumstances. In the utopian limit, all are entitled to whatever rights are validly assigned the general human condition—for instance, when suitably globalized, those of *minimum bonum* and *summum malum*. Equality, therefore, is not an initial postulate of all valid moralities (if it is not interpreted as consistency of usage). It is, rather, a utopian leap, under globalized possibilities, of other contextualized policies writ large—in particular, what, in the final chapter, I shall discuss under the heading of *humanitas*. In the abstract sense *humanitas* signifies, every person is *unum inter pares*, but not literally equal. The first distinction avoids arbitrariness in a formal way. The second concerns actual contexts of societal life construed *rationaliter*.

HUMAN SELVES AND MORAL AGENTS

[I]

The picture that is taking form is a picture of a moral world that legitimates itself by dialectical means alone, that eschews cognitive and rational privilege, that treats *sittlich* practices in a conserving spirit, and that proposes to pursue reform principally by altering, *rationaliter*, the embedded concerns of our *Sitten*. I view any such effort as the slimmest possible moral proposal we can imagine, one that avoids arbitrariness as well as the presumption of cognitive and normative privilege, one that never pretends that what it yields, constructively, *is* simply right or good or obligatory *sans phrase* — or best in any way. It proceeds by comparative means alone: it holds that it can match the plausibility of any would-be objective claim about the right norms of moral life by constructing sparer norms of comparable or greater plausibility than its canonical rivals. It affords no more than a conditional morality — a second-best morality, as I say, though one capable of genuinely substantive constraints (where wanted) without additional normative pretensions. And it shows, by its own example (by its ease of construction), that the tradition of Western moral philosophy is conceptually bloated, profoundly question-begging, and arbitrarily confident about the scope and power and conviction of what can actually be demonstrated.

There are certain immediate lessons to be collected, therefore. We must scale back our conceptual expectations regarding how much can actually be shown to be objectively valid in the way of moral judgment, and, where objective discipline is admittedly possible, we must acknowledge that in contexts of normative reform,

we cannot show that legitimation demands or can always support determinately unique solutions—or need never accommodate solutions that depart,
coherently and validly, from the familiar constraints of a bivalent logic or admit incompatible or relativistic solutions. I have explained both lessons, in
part, in urging the rejection of the rigid propositional model and the adoption instead of the (logically benign) holism of a *modus vivendi*, one capable of being validly instantiated in plural, incompatible, possibly opposed,
and even incommensurable ways in accord with the informal conditions under which acceptable such resolutions may be confirmed (if, indeed, any
may be).

Oddly, what I have neglected to provide, in pressing these matters, is the
analysis of *what it is to be a moral agent*, although I have noted the same la-
cuna in Foucault's account. I have said something about the culturally constituted nature of a human self: for instance, that selves arise as the "second-
natured" sites of certain (second-natured) powers by which the members of
Homo sapiens are transformed in a unique way through the process of acquiring
a first language and a home culture. *That* single fact affords the strongest argument against cognitive and rational privilege vis-à-vis moral matters (and
more). On the argument I am advancing, selves are cultural artifacts indissolubly embodied, one on one, among the members of *Homo sapiens*, in virtue
of which their cognitive and rational powers are, correspondingly, also artifacts of cultural history.

Notice, please, that if selves *are* constituted in the manner sketched, then
there can be no principled disjunction between theory and practice. All enlanguaged cognitive competence would be grounded in our first mastering
the *Sitten* of our home society. Otherwise, only a prior, prelinguistic form of
cognitive privilege (say, of an innatist or "natural" or nativist or transcendental or Platonist or revealed sort) could provide any basis at all for construing
knowledge or right judgment as the (right) exercise of a determinate faculty
(as in Descartes and Kant), that is, addressed to the discernible features of the
independent world or construed as the application of some invariant normative rule to human judgment and/or conduct.

The artifactual nature of selves requires and supports the notion of a second-
best morality—that is, the idea of our *not* being able to exceed a second-best
morality. If normative matters arise only within the reflexive ken of human
selves (as they in fact do), then there cannot be any objective moral norms
apart from, or independent of, what aggregated selves are prepared to propose
and sustain. Accordingly, whatever we think may be confirmed as normatively
valid will be an artifact of our own artifactual powers (though *not* for that rea-

son conventional or arbitrary or incapable of claiming objective standing). It will, however, affect what moral objectivity might reasonably mean.

At the very least, therefore, reason and knowledge are capable of determining what to count as objectively true or right by constructive or constructivist means. It follows from this that there are no moralities that enjoy second-order validity except that they be second-best moralities as well *and* that they gain whatever standing they do only in dialectical competition with the *sittlich* moralities by which selves are first formed. Stronger moralities can only pretend to have captured some privileged moral insight. (No one has ever advanced the stronger option compellingly.)

I hold, then, that the analysis of morality—or, indeed, the affirmation of what is thought to be morally valid—cannot be epistemically autonomous in any important way. For instance, it cannot ever be shown to be independent of how we suppose scientific claims are rightly confirmed. Furthermore, moral validity ineluctably depends on our conception of *what kind of creature we ourselves are!* In that sense, as I have already suggested, Levinas is surely mistaken: there cannot be any disjunction between our valid ethical concerns and the "metaphysical" analysis of the human condition itself. (That is, if you don't mind speaking of metaphysics.[1] Nothing hangs on the mere choice of a term.) On the contrary, to know anything of our "nature" is to know that we cannot escape being morally engaged. Being engaged in the moral way simply means responding, reflexively, to what is most distinctive in our nature: namely, that we cannot be what we are but for our sharing with other selves the collective (the historically changing, enabling) resources of our formative and transformative culture. (That is what Levinas misses.)

"Morality" is our name for the whole of our coping with the practical implications of that immense fact in terms of the normative assessment of what we and others do. To be a human self, a human agent, is to be poised to act in our cultural milieu, in the company of similarly cognizant selves, in accord with our and their interests and needs and with the conjectured interests and needs of humanity at large (attentive, of course, to the *prima facie* standing of the *Sitten* by which we are first formed). From this perspective, Levinas is obliged to put out of play the second-naturing condition of being fully human—in order to appear to put into play, *prior* to our culturally formed concerns, the ineluctable ethical confrontation with another human being (*l'Autrui*)! The coherence of his maneuver is distinctly shaky, whatever its humane intent. At best, it cannot do more than duplicate, by its own fiction, what is already in place, except of course for whatever privileged implication Levinas means to draw from his own invention. Furthermore, if you admit that we cannot really address another human being without effectively addressing *this* or *that* particular individual (that is, without individuating the "Other"), then Levinas's account must be utterly incoherent and useless to boot. Clearly, if you allow the fiction, then Levinas is free to stipulate—however humanely—whatever he deems to be the moral implication of whatever counts as the originary face-to-face encounter with the Other.

In putting matters this way, I am aware, of course, that, in spite of seeming affinities between Heidegger's notion of *Mitsein* ("being-with" [persons, not mere "things"]) and my own notion of the cultural emergence of selves— that is, *if*, contrary to Heidegger's actual intention, *Mitsein* signified no more than the "natural" reality of the societal life of human selves—the view I offer is as much opposed to Heidegger's conception of ethics as to Levinas's assigning primacy to the ethical over the ontological, which was itself partly directed against Heidegger's insistence on the high primacy of *Sein*. Both views seem to me to be spendthrift visions that lose the human center by exalting it above its conceptual station in ways that are stunningly difficult to paraphrase in any terms as conceptually and practically accessible as the ethical itself. *It is simply unclear how there can be an ethic at all that does not presuppose individuatable and responsible selves*; hence, it is unclear how one can go "beyond" Being (going beyond reference, individuation, and predication, say) without going beyond morality (and minimal intelligibility) as well. Despite temptations to the contrary, we must at all costs confine the human within examinable nature. Whatever is worth saving of Levinas's and Heidegger's visions—relative to understanding morality—must be reconciled with the constraints mentioned, if they are thought to be intelligible at all.

I confess that I cannot understand, for example, what Levinas means by a "person," if persons (oneself and others) escape "beyond being," *are* "otherwise than being" *(autrement qu'être)*—or what another self, the "other" (or "Other") *is*, if such an other is not identified as a competently encultured moral agent (or, as with infants, promisingly included in the world of selves). By a kind of parity of reason, I cannot understand what Heidegger means by *Dasein* beyond what may hold true of different kinds of *seiend* or *Seiendes* (plural entities, say) that are or include the finite encultured agents of human history, or what it would mean to go completely beyond *that*.[2] That is hardly to ignore the difference between a human being and a stone. I concede the importance of attributing historicity *(Zeitlichkeit)* and care *(Sorge)* to human beings as, as Heidegger might say, what belongs to their "existential condition." Still, I cannot see what Heidegger means, if he means to avoid essentialism (as he plainly does), in speaking of such *existentialia* (as distinct from ontic "categories") if they remain at all discursive. The historicity and care that selves manifest are, I would say, internal to the very enculturing process by which selves first emerge—second-natured.

Heidegger appears to mean that the "nature" of a human being—the human kind of "Being"—is utterly unlike whatever may be rightly identified as the "nature" of a stone! I agree. But I fail to see that admitting that entails that the human condition cannot be rightly rendered in terms of the natural world that includes the stone. Heidegger's doctrine requires that we deny that the *Dasein* that is human Being can be conceptually captured by naturalistic categories—possibly on pain of not being able, then, to deny the efforts of reductive science to describe and explain human nature adequately in terms drawn from inanimate nature or biology below the level of the specifically human. If that is his purpose, then Heidegger's entire account is a misguided extravagance ventured on a false assumption. It is entirely reasonable to regard the human world as *sui generis* within the same Nature that includes the stone—without yielding to any reductive or eliminative account—*if*, indeed, reductionism proves to be inadequate to its own purpose, as I believe it does. (In the present context, I waive any temptation to try to understand, with Levinas and/or Heidegger, what we might mean by speaking of going "beyond Being"—of what might be meant by "*autrement qu'être*," for instance.)

I don't deny that standard ontologies neglect the historicity of the human condition and the culturally formed and informed "nature" of human selves. But I cannot quite grasp whether, or in what respect, or on what justificatory grounds, Heidegger would claim (if he *would* claim) that *Dasein*, said to be "onto-ontological," is or is not a being that belongs to, *exists* in, the order of nature. If he admits that it is, then the "care of Being" (which, in Heidegger's opinion, uniquely distinguishes *Dasein*) is itself a natural concern, even if it is an unusual one or one that the philosophers Heidegger opposes have somehow neglected. But if more is meant (and it seems clear that more *is* meant), then I cannot quite see how, precisely, Heidegger characterizes the distinction *vis-à-vis the natural order* (what he calls the "ontic" or the merely "factical" order) or how he validates the distinction he intends.

I realize that he believes an ontic characterization of *Dasein* would be altogether inadequate to the human, but I cannot see how the "ontological" differs from the "ontic" (except verbally) or how it is related to nature or to Being in a way different from the ontic, at least as far as it concerns distinctions in the order of nature or natural Being. But *if* the moral, for Heidegger, implicates the ontological in addition to, as well as in contrast with, whatever belongs to the ontic alone—and also implicates more than the mere anthro-

pological world of human experience, which, Heidegger supposes, characterizes and notably restricts Karl Jaspers's existential concern—then, if the distinction of the ontological is not really given, we will be as unable to recover
Heidegger's lesson about morality as we were Levinas's. (Even these worries
do not go far enough for Heidegger.) The critique of particular accounts of
human "nature" is hardly the same maneuver as that of invoking sources of
human "Being" beyond the space of "nature" itself. I am prepared to say
straight out that Heidegger fails us here.

That leaves us still with the central question of human agency, the agency
of selves. Let me add a few considerations that may temper the objection just
raised against Levinas and Heidegger. For one thing, both are right to refuse
to derive valid moral norms from the independent analysis of essential human nature or of nature at large. That is part of the point of their refusal to
link ethics and metaphysics (the latter confined, in Heidegger's sense, to the
finite contingencies of the "ontic" world). I can only plead that to speak of
the cultural emergence of selves is more perspicuous in isolating the meaning of the moral than the incoherence of Levinas's disjunction and the utter
mystery of Heidegger's ontology. For a second, the account we need, if it is
to make morality intelligible at all, must provide for the initial (the *prima facie*) but not foundational validity of our *sittlich* practices. Heidegger fears reducing ethics to anthropology. Fine. Yet, in accepting Heidegger's challenge,
we may surely counter that we must at least *begin* with the "anthropological,"
or else our view of morality (or "authenticity," if you please) will prove completely arbitrary. Levinas is even more extreme.

Again, a third consideration: emphasis must be placed on the practical competence signified by human agency, which seeks commitments acceptable
or tolerable to whatever particular aggregate of selves it addresses. Such aggregates are formed by common processes of enculturation and are thereby
disposed to act in ways that fit (with whatever individual variation) the collective practices they jointly share, as well as additional or altered practices
they can be persuaded to adopt.

I mean, by "collective," culturally meaningful, normatively freighted, historically contingent, distributively shared forms of life or attributes—as in
shared language, tradition, custom, institution—that can only obtain within
the enabling unity of an encompassing society, but that, though capable of
informing individual acts as the basic formative practices they are, cannot
themselves be shown to have been formed by mere aggregative means alone.
In that sense, they are emergent, physically and biologically irreducible, and
second-natured. No *one* agent or self can produce a first language or tradition

as such, or possess a first language or a tradition, except as a member of a socially viable aggregate of selves that (for the same reason) cannot produce *their
own* first language by aggregative or cooperative or prelinguistic means alone.
Speech, for instance, is, as an act, *uttered* only by individual speakers, but the
sheer uttering of meaningful speech (not mere noise or sound) is a function
of our sharing the collective potentialities of the common language we speak.
Second-natured, we hear and understand language directly and fluently. We
cannot suppose that, as a rule, we first hear sound and then learn (prelin-
guistically) to interpret uttered sound as meaningful speech. *Per impossibile:*
where would the interpretive power come from?

You see in this the inseparability of the theory of what morality signifies
and entails and the theory of what it is to be a self. The "collective" is itself
confined to what is predicable. Effective agents are all individual selves, taken
singly or in the aggregate. There are no collective agents or persons, except
by way of legal fictions or the like—contrary to Emile Durkheim's apparent
doctrine, or, for that matter, the doctrine of the Nazi *Volk*. (It is worth remarking that although Marx spoke of class consciousness, he nowhere appears
to treat socioeconomic classes as collective agents.)

I know no better way of marking the distinction I have in mind than by re-
minding you of the well-established contrast between *Gesellschaft* and
Gemeinschaft—the distinction between an aggregate of selves (a "civil society," say) that may cooperate productively *(Gesellschaft)* and a community
that shares a common language and a common culture *(Gemeinschaft)*.[3] The
latter concept cannot be analyzed solely in the cooperative terms of the former, but it informs (and thereby makes possible) the actual, linguistically informed cooperative powers of the other. *Gemeinschaft* is often construed as
constituting a collective agency, whether in Jean-Jacques Rousseau, Hegel,
Marx, Ferdinand Tönnies, Durkheim, or Adolf Hitler, but the two ideas are
plainly distinct, once you seize the importance of construing *Gemeinschaft*
in predicative terms and *Gesellschaft* in substantive or individuative and ref-
erential terms.

There is compelling evidence, of course, that preindustrial peoples (so-
called primitive peoples in particular) exhibit a more profound sense of
"community" than advanced industrial societies. But there cannot be a human society that is never more than a "community" *(Gemeinschaft)*, if that
means that no members of such societies ever hunt or prepare meals together!
Similarly, there cannot be a human society that accomplishes "everything"
it does by cooperative or aggregative means alone *(Gesellschaft)*: their members would never learn to speak their home language. Human agents—

selves—are individual transforms of the members of *Homo sapiens*, second-natured by way of internalizing the collective aptitudes of their parental generation. *Gemeinschaft* and *Gesellschaft* are functionally inseparable distinctions incarnate in the lives of human selves.

Selves are uniquely capable of Intentional (or culturally significant) acts or behavior—*utterances*, let us say, whether verbal or not—as in art or ritual or war or manufacture. Such utterances are always attributively informed in *gemeinschaftlich* ways (Intentionally), though, as acts, they can be performed or uttered only by individual agents, whether singly or aggregatively, in the *gesellschaftlich* sense—that is, effectively. Failure to perceive the inseparability (at the level of human culture) of the *gesellschaftlich* and the *gemeinschaftlich* produces the famous paradoxes of the contract theory of society (paradigmatically, of language itself), which Rousseau plays with so cleverly in his *Social Contract*. It is also what is meant by characterizing the reflexive understanding of a society of selves as *hermeneutic*, that is, as intrinsically interpretable within the historical and *gemeinschaftlich life of an entire society*. The bearing of these distinctions on moral matters rests with the *gemeinschaftlich* nature of our formative *Sitten*.

This goes utterly against Levinas's line of thinking, of course, and, at the same time, it exposes the unexplained mystery of Heidegger's account of the "ontological" *existentialia* of *Dasein* that cannot (apparently) be accounted for in terms of man's mere "ontic" nature (that is, by way of the *categories* of our second-natured concepts). Levinas's mistake is simply the polar opposite of the "analytic" mistake of thinking that language itself arises as a "convention"—hence, as a cooperative agreement of some sort among pre-linguistic agents. That cannot possibly be true, for it implicates the very powers it pretends to create.

What is morally significant about our lives bears, then, on what we individually do. What we do, however, is morally valid only as a function of the collectively shared norms that inform our individual acts. That is precisely what saves morality from mere arbitrariness. Moral sensibility is already a collective matter among our formative *Sitten*; it must remain collective in our would-be second-order reforms if it is to preserve the *ethos* we mean to change *and* if it is to do so effectively. Read this way, Hegel's speculations about the state may be as extravagant as Heidegger's invention of *Dasein*'s onto-onto-logical mode of Being. Both, however, belong to the order of Nature.

The idea that selves are cultural "artifacts" because they are so remarkably transformed by the natural acquisition of a home language and a home culture suggests very clearly why Levinas's and Heidegger's extravagances are so misleading. Hegel's own extravagance, also unnecessary (and confusing in its own way), comes from an attempt to treat the *geistlich* (collective) dimension of human life in terms of its own distinctive history viewed as an adequate replacement for the whole of Kant's entire transcendental order. *Geist*, I suggest, is a heuristic and mythic device that Hegel introduces in order to isolate the collective cultural significance of the historical life of an entire society or age that informs the thoughts and acts of the aggregated individual members of that society, often beyond their own capacity to understand the full import of what they themselves do. Moral life and political life share the *geistlich* dimension of meaning, which we construct reflexively, unendingly, diversely, by our historicized interpretations of our own life. This provides, we may say, the *sittlich* ground for the only kind of objectivity science and morality can command.

In short, the very nature of cultural life sets conservative (or conserving) limits on what an entire society can effectively support in the way of a potentially radical change of practice. This is perhaps what Akhenaton failed to grasp—and what the Nazis triumphantly demonstrated was far more manipulable than might be supposed. This is also close to the sense of what Heidegger means by "being-in-the-world" (*in-der-Welt-sein*) as well as what he means by *Mitsein*, except that, for Heidegger, moral sensibility must always address Being or finite existence in terms of Being rather than merely the specific finitude and contingency of human lives and human practices themselves. It's in this sense (somewhat against Heidegger) that moral agency may be said to feature a determinable *modus vivendi* more than an ontological surd or bloodless proposition. Putting matters this way obviates the need for Heidegger's reliance on the murky and privileged distinction between the "ontic" and the "ontological"—or what might exceed any such division itself. Whatever of prime importance that is marked (by Heidegger) as "ontological" must already be implicated in what he treats as the "factical" or merely "ontic," although, in saying that, I may well be distorting Heidegger's intent. I certainly agree that the specifically human is *sui generis*—though not, for that reason, "beyond" nature.

I see no other possible idiom for capturing the human. If Heidegger intends something more fundamental, then he runs the risk of being unable to distance himself from Kantian transcendentals—which, of course, he opposes. To my mind, if he has another option, he has never rightly said what it is. I doubt there is another intelligible possibility, unless it is to present something close to what I've sketched but in terms of its existential pathos. In any case, I cannot make sense of any conception of the human in which selves lack (or are not) "living bodies," or in which, as living bodies, they do not achieve their characteristic powers by way of some initial enculturing process. I can admit that there may well be exalted questions that query the ultimate source of this—and "everything." But I cannot see how they might displace the considerations before us now without disallowing the meaning of those glorious questions themselves!

I collect the import of all this, as far as concerns moral matters (though it informs the factual and scientific as well), by noting that *selves* are: (i) hybrid beings, at once naturally and culturally endowed; (ii) indissolubly "embodied" in, but culturally emergent (emergent *sui generis*) with respect to *Homo sapiens*; (iii) second-natured *qua* emergent, possessing the powers of *agency* in the way of languaged thought, speech, intention, choice, deliberate action, knowledge, the acknowledgment of responsibility, and whatever else depends on the mastery of language and cultural practice (feeling and emotion, the sense of mortality); (iv) formed and transformed by the contingent processes of Intentional, *gemeinschaftlich* history; (v) in possession of powers that are themselves also artifactual, hybrid, second-natured, indissolubly "incarnate" in the biology of *Homo sapiens*, forever subject to further historied, Intentional, transformative change; and (vi) singly and aggregatively apt as effective moral agents, continuing to alter themselves and others in historicized ways by their own effective "utterances" and interventions.

As I have already remarked, whatever belongs to the culturally significant, in the manner collected as items (i)–(vi)—the linguistic, the semiotic, the significative, the representational, the expressive, the traditional, the institutional, the rule-like, the historical, the intentional, the purposive, the normative—I call the Intentional.[4] In short, *the Intentional = the cultural*, in the sense of all that is intrinsically interpretable (as art, language, history, and agents' deeds). It follows at once that *(a)* moral agents are capable of knowing the lay of the entire world, both natural and cultural, in which they act; *(b)* rightly informed, they act with the knowledge that they cannot legitimate what they do, beyond the resources and limitations of one or another second-best morality; and *(c)* they know they act under the conditions of an evolving history, their own *sittlich* formation, their partisan commitments, horizoned understanding, and the impossibility of avoiding conflict with the normative convictions and partisan commitments of other agents differently formed and informed. The effective exercise of their aptitude as agents, as in judgment and commitment (or in art and manufacture and speech), I call "utterance." It is primarily our utterances, then, Intentionally informed, that are the objects of moral review. In short, I ask you to think of 9/11 in these terms before you spring to judgment.

[II]

Seen in this way, there is no principled disjunction between the moral and the political—and hence among the moral, the legal, the economic, the religious, the interpretive, the practical, the cognitive, the legitimative, and the culturally real. All of these distinctions "arise together"[5] within the holism of our understanding of the world and of the ways in which selves live in the world. But they live not only in substantial ignorance of the causal linkages among the innumerable physical and biological processes that affect or can affect their practical plans and prudential interests, as when an unsuspected disease takes the life of someone essential to one's own life and world, but also in ignorance of how their own interventions ramify (in causal ways) through the hybrid lives of their own and other societies. (Think, for instance, of the Americans' enthusiastic support of the Taliban during and after the Cold War—but before 9/11—or of Saddam Hussein during the war between Iraq and Iran.)

Not only that, but, more consequentially, individual and aggregated selves act with very little understanding of their own second-natured "natures." They are indeed aware that they and those they affect are profoundly changed, reflexively, as a direct consequence of what they and others do — *but they cannot know precisely in what way they will have been changed in historically and Intentionally pertinent respects.* They *cannot* know, because what we mean by "knowledge" here—which bears on what we also mean by moral responsibility—entails what their own agency and the agency of others *will* yield in an extended future that will need to be judged in order to judge what they now do in the present! This is perhaps what is most arresting and important about the "terrorism" we now identify as "9/11." It begins to explain the meaning of the great variety of (and conflicts among) human norms and, even more deeply, the meaning of the argument that draws us in the direction of viewing life *rationaliter* in accord with a second-best morality.

We cannot rightly know—though we may guess—the historicized changes in our own "nature," the thread of our own "career." Creatures like ourselves— the second-natured cultural artifacts that we are, hybrid entities whose own powers of agency are transformed through our own utterances and responses to the uttered agency of others—cannot fail to see that the moral import of every present challenge *includes*, in a public way, the evolving, open-ended, future interpretations of how we respond *now* to how our present appraisal of the present informs our present acts! There you have the pathos of morality itself: the longing for fixed principles and the clear perception of their inevitable inadequacy for the task they set themselves. I see no principled difference between such transformations and, say, the conversion of Saul on the road to Damascus, except that Saul apparently believed that he was made instantly aware of the essential meaning of the transformation he had undergone and hence the altered meaning of his past life. By comparison, *we* understand (correctly) that the "full meaning" of 9/11 belongs, interpretively, to our future history and cannot possibly be made out *yet*, though it will surely alter the meaning and our capacity to understand the meaning (not simply *add* to the meaning) of past and present history. The changes we undergo are "unconscious," subterranean, fluent in an unsuspected way—in effect, "historical" in that sense in which, more ambitiously, Hegel takes note of the "world-historical" roles that figures like Napoleon and Alexander play, without *their* grasping (as Hegel claims he does) the Intentional meaning of what they do! Also, of course, morality yields to reasoning *rationaliter*. Paul would not have acquiesced in such constraints.

The meaning of history is itself constructed, artifactual, determinable, yet not strictly determinate.[6] Still, history is thoroughly realist in the cultural sense, in being open to description and interpretation that, from time to time, cannot be made to conform to the strictures of a bivalent logic, obliged to be hospitable (to be realist at all) to relativistic, incommensurabilist, evolving, historicized appraisals and reinterpretations.

Furthermore, the continuing reflexive interpretation of prior interpretations may be as efficacious as the latter—again, subterraneanly—so that, as a consequence of having acted and of having interpreted what we have done, we are no longer quite the "same" agents we were when first we acted. Our sense of our own agency will have changed. We will have changed in "nature" or "history," though *not* in "number"—an idea the Aristotelian canon would never countenance. Entities like selves—culturally emergent agents, Intentionally qualified—are, I suggest, *living histories*. Acting as they do, they alter themselves (and other selves) both in terms of their interpretable natures and in terms of their perceived powers as engaged agents. Think of the blind Oedipus transformed in Sophocles' sequel to the *Oedipus Rex*, or Macbeth—or, for that matter, anyone who has reflected on having carelessly caused another a great harm that might have been avoided. We are, in short, what we utter (or, perhaps better, what we and others utter) and we are at least dimly aware of this truth. (I trust you see that I am inventing a use of a thoroughly naturalistic idiom that Levinas and Heidegger reject in advance of any such effort. I take the liberty, therefore, of inviting their admirers to identify what is missing or unacceptably distorted.)

Our lives—our careers, which are the longitudinal unities of our hybrid "natures" deployed in time as histories—are never mere histories but are, at least incipiently, *histories historicized*, in the sense in which the Intentional meaning of what we think and do *now* is artifactually altered by the *further* events and interpretations within the same cultural world. These further events and interpretations signify a formative or transformative change *in the conceptual resources and cognitive horizon* within which we continue to think and act. In fact, we act *now*, knowing that such changes will happen *then!* We are aware that our own powers of understanding are altered under the condition of our evolving cultural experience—and we act, anticipating such changes.

Very few complexities of these sorts are regularly analyzed in English-language moral philosophy (or, for that matter, in continental European thought), though their acknowledgment must color in the profoundest way the validity and merit of moral assessment itself. Here, "historicized" means not only "historical," in the sense in which human events are rightly ascribed Intentional import reflecting (as Hegel says) "our own age remembered in its time," all the while subject to historical changes in our cognitive and active powers affecting the ongoing interpretation of history itself (which is what Hegel clearly had in mind), changes in the very operative concepts and mode of understanding by which we continually adjust our sense (subliminally) of moral and scientific objectivity in the face of changing history. In our own time, Foucault is probably the most compelling master of large changes of this sort tracked among the *epistemes* of Eurocentric history. But as far as I know (and I may be mistaken), Foucault does not track the thought of an agent who acts with a sense of the transformation to which his own act contributes. That, I believe, is the startling sense of Kuhn's discovery of "paradigm shifts." (I suggest that we are in the middle of such a deep shift, responding to 9/11.)

The Greeks had their admirable Thucydides, of course, but they could not have had a Foucault. Yet Foucault rarely explores (in the way Nietzsche does, for instance) the complexity of moral judgment and commitment specifically under historicized conditions. Typically, Foucault emphasizes that *epistemes* have changed as a result of ongoing history—but he does not pause to analyze the historicizing process itself.

Nietzsche unites, as Foucault does not, an implicit grasp of the deep risks of the ineluctably anthropocentric nature of moral reflection and the artifactual and historicized nature of human agency itself incarnate in the unfathomable *conatus* of the race. Foucault makes agency an almost impossible attribute — one pointless to speak of ever exercising. Nietzsche, on the other hand, tempers the very exercise of responsible agency with a constant reminder of the cosmic comedy within whose terms we always act. Heidegger cleaves to the pathos of the human condition, though he also risks (notoriously, you remember) subordinating that pathos to a Volkish destiny. I see no evidence that what Heidegger says in his best moments cannot be recovered, in the way I've sketched, within the boundaries of intelligible nature.

My own intuition is that, as a result of ongoing historical changes triggered by events not yet perceived in the operative present and possibly not even evolved as yet, the remarkable transformative force of events like 9/11 — in effect, the *geistlich* "present" event around which the interpretation of the present *is* being transformed — may now actually be seen, not only in the way of normal evidence but also in terms of altering our cognitive resources and our horizon of understanding in a historically evolving way.

I mention these contingencies because they confirm a number of important theorems that often go unnoticed, viz.: (i) that disputes, however centered on the acts of individual persons, are inseparable from larger political and ideological contests; (ii) that, in the globalized setting of the most pressing moral/political disputes of the day, it would be hopeless to believe that resolutions arrived at *rationaliter* could rightly presume that the contending parties *will*, in time, converge on the same ideologies and convictions; and (iii) that some sort of normative universalism or essentialism or invariant rules of reason will probably become apparent to all involved. The tally begins to collect the elements of our grandest utopian delusion. But I must add now: (iv) that distinctions (i)–(iii) confirm the odd ("metaphysical") fact that the Intentional meaning of whatever obtains in the cultural world is determinable rather than determinate (in the sense usually accorded physical nature) and is subject to historicizing forces. This helps explain the significance of drawing the theoretical out of the practical, of construing the practical in terms of a *modus vivendi* rather than of determinate propositions or principles, and of acknowledging the pertinence of relativism in every form of human inquiry and commitment.

The Intentional (that is, the cultural) tolerates (consensually — in effect, interpretively) the objective meaning of whatever obtains in human circumstances as a consequence of the evolving historical novelty of human interaction. Our future fixes in a constructive way the objective meaning of what we have already done *in the past*, because the meaning of the past is determinable, actually open to alternative interpretations in the evolving present of societal life, alternatives that could not be convincingly imputed (within unfolding history) until consensual tolerance admitted them. Imagine, for instance, construing class relations in the Marxist sense in ancient Greece, before the Industrial Revolution made it possible to assign objective standing to such an attribution.

We cannot afford utopian dreams that are not anchored in culturally immanent possibilities. And yet a very large part of Western moral philosophy is committed to one or another improbable version of universalism or facultative competence keyed to moral cognition or a general aptitude for objectivity (possibly even neutrality or disinterested judgment) capable of discerning what "any" informed observer is "bound" to find. Otherwise, you cannot even make sense of the master themes of the strongest versions of Kantian and Aristotelian and empiricist and intuitionistic moral philosophies. Frankly, the world is too dangerous a place for such pretensions. Could that have been a part of Nietzsche's lesson?

Viewed even more narrowly, the larger moral/political disputes of the day confirm the sense in which so-called international law is, for the most part, either the law of victors in war or of states powerful enough to impose their will on other states, which returns us to the Thrasymachean challenge writ large. One sees this very clearly in the war crimes tribunal's handling of charges in Kosovo, in various feints (in the American "war against terrorism" in Afghanistan) to forestall invoking the Geneva Convention concerning so-called detainees not yet classified as "prisoners of war," in the awkward lengthening stalemate of UN resolutions affecting Iraq's economy and quality of life before the second war against Iraq, and in the threatening chaos of the entire Middle East (and with it the threatening chaos of the world).

I acknowledge that there is no effective alternative to the dubious model of international law. But to admit the fact invites a change of moral/political theory—more than a protest in the name of neutral justice.

I do not wish to deny the importance and even the defensibility of UN intentions and resolutions in the name of justice. Rather, I wish to draw attention to the plain fact that the appeal to international law is hardly comparable to the procedures of established courts within the jurisdictional authority and competence of well-defined states. It seems fair to say that the very threat of conflict capable of destabilizing the global community of nations undermines the would-be function of international courts just when they are wanted. In that sense, appeal to international law is an exercise in political morality disposed to model its would-be resolution of relevant conflicts in terms of legal and quasi-legal procedures and precedent, even where resolution is plainly ad hoc, distinctly ideological, favorably skewed in the interests of strong states that are themselves aware that great powers cannot be "governed" by an independent court and will not willingly submit to adverse findings. Think of America's intervention in the affairs of Nicaragua and its fear that its own participation in UN peacekeeping in Bosnia (if not also, eventually, in Iraq) may open the way to its being held answerable to war crimes charges. It is historicity—not merely history—that overtakes the search for stable principles of law as well as would-be interpretive norms of objective morality. It may even be plausible to believe that nations guided, but not governed, by the impossible dream of a valid international law yield frequently enough to consensual pressures against unlimited brutality, victor's justice, genocide, and the like that they half-persuade themselves of the rational benefit of their self-deception and inconsistencies against the endless threat of the instabilities of power.

The American Civil War is sometimes cited as a war that actually preserved (and was intended to preserve) the constitutional integrity of the nation, not to change its essential structure or allow it to be changed. But, of course, in doing that, the Civil War *did* change the country in the profoundest way. It changed the *geistlich* prospects of its own people. So did the Second World War. So did the Cold War. So did the Gulf War. So will the war on terrorism, we may conjecture. Actual history changes the capacity for further history— and our capacity to understand and judge it. The process is only dimly perceived, reflexively: the demands of continuously assured coherence, collectively as well as personally, obscure the flux of history itself. That, frankly, is what is at once so remarkable and preposterous about America's penchant for believing in the interpretive fixity of its living Constitution.[7]

To be a moral agent is to act and be vulnerable to a change of Intentional "nature" as a result of being an active agent. There is nothing comparable in the whole of physical nature, not even in biological evolution (on the standard theories). Reductionists are likely to say, therefore: "So your theory of agency is false, very probably incoherent." My suggestion is that our understanding of ourselves—and the world we inhabit—is itself second-best, a series of constructed, provisional, locally grounded, heuristic, proliferating, not easily generalizable models of how to understand our "nature." These models are produced, in some measure, by partisans and ideologues concerned to vindicate their own judgments and commitments, by which *they* mean to influence and alter human affairs and the world—*and* our understanding of what has already been wrought.

The entire argument rests on the irreducible uniqueness and novelty of the

Intentional complexities of historical and cultural life. I claim that there would be no moral issues at all if that were not so; I claim further that moral philosophy has rarely acknowledged the connection. Its strongest intuitions are surely Hegelian, but its subversive possibilities were hardly regularized before Nietzsche and Foucault. I admit I find them already implicit in Plato's dialogues and the work of the Sophists (but there they lack a clear account of the relationship between the natural and the cultural or of the force of historicity).

So the theory of human agency can hardly fail to be heterodox. It makes sense, conceptually, only in terms of a *sui generis* form of actual (real) emergence—cultural or Intentional emergence, under the speculation already ventured. Otherwise, it has to be displaced, one way or another, by alternative models of a very different kind. I have already signaled that Heidegger and Levinas were aware of the potentially unwelcome consequences of confining human selves *to the order of the "naturalized" world* (not to be confused with the "natural" world, which includes the hybrid human world, coherently enough).

"Naturalizing," as in the current analytic idiom, signifies an inclusive causal order "closed" within the terms of the physical and biological world alone.[8] In its strictest form, naturalizing is deterministic; hence, it obviates the bare admission of moral agents. But Levinas's and Heidegger's own efforts were, as I have suggested, either arbitrary or conceptually extravagant or incoherent or simply impenetrable. The same may be said of efforts to make more of the supposedly transcendent or transcendental powers of rational competence that cannot be confined to the merely human, as in Plato, Kant, the post-Kantian Idealists, Edmund Husserl, and possibly even (by default) John Rawls and Jürgen Habermas. (The latter two pretend to locate an alien power of "reason" *in* the natural world itself, though they assign it a competence it could never acquire or manifest in a merely human world.)

A similar motivation appears among the Francophone structuralists, whether linguists, anthropologists, historians, or Marxists (as with A. J. Greimas, Louis Althusser, Claude Lévi-Strauss, Jacques Lacan, and Michel Foucault at times, despite his pertinent demurrers). The self is reinterpreted, there, as a kind of abstract node at which structured *relata* within a relatively closed system of formal processes (operating on such *relata*) are alleged to yield admissible transformations under which we may then interpret what, in the conceptually unruly human world, would be inexplicable otherwise (as Ferdinand de Saussure affirms). The structuralists thereby detach and hypostatize in their own extreme idiom what really would make sense, in a predicative way, only in a world of human agents.

The conceptual needs of a theory of agency begin to dawn easily enough. Selves or agents must be actual entities apt for agency. That's all! Otherwise, moral/political questions, practical questions of any sort, and even questions regarding the human competence to pursue scientific inquiry would make no sense. Lacan, for instance, is a genuinely—if maddeningly—ingenious theorist bent on elevating unconscious processes, semiotically, to the effectively real level of psychoanalytic description. Read literally, Lacan's account is never completely intelligible, because it denies the existence of actual selves or actual agents. But Kant's account is not altogether dissimilar, if you take seriously Kant's conceptual disjunction between the noumenal and the phenomenal—the disjunction on which his account of morality depends.

Selves are the denotable sites of moral and scientific agency. To admit that a scientific or moral or medical inquiry "is under way" *is* to acknowledge the realist standing of selves. Otherwise, we are the victims of paradox, forever speaking of selves (ourselves) "in other ways": *autrement qu'être* (Levinas), "ontologically" (Heidegger), transcendentally (Kant), as a structuralist *relatum* (Lacan), fictionally (Sellars), eliminatively (Paul Churchland), and so on.

Sellars, for instance, speaking directly of moral agency—frankly, no one can be quite sure how such a posit fits with the rest of his speculations—treats persons as no more than functionally assigned fictional ascriptions, or roles. "Assigned to *what?*" you may ask. Well, it must be some congeries of microtheoretical entities that could be plausibly *assigned* such a role; all the while, we tactfully avoid asking just what *our* making such an assignment might entail! (That is the very demon Heidegger means to exorcise. But does he succeed in his own right?) Extraordinary that there should be so much uncertainty about our own nature.

I take it to be reasonably certain that no one has been able to make conceptual sense of speaking a language, making a choice, deciding on a commitment, paying a bill, or fighting in a war, say, without admitting the realist standing of selves possessing certain powers that *(faute de mieux)* can only be explained, as we now understand matters, in terms of cultural emergence. To admit that much, however, is to treat selves as culturally constituted: "artifacts," if you like, of some naturalistic (but not "naturalizable") process of social construction, as by internalizing the language and culture of one's home society. In that sense, selves are second-natured entities to which we predicate the emergent Intentional aptitudes that, we say, distinguish selves from whatever is confined to physical nature alone—including the members of *Homo sapiens,* which the enculturing process transforms into selves. Alternatively worded, what I mean is that Heidegger might have viewed *Dasein* as a thoroughly "natural" entity if he could have been mollified by something like my distinction between the "natural" or "naturalistic" and the "naturalized" or "naturalizable." Instead, he makes a mystery of *Dasein* itself. The result is an extravagance with which serious moral theory cannot possibly be satisfied.

A fully formed account of how all this obtains would explain the original emergence of common culture. I see no principled difficulty there—only empirical uncertainty. My thought is that prelinguistic communication must have begun to develop incipient linguistic features somewhere in the evolutionary sequence of prehuman life (for instance, among intelligent monkeys and primates, by making possible reference to different kinds of danger, here and now, by different calls). The unique placement of the vocal cords in humans permitted a very fine-grained articulation of sounds that could have been incipiently fixed for certain primitive grammatical functions (reference, for example) that might have remained unformed until some marvelously inventive hominid moment.

Once a certain threshold was passed, however, which might have been approached through very small increments below the level of true language, the cultural world was on its way to emerging full blast. Retrospectively, only when proto-language achieved a certain critical complexity (we may suppose), only when the creatures who could "speak" actually began to speak and, "speaking," began to refer to and identify themselves and others and the sites of danger, food, and other creatures, could *we* say that the emergent world of human culture must already have existed. How so? Well, *if* we are *now* able to speak and do the things we plainly believe we do, then there must have been some continuous process at the level of primate and hominid life when evolution made possible small changes sufficient to permit the entire flowering of human culture. You cannot have the one without the other. That is all that is meant by the "second-natured" nature of cultural life. The rest is empirical detail.

In this sense, it would be absurd to deny that selves are actual beings—and absurd to deny that the cultural world that includes selves and what, in the Intentional way, they "utter" (do, make, say, create) *is* as real and as causally efficacious as the physical world. Indeed, it is inseparable from it: "embodied," as selves are, in *Homo sapiens*, and "incarnate," as speech and thought and production are, in physical and biological attributes. That world, I have been at pains to explain, is the very world in which, and in which alone, *we* function as moral agents. It is worth remarking that if we admit the emergence of the cultural world, the causal closure of the physical world will be threat-

ened. I have no doubt that that possibility has had a sobering effect on speculations in the emergentist direction. It is obviously a cousin to Kant's reflection on the determinism of the natural world. The entire argument rests on
the strategic finding that the cultural world *is* a real world—and *is* irreducible
to the physical. (Does Heidegger require more?)

[III]

I insist, however, that although there is no viable philosophy that does not admit the existence of selves and the reality of the world of human culture, which
must have arisen by some *sui generis* process in a manner close to the one I've
sketched (a thesis I name "cultural realism"), I do not conclude from that that
my own view of what a self is, of what the Intentional signifies, of what the
hybrid ontology of the cultural world is like, or of what we should understand
by "history" and "historicity" *is* the only or best or minimal or discovered truth
about the human condition. Not at all. I *do* regard my account as a not implausible example of a very large, diverse set of possible solutions to the question of the relationship between physical nature and human culture (between
the members of *Homo sapiens* and apt selves) and what it is to be a causally
efficacious and responsible agent.

There are strategically placed considerations here that would favor the
choice of a second-best morality somewhat along the lines I've developed.
My conviction is that we're pretty well driven to such a choice. My principal
caveat is that any such theory should be as spare as possible, should avoid all
suppositions that smuggle in substantive views about objective norms, should
be coherent, and should address all the familiar puzzles that are known to
defeat unwary proposals (for instance, scandalous dualisms, inconsistent logics, unsecured metaphysical or epistemological forms of privilege, adven-
turous departures from the natural world). Apart from all that, I see no reason why there should not be a sizable number of alternative such proposals,
which need not, of course, be compatible with one another. On the contrary, if what I have been urging is reasonably correct, the construction of a
philosophical theory of agency (and selves) is bound to be a second-best conjecture of its own.

In any event, it may be helpful to collect the most important themes that
have informed the sketch of agency I've been developing. These cannot fail
to affect the kind of moral theory that might be ventured, but they have application beyond the moral question: they affect the prospects of a viable theory of science, too, and for the same reasons. That is indeed what motivates
my account: namely, (i) that the same spare conceptual constraints imposed

on science should obtain as well in moral matters (and vice versa); (ii) that the same cognitive resources should be applied more or less in the same way to moral and scientific data; and (iii) that our cognitive resources should not exceed what we can reasonably confirm without invoking privilege or fictive necessities or anything of the kind.

Kant, it seems, meets the first two constraints only in part, but not the third—and therefore not the first two either. The disjunction between the "heteronomous" (empirical human nature) and the "autonomous" (human freedom and reason as a self-legislating power "beyond" empirical nature) in Kant's account is patently contrived, indefensible, and pointedly inadequate as a theory of agency. (Ultimately, Kant has no realist theory of agency at all. He is not entitled, therefore, to claim a moral theory.) Aristotle is more successful, although, finally, we hardly know how to construe the argument of the *Nicomachean Ethics*—if, through the passage of centuries, the *Ethics* is still pertinently addressed to us! We are, however, clearer about what Kant thinks is fundamental to moral validity and why *he* cannot make his case a compelling one. If you read Kant carefully—in almost any text of the Critical period— you realize that, though he has a clear account of the conditions for the objective validity of every kind of judgment, he cannot formulate an account of the functioning unity of a moral agent or, more generally, an integrated human self! He "approximates" to such a theory, and cannot do better, by identifying the *separate* strata of experience, imagination, understanding, and reason that enter into any well-formed judgment. His human beings, though, do not quite live or commit themselves in the actual world as actual agents. They cannot understand themselves in such terms. To claim that they do would produce insuperable paradox; it would require combining, impossibly, autonomy *and* its palpable "contradiction" (actual human life) as ingredients in what makes us effective agents. The result is a kind of philosophical scandal that would never have been countenanced in a lesser figure.

Here, then, is a tally of some of the more strategic themes I've invoked in advancing the idea of a second-best morality: (i) that the world is a flux, that is, it lacks necessary invariances of any sort, though it is not a chaos; (ii) that there are no valid forms of cognitive or rational privilege in either theoretical or practical matters, or in science or morality; (iii) that, regarding metaphysics and epistemology or any disciplines that address the way the world is and how we know it to be such, or how, knowing that, we should conduct our own lives, there is no principled disjunction or hierarchical order or foundational priority of any kind—for instance, as to whether semantic questions can be settled before metaphysical questions or legitimative questions before empirical ones; (iv) that, as a result of (i)–(iii), the resolution of any philosophical or scientific or practical questions takes a constructive or constructivist form, *faute de mieux*; (v) that selves and what they utter are culturally constituted — Intentional artifacts — and that enlanguaged thought is historicized; and (vi) that, as a result of (iv)–(v), if there is any valid resolution of a given question, in the way of being true or right or taking related values, it is entirely possible that there will be alternative answers of comparable validity that are incompatible or incommensurable with the first.

This final tally, of course, articulates the conceptual spine of the entire preceding argument. But it further yields two extremely important theorems that bear on the advantages of a second-best morality. Each spells out a consequence, largely ignored in canonical discussions, of the perfectly obvious fact that a moral theory (in effect, an account of moral agency) reflects what we regard as a tenable theory of the nature of selves, where, that is, the analysis of what a self is may, but need not, entail actual substantive moral norms. Where there *is* a direct entailment, the resultant theory may be said to be a *realist morality* (in a pejorative sense), because, on the strength of the foregoing tally, metaphysics cannot fail to take a constructivist turn itself.

By contrast, assuming the validity of cultural realism (which is thoroughly constructivist) and admitting the bearing, on the issue of realism, of item (vi) of the tally just given, it would be entirely vacuous to claim that *any* particular moral theory *was* directly entailed in the realist sense. Very nearly any moral theory could then be similarly characterized — and for the same reasons! The issue is not a negligible one, because both Aristotle and Kant are moral realists (of very different sorts), and any willingness to subscribe to items (i)–(vi) of the previous tally would show at once the deep circularity of their accounts. They must show not only the coherence of their respective conjectures but also the necessity of following the line of argument they happen to favor. That now appears to be an impossible task.

Proceeding *rationaliter*, it follows that moral theories are distinguished among themselves largely in terms of their ideological convictions — of what to preserve and what to yield in terms of partisan priorities. A moral agent, therefore, *is* a moral ideologue, though one prepared to debate and act *rationaliter* (say, along the lines of the various strategies laid out earlier in this account). Hence — and here is the first of the two theorems I mean to feature — moral agents are prepared to debate the validity of competing moral judgments, findings, appraisals, assertions, and prescriptives (*propositions*, in short) as an integral part of validating their actual and intended commitments, acts, practices, *engagements*, and partisan advocacy (the various ingredients, that is, of their preferred *modus vivendi*).

In a word, moral agents *bear witness* to the seriousness with which they are committed to the form of life they have chosen—precisely *by* engaging, dialectically, the views of competing partisans in order to expose some plausibly charged weakness in the moral ideology of their opponents. (The better to strengthen their own.) But, of course, to be prepared to assess competing views *rationaliter* is already to share an incipient *modus vivendi* in which objectivist or "realist" resolutions, in the moral sense, are no longer needed. That, I think, must be the principal advantage of a credible moral theory.

The second theorem is the mate of the first. If moral agents lack a "natural-kind" nature, have or are "histories" (still within "nature"), and if their ideologies have probably evolved from their formative *Sitten*, then it would be entirely reasonable that, under the conditions of their changing history, they would be drawn to consider changing ideologies as they change their prudential interests or discover better strategies for gaining the interests they have. Classic Marxism, for instance, was occupied with exposing "false consciousness" among the proletariat, with an eye to preparing the revolutionary means by which to achieve the proletariat's "true" interests. But the evolution of capitalism has outflanked Marxism, in that form at least. Contemporary feminism has pursued the same kind of dual emphasis (though hardly the same objectives), even to demonstrating the inability of the Marxist analysis to capture the intractable implications of "patriarchal" dominance. But the feminists have also found it impossible to formulate a comparably ample picture of the stable prudential interests of women worldwide. ("Woman" proves to be an artifactual distinction as well.)

My sense is that feminism cannot be a determinate ideology, though it is an honorable moral strategy. *Prudentiae* must be construed in local, detailed, historically contexted ways if they are to be effective at all. There is no useful sense, I believe, in attempting to isolate, oppositionally, the universal *prudentiae* appropriate to women as opposed to men. The feminisms of the Western world and the feminisms of the "third" and "fourth" worlds of Africa and Asia, for instance, have very little in common.

I mean by the second theorem, then, something to the effect that agents committed to a second-best morality are, unavoidably, *moral opportunists*. They cannot discover the "virtues" of the moral life in their own restricted "natures," because what distinguishes one society from another are their divergent histories and the changing prudential prospects of their evolving *Sit-*

ten. They cannot be faulted for that alone, however. By the same argument, there cannot be a specifically American or Iraqi morality, except in the anthropologist's sense. I admit that moral reflection and commitment are a partisan affair, but morality cannot be validly or even coherently formulated *as* a deliberately partisan doctrine. It is what it is, *faute de mieux*: it is the work of interested agents, but it also seeks to present itself in whatever way may be recommended as objective. And, to that end, it can only speak in the name of what is generically human. On the strength of the tally given a moment ago, there is no other way to live and think responsibly. It has its dangers, I don't deny, but it is no more dangerous a vision than it has always been. And there is no coherent alternative.

HUMANITY AND MORAL DIVERSITY

I return now to my opening reflections. I had featured the idea that the legitimation of moral judgments and commitments could not expect to be convincing unless we restricted our claims to second-best moralities based on the actual *sittlich* practices of a people—admitting, as *sittlich*, practices that have normative force only in that first-order sense in which anthropologists record the habitual customs of a society's members regarding how they believe they should treat themselves and others. A moral theory, I supposed, was a second-order defense of the validity of some reform or continuation of such *sittlich* practices, one that could (and normally would) generate changes that could be spontaneously absorbed into the *sittlich* stream itself. And because, on my account, selves or persons are second-natured artifacts—hybrid agents viewed as functional transforms of the members of *Homo sapiens*, made apt and responsible by internalizing the language and institutions of their home society—moral legitimation, like selves themselves, could not be other than culturally constructed. Admitting selves to have realist standing (for *who* would be left to deny that they did, if that were disputed?) allows us to speak of moral norms and practices as open to objective validation in much the same constructive or constructivist sense as the sense in which (though for very different reasons) the objectivity of science is also a constructivist affair.

From this and related considerations, I drew a series of findings that argued that an objective moral vision focuses more on a defensible *modus vivendi* than on any isolated act or proposition; that it could never rely on cognitive or rational privilege, because its own assessments could never be anything but *sittlich* constructions; and that it would favor a second-best morality, invoke constructed norms grounded in and applied to our first-order *Sitten*, engage the convictions and commitments of admitted partisans and ideologues, and be guided by considerations *rationaliter*. I suggested that we could proceed here only dialectically and that we could not deny that if there were alternative rationales that could claim objective standing under such circumstances, it would be likely—even commonplace—that conflicting, incompatible, possibly incommensurable defenses might prove valid according to our second-best terms. In addition, I believed that moral validity was more a practical than a theoretical affair; that there could be no compelling reason to insist on the strictures of a bivalent logic in assessing objective resolutions of moral disputes; and that, if so, moral objectivity might have to yield, to some degree, in the direction of historicism, relativism, incommensurabilism, constructivism, and similar doctrines. I took (and still take) these heterodox possibilities to be demonstrably coherent and self-consistent. But, apart from that, these strenuous findings confirm (in my opinion) that a serious review of moral reflection cannot rightly free itself from a sustained philosophical analysis of the nature of human culture and that of the human self—both of which are remarkably problematic matters normally ignored in the usual accounts. That might have been acceptable in other inquiries, but in moral matters, as we have seen, these questions play an absolutely decisive role in crafting the most convincing and balanced account of the entire field. The "metaphysical" options championed in the canonical literature are so directly implicated in the defense of inadequate moral models that it has become well-nigh impossible to propose a fresh analysis of 9/11 without addressing the metaphysics of culture and selves. That fact itself is a warning of some importance.

It also needs to be said that, in characterizing moral/political reflection as "dialectical," I was invoking something close to the general Hegelian/ Marxist emphasis on the consensual or *prima facie* validity of doubts about the adequacy or effectiveness of standing *sittlich* norms—possibly in proposing adjustments or changes *rationaliter* to particular norms—as in learning, when facing some impending *summum malum* or the loss of some acknowledged *minimum bonum*, that advisable corrective action may not be able to restore sufficiently the *status quo ante*. That, I suggest, *is* the Hegelian theme of Marx's conception and defense of class warfare, as well as the key to Hegel's notion of a normative and social "contradiction." What is "dialectical" in this sense is constructed and pertinent to the collective life of an actual society.

But it requires our tolerating—indeed, our validating—a reasoned change in the *sittlich* order. Here, Hegel has invented one of the most plausible clues we possess regarding the objectivity of legitimated norms evolving under historicized conditions, with due emphasis on their practical relevance, while admitting in the frankest way the partisan nature of moral/political reforms themselves. I don't happen to subscribe to Marx's criterial reading of economic determinism. But when class warfare is vindicated as a second-order moral reform rather than a mere proposition of scientific economics—which, in Marx's time, actually acquired *sittlich* standing in the guise of class warfare— it is certainly entitled to a measure of second-best inclusion and may be so included even now. It is actually quite difficult to formulate a better clue about moral legitimation than what may be grounded by the generic idea of dialectical opposition. It must be acknowledged, however, that Hegel's specific version of the clue cannot, except at the price of reclaiming some sort of normative privilege, be converted into a legitimated moral or moral/political criterion of any objectivist sort. Seen in these terms, my own effort in interpreting 9/11 is an attempt to recover the Hegelian insight in the spirit of Plato's elenctic strategy (which I take to be analogous to, but much simpler than, Hegel's own intention). I don't deny that this is a strenuous claim. Put another way, what I offer as a second-best morality is a Hegelian conception shorn of all objectivist assumptions even where applied to the most stubborn challenges of moral and political history.

Granting all this, it seemed to me that where we pressed the question of moral objectivity (particularly where danger arose from the confrontations of opposed partisan aggregates and communities convinced of the exclusive validity of their own extreme measures, as in the struggle over Kashmir and the Arab/Israeli wars), to think of moral disputes as proceeding *rationaliter* was already to have taken a giant step in the constructivist direction: to have identified the *sine qua non* of any viable model of moral objectivity without adopting any substantive moral postulate. I took it to follow from all this that validation of the normative kind must be extremely modest and that most Western moral philosophies (perhaps most of the moral philosophies of the world) were hopelessly inflated beyond any conceptual resources we or they could rightly claim, if, indeed, we proceeded *rationaliter*. In this same spirit, I collected a number of proposals as to how a second-best morality might plausibly gain objective ground—*nullum malum* and *minimum bonum*, for instance—in a way that might also teach us to scale back our philosophical expectations and proceed with more than usual caution, particularly in moral/political disputes where great harm was being risked.

In all of this, I remained convinced that 9/11 confirmed how likely it was that the most important moral/political resolutions of the foreseeable future would be obliged to take into account how extraordinarily difficult it is to move all the members of a given society to a level of moral reflection at which their proceeding *rationaliter* could be taken for granted—or possibly even strengthened or extended to include more and more quarrelsome disputes. In any event, admitting the diversity and frequent irreconcilability of *sittlich* conflicts through the entire history of mankind—adumbrated in 9/11—it seemed more than implausible to believe that the most dangerous moral/political disputes of the day (and of our probable future) could be resolved by invoking the usual doctrinal and facultative resources trotted out in standard moral philosophies.

I should emphasize again, before turning to my final topic, that I apply the term *"sittlich"* in a sense closer to its ordinary use than to Hegel's grander, obviously partisan (and potentially question-begging) use. I take Hegel's account of moral/political questions very seriously, of course. But there surely is no dialectical "method" by which to discern just how the moral/political "ought" arises from the historical "is." (It's always a mystery how Hegel arrives at its objective "necessity" in analyzing any part of cultural history.) Nevertheless, Hegel is also right to recommend that we search for alternative *geistlich* clues by which to display the narrative coherence of an ongoing history relative to our *sittlich* concerns. The "logic" of Hegel's conception of *Geist* nowhere yields a necessary rule of any kind. It is, rather, a mythic representation of a thoroughly contingent, historicized thinking that succeeds well enough (in the informal sense we count as objective) to justify its being abstracted as a heuristic model. After all, it is a strategy for discovery and dawning conviction, hardly a rule of confirmation.

I take history itself to be a reflexively contrived artifact of our evolving horizon, endlessly open to diverging further constructions, and I take Hegel's notion of "absolute *Geist*" to be (at worst) a piece of Kantian-like trickery wherever it appears to impose the language of necessity and objective validity on our constructive interpretations of the *sittlich* itself. Hegel dramatizes in a particularly compelling way just how we think about history and moral/political norms. He is not, however, an authoritative judge of *sittlich* matters himself. No one is. The histories Hegel (and Marx) compose encompass events that, by their very nature, attract diverging and even conflicting normative readings, however much they are constrained in the *sittlich* way. (I am attempting to isolate their "logic" in a slimmer Hegelian spirit.)

[I]

My sense is that we are drifting into an age (if we are not already in it) that will spawn a great number of what may appear to be (but may actually fall short of) religious or cultural wars and confrontations. I am not interested in mapping any contests of this kind, even the most salient. They seem to be springing up everywhere in incipient and opportunistic ways. I do not antic- ipate that they will converge on a grand contest between Christianity and Is- lam, for instance, though the idea is certainly heating up and must be taken seriously.[1] It strikes me as much more important that the very tendency to think along these lines is likely to reduce the effectiveness of pursuing moral matters *rationaliter*, even where we begin to approach doctrinal exhaustion in the middle of extreme danger.

Nevertheless, in the sense in which I have brought the argument to this fresh issue, there can be no objective morality that relies on the revealed va- lidity of the *sittlich* norms of, say, Judaism, Christianity, Islam, Hinduism, or comparable faiths. On the contrary, although I would not deny that there *are* Christian and Muslim moralities (in the anthropologist's sense) that do indeed have their own conceptions of second-order legitimation, they and similarly motivated moralities tend to be strenuously committed to "revealed" rather than "rational" (explicitly prudential) norms, even where they insist, as Mus- lims and Christians often do, that their moral norms are also "rational"— rationally defensible. In this sense, they favor unacceptable norms of "cogni- tive" privilege over provisional prudence, assign objective validity on revealed grounds, and refuse to acknowledge the practical possibility of overriding "truths" of the revealed sort by constructive means applied *rationaliter*. There is a deep divide, here, between conditions favorable to a second-best moral- ity capable of attracting a measure of support among moderate religious co- horts and religion's enormous and largely untapped *sittlich* capacity to mo- bilize the extraordinary kinds of commitment (suicide bombing, say) that we find almost routinely instanced after 9/11.

The point to bear in mind is that there is a seemingly irresolvable contest regarding legitimative resources in moral disputes involving what I have dubbed the rational and revealed aspects of our *sittlich* life. Moral reflection that proceeds *rationaliter* admits the *sittlich* presence and power of revealed practices, though it cannot presume to debate or adjust such practices except on prudential grounds, which committed religionists may not be willing to countenance at all. There's a stalemate there that we must avoid. The only possibility of viable collaboration rests with the plain fact that prudential pressures tend to oblige the champions of revelation to yield often enough *ratio-naliter,* even in the defense of their own revealed interests. The internal po-litical life of contemporary Iran affords an excellent example: witness Iran's willingness to allow an international inspection of its nuclear facilities. The practices of the deposed Taliban count as a more uncertain case. If these are not fair examples, then moral reasoning in the second-best sense may be wor-risomely easy to stalemate. Western religionists have, by and large, reconciled themselves to a viable collaboration. But I venture to say that, despite enor-mous resistance within the Muslim world ranging over a larger portion of moral/political questions than the West would favor, there is no evidence that concessions favoring rational disputes are unlikely anywhere. Consider the slow but definite progress in the way in which the fate of Jerusalem is being weighed by the Palestinians and the Israelis. This, I insist (against Rawls, for instance), shows no tendency *anywhere,* among diverse cultures, to be won over to the "decency" of the liberal ideologies of the West. (Rawls's naiveté has a decidedly dangerous self-deceptive side.)

Hence, in speaking of an age of "religious wars," I admit I am advancing little more than an alarmist conjecture. It's a conjecture we dare not neglect, however. I mean, primarily, the potential increase in the reliance, on the part of desperately disadvantaged populations, on forms of *sittlich* legitimation that are bound to turn away, if they can, from resolving moral matters *rationaliter.* At any rate, to proceed *rationaliter* entails, wherever possible, weaning large populations from such uncongenial practices—say, in favor of policies like *summum malum* and *adaequatio.* Here, the entire fabric of morality is put at risk: the tension between first- and second-order values is bound to be at its most trying. In effect, moral reasoning is centered on the prospects of second-best moralities, but its own practice requires a siege mentality alert to the pos-sibility of being overwhelmed by legitimative convictions whose sources it can-not possibly legitimate. It can do no more than reach provisional or piecemeal alliances on particular commitments in the name of a *modus vivendi* that strad-dles common prudential interests across insuperable divisions at the legiti-mative level. Consider, for instance, the plausible need to cooperate in the control of AIDS or SARS or an entire raft of new infectious diseases spread-ing through the world by means of changing patterns of world travel. Here, one begins to see an obvious need for tighter forms of global cooperation than any local form of revealed legitimation could possibly secure.

I believe ours is a time of momentous change. At this moment of writing, as far as Eurocentric interests are concerned, the gathering conflict appears only at flash points but may not be far from the center of a potentially unifying contest: I mean, for instance, the mutually destructive wars between the Palestinians and the Israelis and the potentially explosive conflict between the Indians and the Pakistanis (both of which keep changing and both of which seem open to deliberate manipulation that threatens to exceed any rational constraint).

Direct struggles between Muslims and Christians have appeared only sporadically, though ominously, in many countries. But their hint of a coming religious war may be misleading—may, in fact, deflect us from the deeper sources of moral and political chaos that now threaten to engulf our globalized world. It is quite possible that the mounting threat of pandemic disease, hopeless poverty and starvation, exclusionary monopolies of markets and raw materials, ineliminable unemployment, dangerous levels of pollution, genocide, and political anarchy, hegemonies of affluence, and similar ills may yet persuade the more fortunate West and its allies to consider that the fear of a religious war between Islam and Christianity is no more than a dawning sign that events like 9/11 are a plea and a demand for corrections along the lines of something akin to the policy of *liberalitas* favored by moral speculation constrained *rationaliter*, if the forms of "terrorism," construed as neutrally as possible, are not to worsen or become more frequent and more destructive.

If that is a reasonable prophecy (and I think it is), then our perception of the struggle between revealed and rational legitimation may be distorted by the dismal facts themselves. Even the opportunism of invoking the crusade and the *jihad* suggests that the real moral/political struggles are grounded in prudential matters (contested lands, markets, resources), which I take to be the most hopeful feature of the "religious" contests. These concerns suggest a more tractable strategy by which religious and ethnic hatreds and fears are being harnessed *rationaliter* even by the advocates of would-be revealed legitimation. I also see this way of thinking as a plausible example of Hegel's "method" of searching for the *Geist* of an age. In fact, if you think carefully about what I've just been saying, you will see that I've been juggling three (at least three) alternative "applications" of the Hegelian/Marxist model of dialectical opposition: first, as a religious war between Christianity and Islam, which I think to be quite improbable; second, as a contest between "revealed" and "rational" ways of pursuing moral/political conflicts, which seems to me to be a perennial ingredient in any large confrontation, but almost never more than that; and third, as the opposition between the "haves" and the "have-nots," perceived as polarized in increasingly extreme forms that reach to broaches of *summum malum*, *minimum bonum*, and *adaequatio*, which most resembles Marx's notion of class warfare. I think the third sort of contest is the one that principally informs 9/11 (suitably laid out) and is the most likely of the three to be the *geistlich* engine of a "Hegelian" moral/political history of the future. If so, then Marx's moral conviction—not Marxism in any familiar form—is likely to have an important second inning in our time.

Frankly, an effective and scrupulous morality that might claim to be objective in the manner I have been trying to sketch must confine itself to rather modest prospects. Western moral philosophers are in the habit of speculating quite grandly from within one utopian conceptual bubble or another. The principal energies of the peoples of the world are almost never attracted to academic moral philosophies. They are more likely to embrace the *sittlich* power of one religion or another, however uncompromising its requirements may be. For all that, the almost assured chaos of what an intransigent religious war would be likely to entail (in a technological age like ours) must surely oblige even the most extreme states and movements to contrive a channel of accommodation with their enemies in favor of proceeding *rationaliter*. Moral/political philosophies of the kind I am urging will have to mobilize their best skills in order to occupy the shared space that is thus created. They will improvise endlessly varied scenarios of prudential woes that our troubled age can hardly ignore—think of Lebanon and the Gaza strip. But think also of that other extraordinary (and possibly more instructive) dialogue between the United States and North Korea regarding the inseparability of the production of nuclear weapons and the assurance of an adequate *modus vivendi*. I would say that the North Koreans are pursuing a risky strategy of *adaequatio*. The best we can achieve under threats of destructive stalemate rests with some second-best conception of a larger *modus vivendi*.

You see how likely it is that stalemate will prove intractable wherever it incorporates fundamental religious, ethnic, tribal, and similar differences (involving, however they must, common *sittlich* and prudential interests) if you review, even lightly, Northern Ireland, Kosovo, Kashmir, the Arab/Israeli conflict, and the festering wars and disasters of black Africa. The endlessness of relying on a literal reading of any largely revelatory idiom, the carnage and exhaustion of stalemate at that level, cannot fail to oblige the parties to such contests to find (however haltingly) a *modus vivendi* that they are prepared to cast *rationaliter*. If they do not succeed in this (and some may well have failed), then, in our technologized age, they will destroy themselves, combating their enemies. The Palestinian question is a textbook case. The failure of both parties to escape the futility of their own ideologies is not a failure intrinsic to moral understanding: on the contrary, their potential self-destruction (arrested from time to time) actually vindicates the essential argument. For how is it possible to be unable to invent a morally valid solution if all such solutions are constructed? Failure can only mean, as it *may* well mean in the Arab/Israeli conflict, that the parties to the dispute have risked their doctrinal loyalties in such a way that they can no longer adjust them *rationaliter*. The argument suggests that it is already utopian to judge such conflicts in terms confined to the "terrorist" acts of local groups. Only the ampler space of a regional *modus vivendi* begins to provide an adequate context for pertinent rational reflection. We must change our frame of reference — our habits of appraisal and condemnation. Both the Palestinian/Israeli conflict and the Indian/Pakistani conflict are, as it happens, actually cast in large measure in secular terms: that cannot be gainsaid. But no one doubts that unmanageable religious strains may suddenly gain the upper hand in either setting.

I add at once that I do not mean by these caveats to favor (in any sly way) one side or the other in any of the terrible political stalemates of our age. My thought is that the loss of life alone (on the scale the Palestinian/Israeli conflict has generated, for instance) signifies that a negotiated solution cannot possibly be cast in terms of the serial rights and wrongs of all the running skirmishes. It must instead be cast in terms of larger notions of the viability of the two peoples (and the viability of an even larger region), which the strategies of a second-best morality are particularly well-suited to pursue. Of course, the forces arrayed against success have easier opportunistic targets. But the co-operative work of ordinary people across the two populations, as opposed to the destructive efforts of doctrinaire governments and intransigent factions, still shows the way to what may be needed *rationaliter*. It is hardly my place to spell out any fair or final solution.

Nevertheless, terrible as the struggle has been on both sides of the Arab/Israeli conflict, we are not yet at the end of patience. We see something of what is still lacking in the way of powers and resources beyond the local struggle, and we all realize that the struggle itself is not primarily a contest between revealed principles and rational interests. It's quite possible that conflicts of these sorts demand generations of great pain before they can be resolved at all. No one in Europe during the interval from Napoleon to the end of World War II could possibly have foreseen anything like the present relationship between France and Germany. Historical forces are clearly altering the context in which the resolution of the Arab/Israeli conflict may be fitted into a changed Middle East. Even the American strike against Iraq, which bears in a decisive way on the resolution of the Arab/Israeli struggle, is bound to be altered by historical forces that it has, uncomprehendingly, doubtless set in motion against its own purpose. Moral/political resolutions of the order required must be extremely gross-grained if they are to succeed at all. Canonical moral theories have ignored this obvious truth.

Academic moral philosophy in the West has overwhelmingly pursued one or another single-barreled conceptual model, as if it had discovered the true morality at last, almost in defiance of the obviously intractable differences between disputing parties. That luxury is now impossible to sustain. More than that, we positively require a conception of moral objectivity that concedes in the frankest way just how deeply and intractably culturally diverse societies, mingled in global affairs, oppose one another in normative terms—and how devotedly they are prepared to favor war and even death in the service of visions the West finds entirely alien, if not downright repugnant and irrational. Such confrontations are readily remarked in past ages. But it comes as a surprise to the West (and to Americans in particular) that they arise just as naturally in an "advanced world" like ours in ways that are not entirely legible in prudential terms (not confined, say, to territorial terms or to those of class warfare or the control of markets and natural resources). They harbor a hostility deeper than we may imagine *rationaliter*. On a small scale, the Bosnian horrors might have warned us. All this signifies the eclipse of the ideal of a "best" morality, of the conceptual convergence of all *sittlich* norms, the sufficiency of a bivalent logic in moral matters, the presumed validity of any entrenched normative hegemony, the very idea of reaching moral truths by cognitive discovery or rational decision. That dream was a delusion from the very start. Still, it hardly defeats the resources of a second-best morality.

I admit the propriety of asking me directly to explain why the privileged *Sitten* of so many fevered societies should yield to the kind of prudential reckoning I am recommending. I concede that they need not and may not do so, but it is very nearly the only "rational" alternative we and they have. In our globalized world, the very existence of a human population possibly exceeding six billion souls, grown from an estimated half-billion at the start of the sixteenth century, makes it very clear that the only way to avoid utter catastrophe—*summum malum* on an unprecedented scale—will probably require the effective, even if no more than partial, displacement (or congenial paraphrase) of Jewish, Christian, Muslim, Hindu, and Buddhist doctrines and the doctrines of a mountain of minor (lesser known but not less zealous or less extreme) cultish and tribal longings disposed to yield to the uncompromising authority of their own revealed truths. The new technologies of warfare have, indeed, strengthened the hand of radical ideologies of otherwise negligible sects (or even single individuals). There are no longer fringe groups too small to be taken seriously. We have, in short, "capacitated" destruction worldwide before we have capacitated the possibilities of human well-being.

At the moment, if we reflect on what is happening in very different ways in Afghanistan, Pakistan, Iran, and Turkey, it is difficult not to suppose that a large part of the Islamic world, at a distance from Arab sources of solidarity, is struggling to define a political system somewhere between a thoroughly theocratic state and a complete accommodation of the prudentially centered moral/political visions of the West—a struggle that, in the global setting, will demand an encompassing *modus vivendi* in any event. In the West, on a smaller but not insignificant scale, the monarchomachic experiments of the sixteenth century and the work of figures like Jean Bodin presaged the rise of the prudentially oriented moralities that have dominated Western politics and philosophy from that time to the present (without eclipsing, of course, the West's own deeper "revelations"). I cannot deny that what I have been trying to formulate is not much more than the "next" small step in a legible progression of consistently globalized moral visions. (It is also, perhaps, both more and less than a "first" step.)

That perception is in fact an important part of the rationale for the effort itself. Turkey, for example, is viewed by the West as the prime instance of the reconcilability of the seemingly intractable claims of religious Islam vis-à-vis the secular, market-oriented, "rational" concerns of the West (with which, of course, Christianity and Judaism share a workable understanding). The rise and fall of the Taliban *and* its resurgence in protean forms, however, signify the permanent threat of the "final" intransigence of the Muslim world. (That is, of course, an important factor in specifically American, Western, and Christian fears.) The Jews are too small a people to count for much on the world stage, except for the fact that they are currently in control of sacred Jerusalem and occupy a forward position in the struggle for oil. If you read history in terms of an impending (or existent low-grade) war, they are, willy-nilly, the loyal outpost of the engaged West—although the Israelis are always at the point of outstripping their Western handlers *rationaliter*.

That is surely how the Islamic world reads Western history, and the Muslims have the perfect symbol now for the possible unification of their scattered might—namely, the recovery of Jerusalem, the "restoration" of Palestine, and the purification of Arabia. In that same sense, the American victory over the Taliban (less clearly over al Qaeda) and the institution of a modest Western-oriented government in Afghanistan (if it will finally succeed), the problematic victory over Iraq, and the penetration of the entire Middle East to a depth at once too deep and too shallow for comfort signify the first great skirmish, post-9/11, of what a growing number of commentators see as in-volving both a crusade and a *jihad*—never mind the accuracy of the epithets. I encourage the speculation, I suppose, though my argument hardly depends on its accuracy. It dramatizes the significance of proceeding *rationaliter*, be-cause it addresses the essential threat to its general adoption. It avoids the bloodless consistencies of utopian doctrines, but it also admits the permanent vulnerability of any victory of rational forms of legitimation over revealed forms. What 9/11 confirms is the impossibility of a final technological defeat of technologized terrorism.

There is every reason to suppose that the prospects of a strengthened moral/political vision of the sort I have been sketching (a second-best moral-ity) will be greatly diminished just where events approaching *summum malum* become more likely. The irony is clear. But, from another perspective, peoples like the Israelis and the Palestinians can hardly be more than client populations. Very probably, they must be brought to heel in their own inter-ests (as well as in the interests of a larger world). This is not to recommend an actual policy but to acknowledge the real-world implications of a prudential vision. The idea (writ large) is close to Sophocles' notion of the restoration of a cosmic order at a very high cost to its divisive human parts. (But that anal-ogy is also, finally, obviously inapt.)

This also bears on the sense in which I claim no skill in the kind of "en-gineering" that will be required if the West (which is hardly committed to an American crusade for oil) commits itself to proceeding *rationaliter*. I will, how-ever, permit myself one prophecy: at its peril, the West will fail to make a con-vincing case if it fails to endorse a sufficiently large conception of the global economy (which is not yet a moral matter), in virtue of which it may then ex-pand its own "rational" policies *liberaliter*, and, by so doing, offer an exam-ple not only to the Muslim world but also to the great third and fourth worlds of disadvantaged Africa, Asia, and South America. I mean that we now begin to see that the prudential interests of the affluent world are likely to be served, increasingly, by a policy of *liberalitas*: that, say, the technologies of what it chooses to term "terrorism" convey a warning to the effect that the disadvan-taged world may be prepared to tear the other down, no matter what the cost to itself. This is not a satisfactory rationale for global life, but it signifies the need to correct the effective model of life favored by affluent America (and other parts of the West) that draws the extremes of power and powerlessness and wealth and poverty so callously that it must begin to look to the dangers of unstoppable threats to its own hegemony. I see in all this a clear sign that the principled disjunction between war and peace—in the idiom tethered to the just war concept—is very likely exhausted. If true, it must count as a change of the profoundest sort. (Again, I take that to be part of 9/11's lesson.)

Ours is the first age in which moral/political thinking *can* actually address the world in a genuinely global way without being utopian. Its vision could in fact be more realistic than Marx's reading of the class struggle, both because it would be explicitly moral rather than predictive and because it would rely on an existing technology rather than an uncertain doctrine of class warfare. But it would still be a vision of the same kind. Imagine, for example, that black Africa, acting out of political despair and an apocalyptic vision, invents a simple, immensely successful alternative to suicide bombing, which it applies to the entire affluent world. (I have some plausible scenarios in mind.) What then?

Presumably, what explicitly links prudential commitments and those of the great religions is that they already share a common objective—namely, *humanitas*, the well-being of the whole of mankind, however differently conceived. But to say only that is to fail to define the second-best meaning of the term. By *humanitas*, I understand no more than an unrestricted concern and respect for human life and its care: that is, the refusal to permit any part of the human race to be excluded or ignored in our moral deliberations.

The universality of *humanitas* is, initially, empty. But because the second-best morality that I've been urging begins, *rationaliter*, with the *sittlich* practices and *prima facie* norms of every home society, *humanitas* signifies (without imposing additional norms) a substantive respect for the diversity of all such *prima facie* values. Its formal universality, therefore, instantly divides in favor of the diversity of the forms of life of every historical society. That is, its universality, which amounts to a vacuous equality, is no more than the avoidance of unearned normative advantage. If there is no natural or rational rule of legitimation to affirm other than to acknowledge that *we* ourselves begin (as we must) with our own *sittlich* practices taken *prima facie*, then, plainly, we cannot disallow the same beginning to other societies. That is *humanitas*. But then, for the same reason, we cannot presume to derive from *humanitas*, directly or objectively, *any* self-validating legitimative strategy. There is none to be had. Hence, if *humanitas* supports universal norms in any substantive regard, it can do so only in a utopian spirit—for instance, by favoring one or another form of the "capacitation" (in Sen's sense) of some set of universalized *prudentiae* or *providentiae*. That, I would say, is precisely what the doctrine of "human rights" amounts to. It makes a genuine contribution in forming a moral vision, but it cannot claim to take precedence over would-be reforms that address the piecemeal improvement of the *Sitten* of actual societies. Its strongest contribution depends on its being compared with more substantive policies—for instance, that of *adaequatio*, as in noting and being prepared to alter the growing disparity between the capacitating resources of the affluent world and the utter despair of most of black Africa.

The point of featuring alternative conceptions of *humanitas* is to draw attention to the most compendious way in which we may compare different moral doctrines. Every moral vision ultimately yields a unifying conception of the moral significance of simply being a human being. Nevertheless, the vacuity of the bare concept *(humanitas)* is hardly more than the implicated lesson of Plato's elenctic dialogues, which never tire of admitting that we cannot say what the function of a human being finally is. Saying that, you will remember, never seems to have discouraged the human search for what to count as the best working notion we can construct.

We cannot construct a uniquely valid account of *humanitas*, and we cannot discount any of the *sittlich* clues the peoples of the world have actually favored. *Humanitas* is the ultimate (or generic) form of respect for the human condition, in which whatever humans have ever believed was their best moral instruction is entitled to its *prima facie* inning. It is too much to say that life is sacred or inviolate if we destroy life as easily as we do in the endlessly diverse ways we do. But it is also too much to pretend that we would be willing to forgo, in the face of an insistent public demand, the need to validate the deliberate taking of a life, our own or another's, or (say) indifference to conditions that begin to approach *summum malum*. *Humanitas* is the tension between these two considerations, without prejudice to any substantive proposal. But if so, then (read metonymically) both Aristotle and Kant are profoundly mistaken. To treat a person "as an end, and never a means only" is a purely formal, completely vacuous formula. Is a mother's sacrifice, or patriotism unto death, or the love of God, or even prostitution as a rational profession consistent with Kant's formula? There can be no assured answer. No more is there an assurance of what, nontrivially, contributes to or defeats Aristotle's formal conception of the good life. *Humanitas* conveys the lesson that, if moral reflection marks a concern for the right treatment of "another," any determinate exclusion within the human fold will risk being arbitrary to a fault. That is all we mean by the humanity of all.

Humanitas, then, is abstractly universal but empty. It is not an unconditional or supreme or greatest good. It is not a revealed good or an indubitable good or a self-evident good of any kind. It imposes no categorical obligations on us, and it captures no essential virtues. It is hardly more than formulaic. But it does signify a willingness to permit no substantive moral, political, religious, revealed, rational, or otherwise privileged norm to be entitled to any indefeasible or fixed priority over whatever may be intended, contingently, to give content and context to the respect and concern that it signifies. It is, in this regard, the mirror image of the abstract policy of the equality of all: parity more than equality, a placeholder more than a doctrine. Its intent, *faute de mieux*, is to oblige all would-be moral/political partisans to admit the need to cast their normative proposals in congruent accord with its open-ended notion—and hence to facilitate, *rationaliter*, comparisons across the entire human world. It is, in a way, a moral analogue of the bilingual competence of every people.

Any moral/political vision that would oppose such an accommodation would be committed to some form of privilege that it could never, in principle, defend beyond "preaching to the converted." Because, on the foregoing argument, there is no basis *of any kind* for normative privilege, the pretense that any society can actually justify its would-be privilege above *humanitas* must exceed the limits of moral objectivity in the second-best sense. The point may be put more directly: there can be no theoretical reconciliation between revealed norms and proceeding *rationaliter*, though there can, indeed, within uncertain limits, be a *modus vivendi* between religiously informed and prudentially paraphrased *Sitten*. This is just as true of Judaism and Christianity as it is of Islam. To say, for instance, that Christianity is committed to "democracy" *cannot* mean that Christians would allow, as a matter of course or principle, a "democratic" rejection or violation of their sacred creed or practice. Hardly! But that means that the universality of *humanitas is* consistent with the differential treatment of given populations for cause, even unto the taking of life. It holds as easily for the defense of war and abortion and suicide and self-defense as it does for the distribution of food and medicine. In the same spirit, we find in the West a growing tolerance, *nullum malum*, for extending something like the marriage contract to homosexual unions, without disparaging or supporting the biblical condemnation of homosexual practice. I take this to be a sign of a profound admission of the ultimate risk of arbitrariness in enforcing our revealed *Sitten*, come what may—*not*, let it be noted, a repudiation, as such, of whatever is thought sacred. Mere intransigence may be a form of piety (consider the Taliban), but it also has its stupid side. Revelation is not any kind of argument, even among its devotees.

In our age, moral matters arise in ways that often presuppose doctrinally diverse peoples who must live together with a measure of tolerance and good will. Normally, they cannot expect to succeed by privileging their own exclusive norms or *ethos*. What they do, characteristically—and effectively—is segregate the domain of public policy ranging over populations of diverse conviction and some more limited space (some form of privacy, the family, for instance) where indemonstrable doctrine and practice can be kept from interfering with or violating the other. That is, in fact, the general nerve of political life in the West from the sixteenth century to the present time. It also identifies what the West fears Islam will ultimately not accept. Moreover, it is, paradigmatically, the only way the West has apparently yet found to reconcile what it views as its principal forms of democracy and what is now called multiculturalism. Admittedly, it is an uneasy and sometimes makeshift truce. That is, it is a truce between a *modus vivendi* and the attempt to capture the "rule" of any such practical solution in theoretical terms—but it cannot be more than makeshift.

A similar fate affects what is called liberalism (which is *not* what I was just describing). If "liberalism" means no more than the advocacy of some doctrine of individual "human rights"—the American Bill of Rights, for instance, or the French Declaration of the Rights of Man and Citizen, or the UN's Universal Declaration of Human Rights—then liberalism is no more than a specific version of *humanitas* cast entirely in prudential terms. But if it is a doctrine of what is essentially or inviolably (or "metaphysically") human, as in accord with a theory of rational autonomy or of the absolute priority of some substantive norm of life over every other *sittlich* value or societal bond, or of an unconditional injunction against the taking of human life (as in capital punishment, suicide, euthanasia, physician-assisted death, or abortion) or, indeed, in more attenuated terms (as in imposing an unconditional taboo against cloning or fetal cell research), then it is hardly more than a narrow analogue of some revealed normative truth. You see, here, the likely collision between revealed and constructed norms. *Humanitas* is the extension of public tolerance, *liberaliter*, among any plausible second-best conjectures of partisans and ideologues of any stripe, within whatever *sittlich* or second-order limits may be defended *rationaliter*.

In the seventeenth century, Holland—having, with English aid, successfully resisted the Spanish masters of the Netherlands who sought in the most brutal way to impose Catholicism on a Protestant people and who had already sought, in Spain, to root out Islam and Judaism—provided the first generous asylum in Europe for the tolerance of the private practice of all religious faiths. In doing that, Holland gave form to a European sense that there must be an effective separation between the terms of political morality governing a trading people of diverse origins and the "private" religious practices of the peoples they governed and protected (which those peoples often believed to be revealed and binding on all). The Dutch, of course, sought to protect Catholics as well as Jews. But they could not have advanced a completely open policy that would have destabilized the very protections they intended to provide. If, of course, the supposedly revealed norms of life could be confined within a private world (no matter how generously construed), the legitimative problem would have been greatly eased. But no religious people would be unconditionally willing to allow such a thing. In Western eyes, the Muslim world threatens to include too much of the public world within the scope of its legitimative authority. I note here only that this is an example of the distinctive power and promise of a second-best morality. It helps explain the profoundly important historical indeterminacy of the meaning of one of Jesus's essential lessons: "Give unto Caesar the things that are Caesar's and unto God the things that are God's." The history of Christianity offers an example for nearly every conceivable interpretation of this single dictum.

I may as well add, if it is not already clear, that I feature the challenge of the Muslim world because it is encapsulated in 9/11, counts as the single largest exposé of the false closure and false adequacy of Western moral/political concepts, introduces incompatible and incommensurable norms, confronts the entire West with forms of resistance that stalemate or subvert the validity and viability of Western forms of self-defense, and presage the possibility of even deeper challenges of such sorts. I can imagine that both black Africa and an emerging China will, in time, confirm the brittle inadequacies of Western moral visions, but I cannot see how that phase of history will yet play out. The Muslim challenge lies before us in the clearest way—but it hardly speaks for all.

The larger moral objective has never been frontally addressed in the West in the deepening way 9/11 now obliges us to consider. That was the problem posed in miniature by and within contemporary Sarajevo. In the United States, it was originally "solved" by the "separation of church and state" and the provision of a *modus vivendi* among the factions of what was cannily judged to be a single "Judeo-Christian tradition." The Islamic challenge concerns both the separation, in global terms, of "rational" political policy from its widest application to alien ethnic practice and the possible inclusion of Islamic states within a company of so-called democratically committed states—which, from the Western point of view but not easily from the Muslim, signifies a domestic separation between political morality and private religious conviction. I leave the analysis and dialectical defense of democracy to one side here. Islam is simply not a religion of private conscience in the way the Protestant Reformers made central to their teaching (though hardly to their practice), nor is it committed to any notion of personal autonomy liberally conceived within the increasingly loosened constraints of something like a single Judeo-Christian tradition. For the time being, the Islamic community in the United States has proved to be much less radical politically than its counterpart in western Europe. But the fact remains that the accommodations of multi-culturalism are practical, often ad hoc and transient, not theoretical in the determinate way the authors of constitutions and legislation are fond of believing. The point is this: proceeding *rationaliter,* reforms must follow (to a significant extent) the *sittlich* pressures of the societies to which they are to be applied. The very notion of "liberal" or "liberal democratic" reform tends to find any such advice utterly benighted.

The solutions that will be needed have still to be invented. The inchoate American fear, which is only distantly connected with Muslim immigration, rests with the fact that, for the first time in U.S. history, the large influx of diverse peoples who have no sustained or original connection with the traditions that first spawned the liberalism of the eighteenth century could, conceivably, in time, fundamentally alter the salient *ethos* that has guided the resolution of America's moral/political concerns. If such a change occurred, then, of course, the seeming self-evidence of the liberal ideology that dominates American thought today would falter and begin to dissolve irretrievably. But surely the very idea of historicizing moral/political reflection cannot be defeated by the contingencies of the moral history on which it must depend. (That is the key to Rawls's intransigence.)

[II]

If we entertain conjectures about what sort of constructed moral vision might accommodate *(rationaliter)* the differences between Western moral/political intuitions and those of the Islamic world relative to the grievances of each, it is not clear in the least that we can see our way as yet to any improved *modus vivendi.* The question here is not one of merely satisfying the actual grievances of one side or the other but of formulating a conception of legitimated practices (conceded by both sides) in terms of which the resolution of such grievances may be fairly adjudicated. The former Shah of Iran thought to bring his regime into accord with certain Western powers by "Westernizing" his country as rapidly and as ruthlessly as possible. Khomeini's revolution signified, at the very least, that the Iranian form of Islam could not be reduced to a matter of private conviction in the "liberal" mode. Iran's *sittlich* interests simply rebelled (and are rebelling again). Atatürk's achievement of a secular Turkish state was largely serendipitous: Turkey was able to separate itself quite quickly from the faltering Ottoman Empire in the wake of World War I. Whatever Hamid Karzai's government may still achieve in Afghanistan, it is unlikely that it will be able to abandon or eliminate the model or themes of Islamic *sittlich* life—or, indeed, control much more than a part of Kabul. In fact, all Muslim societies are now increasingly caught up with the gathering sense of an embattled people within the alien constraints of an unsympathetic, largely Christian-capitalist hegemony.

Forces responsible for an increase in the incompatibility and incommensurability between Western and Islamic moral/political visions may actually be expanding in parts of the Muslim world as a direct result of the American strike against Iraq and its new penetration of the Middle East. If so, then "terrorism" may prove to be a blunderbuss category for new forms of political resistance, under the condition of a substantial loss of conventional military and political power, which Western conceptions of valid defensive actions would never willingly allow but which they could never compellingly outlaw or control. Even the concept of a guerrilla war in Iraq has been contested by the United States, despite its thoroughly conventional and obvious presence. There could well be an endless, even alarmingly effective campaign of "terrorist" measures (think of Chechnya) that might ultimately reverse the American victory in Afghanistan and Iraq. Time may be on the side of Muslim "extremists" here, as far as legitimation is concerned. But what is the rule by which the categories of legitimate war and defense are rightly expanded under conditions of changing technology and international relations? Whatever the answer, it must surely accommodate the deepening inequities of political and economic power; if so, then the answer must also yield, in our time, in the direction of accommodating radically diverse, even incommensurable, moral/political visions. Western conceptions of legitimation are hardly prepared for that.

Seen in this way, it is not a mark of the failure of a moral vision that, in the span of local history, an aggregate of Western and Islamic states, harboring mounting grievances against one another, cannot yet find a *modus vivendi* that would resolve those grievances in a way that could be legitimated in the eyes of both, relative to their own *sittlich* concerns. It may simply not be possible in any immediate future. Would-be moral solutions may require more patience than societies can expect. My own opinion is that brute force will not work any longer, because the Muslims have shown a remarkable willingness to sacrifice their lives in what, more and more radically, they have come to regard (perhaps inaccurately but surely in the popular mind) as a *jihad* against the West—*and* because the miniaturization of the technologies of war, of "weapons of mass destruction," and of "terrorism" and the randomizing of targets and occasions of opportunity *and* the contagion of a heartfelt mistrust spreading throughout the whole of the Islamic world and beyond cannot, we realize, be completely controlled or denied a measure of legitimation. In truth, changes in *sittlich* history bring changes in legitimative vision in their wake. Second-order arguments must draw on *prima facie* practice, but first-order practice has its own history. One begins to see here a dawning ideological analogy between the Palestinian/Israeli conflict and the import of the American presence in the Middle East at the present time—viewed through Muslim eyes. That is not an implausible reading of the perceived implication of 9/11.

We must ponder the point, because the prevailing assumption in Western moral theory seems to be committed to the comforting idea that all reasonable *sittlich* norms—which may still compete or clash with one another in particular circumstances—may be counted on to fit consistently with some single encompassing conceptual scheme that correctly monitors the legitimation of all such candidate options. The idea cannot be confirmed if we reject the thesis that the one true morality (the ideally "best" morality) can be straightforwardly discovered or rationally determined.

If we abandon all that, and if we treat selves as second-natured moral agents, then it must dawn on us that *sittlich* norms—*a fortiori*, the would-be second-order reforms or adjustments of such norms—may be viably linked to practices and forms of legitimation that are not only incompatible with other *prima facie* norms but deeply incommensurable as well, in the way in which Western and Islamic *sittlich* interests and defensive actions may, according to their respective convictions, seriously conflict. I believe that that *is* true of what lies at the heart of the meaning of 9/11. If so, the finding cannot fail to inform what, finally, we should take to be "the human condition" behind morality itself—what I have been calling *humanitas*.

Certainly, there are reasons for thinking that the *sittlich* visions that distinguish Islam and the West are partly commensurable, partly in conflict, partly incommensurable. What a more unified, more militant confrontation between a "greater" Islam and a good part of the West might involve remains to be seen. But it is not absurd to think that the quotient of incommensurability may greatly increase. Afghanistan and Pakistan are, in a sense, the setting for opposed forces within the Islamic world itself. *Their* futures are likely to help us prophesy how the language of moral/political discourse on a global scale may have to change. Everything points to a converging radicalization of the scattered parts of Islam (without yet constituting an actual religious war).

Here, we are up against a problem that has been all but neglected in mainstream ethical theory, though something very much like it has been aired and prematurely dismissed in analytic philosophies of science. The closest philosophers have come to the issue of incommensurable moral norms (incommensurabilism) appears as the problem of moral relativism. Relativism in general is also an important (and neglected) question, of course, but incommensurabilism, which may be regarded as an extreme form of relativism, is almost totally ignored in the West. The matter would certainly be worth examining if, indeed, it proved to be true that the al Qaeda *jihad* was morally incommensurable with standard Western views of how, objectively, wars validly provide for the "defense" or "protection" of a people and that people's sacred *ethos*. (This bears on the erasure of the line between war and peace.)

It is not merely that the normative categories involved are incommensu-*rable* in the elementary sense in which, say, the description of the colors and lengths of different swatches of cloth are predicatively incommensurable without being incompatible. Rather, the pertinent categories are themselves of a deeply incommensurabil*ist* sort, in that we lack any inclusive *prima facie* practice or accepted explanatory theory in accord with which we may rank the *moral* priorities of revealed and natural norms *by the same metric*. We can indeed understand all this, and we can even compare the differences (in prudential terms) between bin Laden's defense and, say, the American condemnation of 9/11. But we cannot, as things now stand, *commensurate* the two assessments in terms of any *sittlich* form of moral legitimation. That is the point, in moral contexts, of distinguishing carefully between the practical and the theoretical, between a *modus vivendi* and a verdict, between a revealed and a second-best form of legitimation.

You must bear in mind that incommensurable judgments and norms are neither unintelligible nor incomparable. They are simply incommensurable — which is to say that there is no single encompassing conceptual scheme or metric common to all descriptions, comparisons, and appraisals that yields an inclusive sense of legitimating the very norms we may apply to all the commitments of every moral agent. In a word, incommensurabilism advances the second-order thesis that first-order incommensurabilities may, viably, depend on deeper cognitive or rational incommensurabilities! That is my reading of the doctrine Kuhn broached so startlingly in the context of the physical sciences.[2] I find it even more common in the moral/political world.

The classic example of first-order incommensurability, of course, is that of the comparison of the lengths of the sides and the hypotenuse of a right triangle. Descriptive and appraisive incommensurability is no more than a garden-variety phenomenon, entirely benign as far as our present question is concerned. But incommensurabilism is a deeper matter. Incommensurability is no more than a first-order distinction; incommensurabilism is a second-order theory regarding some subset of the other. The first arises wherever paired categories are not subsidiary distinctions within one or another single first-order descriptive or appraisive scheme. The second arises wherever distinctions of the first sort are due to the absence of a conceptual schema that links them by means of the same cognitional or rational means. Each can appear in both theoretical and practical contexts. (I have been tracking the moral/political import of these distinctions.)

As already remarked, the incommensurabilism question was raised in a powerful but abortive way by Kuhn in his well-known account of the explanatory dispute between Priestley and Lavoisier regarding combustion. Kuhn was unable (or unwilling) to sustain his own discovery; it has, in fact, been all but dismissed by the academy. Nevertheless, it continues to nag, because, of course, the history of science is on its side and because, despite the severest challenges, it is obviously a coherent possibility. And yet, incommensurabilism may be straightforwardly overcome by merely providing a common rule or evidentiary ground (applied to propositions or actions) by which to ascribe and confirm otherwise incommensurable attributes. The trick is to invent a common ground where there was none before. I have been claiming that 9/11 effectively confirms that our moral theories have not come to terms with the threat of (moral) incommensurabilism. My own notion of a second-best morality is meant to explore the possibility of providing a reasonable basis for obviating the dangers of just such practical impasses. Remember that our findings are objective only in the constructivist sense. We thus cannot rule out the objective standing of suitably opposed *sittlich* or legitimative claims, which (for evidentiary reasons) might, if read incommensurably, have actually favored, for a time, Priestley over Lavoisier and (beyond Kuhn) bin Laden just as easily over George W. Bush.

It's true that, in the physical sciences, a convincing argument was finally advanced in favor of a disjunctive (bivalent) finding in the Priestley/Lavoisier dispute. *But there are no comparable constraints* (constraints like prediction and technological invention) *in matters of moral dispute.* Where the scientific argument against Priestley proved decisive, it actually honored and built on (rather than outflanked) the incommensurabilist complaint. The compelling evidence was never neutral; it was always infected by the explanatory visions themselves. That is a fact often ignored. It is precisely what is ignored in the easy condemnation of 9/11. I have no wish to vindicate bin Laden—or Bush, for that matter. I am concerned, rather, to raise a fundamental problem about *any and all* of our deepest moral judgments in the face of an alien challenge of the relativist or incommensurabilist sort. In what sense, I ask, do we ever actually *find* that opposed assessments and commitments of the moral or moral/political sort *are* either right or wrong, disjunctively, or are rightly read as bivalent propositions?

The difference between moral relativism and moral incommensurabilism — or the difference between moral relativism and moral relativity—may still elude you. Some terminological distinctions may help. Moral relativity (or cultural relativity in general) signifies no more than first-order divergences in normatively freighted preferences. Moral relativism admits second-order findings that cannot be brought under a bivalent logic; that would, if construed bivalently, count as a conflict or incompatibility in the grading or ranking of pertinent options; and that are, nevertheless, taken to have objective or valid standing.

Not all relativisms need take an incommensurabilist form. So "relativity" and "incommensurability" signify only certain forms of first-order difference and divergence among different societies or even within the same society, as of interest, taste, preference, belief, judgment, norm, and the like, in ways that do not yet bear on claims of truth or validity or the like—really, second-order claims—favoring relativism or incommensurabilism. For instance, what passes for personal beauty in one society may be dismissed out of hand in another. That would be a form of "cultural relativity" but not yet relativism; relativism would require that the validity of such a first-order preference (viewed as a defeasible epistemic or rational claim) would not, as such, preclude the validity of other preferences that, on the basis of a bivalent logic, would produce inconsistency or contradiction. A relativistic logic would allow that some incompatible pairings of this sort could be coherently and consistently confirmed. (You see the bearing of such a notion on the moral/political world.) Correspondingly, different ascriptions of colors and sizes to different swatches of cloth would be incommensurable, in the obvious sense that there could be no common scale in terms of which both color- and size-ascriptions could be generated from the same metric (or concept or category) without touching on incommensurabilism. (I have already characterized incommensurabilism.)

The fact is, mere cultural relativity may not and need not support cultural relativism at all. That is certainly the standard conviction in contemporary analytic thought. Indeed, it is often thought that relativism and incommensurabilism are demonstrably incoherent or paradoxical or self-contradictory.

All sorts of puzzles arise here. But, in addition to the terminological distinction just laid down, two items need to be noted. First, admitting relativism in one domain of inquiry (say, moral relativism) neither entails nor precludes relativism in another domain (say, aesthetic or scientific relativism), nor, similarly, does admitting relativism with regard to one kind of judgment (say, moral judgments about personal lifestyle) entail a relativistic treatment of any or all other comparable kinds of judgments in the same general domain (say, legal judgments within a given jurisdiction). Second, all judgments that take truth-values or truth-like values of any kind are rightly assigned such values "relative to" the supporting evidence, but this, though itself a second-order matter, is entirely neutral as between relativism and (say) a bivalent policy and is not, as such, meaningfully characterized as a form of cultural relativity (or relativism) at all. The important point to keep in mind is simply that nothing yet said settles the analysis and legitimation of relativism as such. But I do apologize for having to dwell on these technical matters.

The issue is of considerable importance because, in moral/political matters, the threat of relativism (say, affecting 9/11) is a source of danger and instability that the world can ill afford. I claim, in fact, that an adequate moral and philosophical response to the meaning of 9/11 positively requires the elaboration of some suitably developed account of a relativistic model of judgment and commitment. The entire foregoing argument is meant to provide just such a brief. Of course, I concede at once that if the argument is at all convincing, there are bound to be other substantive moral models similarly entitled to objective standing despite their diverging from, or being in conflict with, or being incommensurable with the moral policies I've favored. I don't believe that the argument supporting relativism need, however, be relativistic itself. I see no paradox there. But I must make a small detour in order to secure the sense of relativism's coherence and consistency. The issue is not a strenuous one, but it does call for a bit of care. I need your patience here.

There are at least three (and possibly four) notoriously indefensible "versions" of relativism that, according to the doctrine's opponents, are the only versions worth considering.[3] (Confining discussion to these versions would, of course, make short work of the offending doctrine.) One holds—as Aristotle does, citing Protagoras—that a judgment or truth-claim of the relativistic sort is both true and false, a palpable contradiction. A second holds to a "relational" analysis of "true," that is, that "true," rightly understood, means "true-for-x," where x is a person or a person-on-a-particular-occasion or a society or the like, so that what is "true" is never more than "true-for-x-at-time-t" or something of the sort. Hence, no two speakers, possibly not even one speaker at two different times, can mean the same thing by "true" (by affirming that this or that is true). Many have drawn this doctrine from Plato's *Theaetetus*, from the episode in which Socrates worries Protagoras's doctrine ("man is the measure"), which some contemporary readers, such as Hilary Putnam, treat as a form of societal "solipsism" (a "solipsism-with-a-we" instead of an "I"). If you separate the "solipsistic" from the "relational," you will have collected three distinct versions of relativism, all untenable: the first, self-contradictory; the second, paradoxical; the third, arbitrary, utterly private, and impossible to share.

To these we may add a fourth, equally untenable: namely, the view that every claim, judgment, or belief is as good as any other, a doctrine often characterized as a form of skepticism (a doctrine trotted out but not endorsed by Rorty.) I reject all four, but I believe that a viable and pertinent form of relativism remains entirely open to us, counts as a reasonable interpretation of Protagoras's doctrine, and may be assigned a genuinely useful function in a variety of inquiries—notably, in assessing moral judgments and commitments. The opponents of relativism—the keepers of the canon, so to speak—almost never risk investigating the possibility of a viable relativism. Extraordinary!

The curious thing is that it would be a scandal to suppose that any self-respecting relativist intelligent enough to grasp that the doctrine must be cast in a way altogether different from any self-defeating analysis *would* ever adopt any of the options mentioned. (There is, of course, good reason to think that Protagoras cannot have been the fool the classic readings of his thesis seem to signal.) In any case, we can explain easily enough how to make relativism coherent—not self-contradictory, not simply arbitrary or private, perfectly worth saving in evidentiary or objective terms—merely by distinguishing between the logical peculiarities of relativistic claims and the substantive grounds on which relativism may be rightly and usefully invoked.

The logical adjustment required comes to this. Relativism rests on replacing (where needed) a bivalent logic by a many-valued logic, in which replacing truth-values (or truth-like values) permits us, on formal grounds alone, to preclude truth-value assignments that, *on a bivalent logic,* would have yielded inconsistent or contradictory claims. That's all! So, for example, abortion may be *validly* defended or condemned on alternative (second-best) grounds relativistically but not bivalently. The trick is this: the denial of the "truth" (or "falsity") of a given claim will not, on a relativistic logic, signify the (bivalently determined, disjunctive) "falsity" (or "truth") of the claim in question. The available options may be taken to be "valid" in the way of being "reasonable" or "apt" or "supportable" or the like within our *sittlich* practices—without, let it be noted, ever needing to deny that some claims may well be flatly and irretrievably false in the bivalent sense. So the strategy concedes that a relativistic and a bivalent logic are compatible, if appropriately segregated in a formal way, and that by adopting logically weaker "truth-values" afforded by a relativistic logic, we preclude the possibility of being forced into inconsistency or contradiction where the judgments thought most pertinent could never be reconciled with a bivalent logic. The schema is self-consistent, easily defended, plainly useful, and nicely matched to the constructivist options of the post-Kantian and post-Hegelian world. (The rest of the details need not detain us here.)

On the substantive side, there are, by and large, two very different approaches to the defense of relativism. One proceeds merely by segregating ad hoc the practices of different societies, so that it *never* appears, say, that moral claims about "the same act" or practice or judgment, viewed from the vantage of two different societies or subpopulations said to exhibit a measure of "cultural relativity," are actually allowed to generate the would-be contradictions that a relativistic logic obviates (by way of admitting "incongruent" claims, that is, claims that on a bivalent logic—but not now—would be inconsistent or contradictory). The other approach, the one I favor, simply admits the threat and resolves it in the relativistic way. This robust approach depends on the actual analysis of the phenomena to which a relativistic logic may be usefully applied: in particular, moral judgments and commitment as well as the interpretation of artworks, history, language, explanation, and competing philosophical accounts of truth and knowledge. Sometimes, of course, relativistic answers depend on evidentiary limitations. But if that were all that needed to be said, relativism would be no more than a stopgap measure waiting to be replaced by bivalence once again. That *is* the usual way of regarding probabilities relative to limited evidence respecting what is deemed to be true.

The robust version of relativism holds, rather, that for determinate reasons—but not for evidentiary deficit or defect—the phenomena in question cannot support more than a relativistic logic. In moral/political matters, those reasons normally have to do with the double fact that moral norms are intelligible only within the space of human culture and that human selves are themselves cultural artifacts. But that brings us back to the intuition with which we began: viz., that if we abandon cognitive privilege in favor of constructivism, then given the argument developed up to this point (that is, assuming strong forms of cultural relativity), it is difficult to see how the resolution of moral/political questions can fail to favor relativism. That now begins to capture the full meaning of 9/11.

Apart, then, from man's inhumanity to man—worked out more fully in terms of the complications of historicism, relativism, incommensurabilism, and constructivism—this *is* indeed what 9/11 now means. It signifies the need to interpret what, *liberaliter*—across all known *sittlich* practices—we may construe *humanitas* to mean. It means at least the search for a convincing union of a minimal or moderate abstraction of what might be offered *rationaliter* to the whole of mankind, between, say, the limits of *summum malum* and *minimum bonum* and in accord with whatever, divergently, may be plurally proposed for the resolution of the grave moral/political problems that confront the separate viable "parts" of our present age. In our own time, then, the answer to the challenge of 9/11 is a contingent and historicized reading of *humanitas*. Furthermore, by the time we reach Hegel's contribution, we grasp the distinction between biology and culture (and the corollary distinction between the purportedly changeless and the historically contingent nature of our norms and values).

In that sense, *humanitas* is the ever-determinable construction of something akin to a *minimum bonum*, addressed to the mature life of the whole of mankind, by way of analogy with what every society is already prepared to propose (according to its lights) for its future offspring. It is not inherently a relativistic notion. But in its intended amplitude, it is bound to accommodate relativistic and incommensurabilist and historicist divergences. It is only slightly firmer than a completely utopian vision, as it must be, because there are no independent natural or rational norms to be discerned. It rests on a reading of the prospects of the hybrid, artifactual, historically emergent creatures we call "persons," "selves," "subjects," or "human agents" (ourselves), cast as well as possible in terms of avoiding every kind of arbitrariness.

Of course, that is precisely where our speculations about universal "human rights" and *nullum malum* lead. It must not be forgotten that no such universalizing can simply override the slow, contingent, partial, prejudiced, contexted, contested, often conflicting resolutions of the grave crises that arise among the different peoples of the earth—hardly the equal of one another on any empirical count. *Humanitas*, then, is the determinable but doctrinally empty universal respect we reserve for the entire human race, which we cannot fail to find historically realized in the moral life of diverse societies. It is a vision that cannot fail to appear to be theoretically paradoxical at the same time it is seen to be practically sufficient. It is, finally, the negative constraint of the only possible vision we can defend.

notes

Introduction

1. I adopt the terms *"sittlich"* (customary) and *"Sitten"* (customs and practices) because of their strong association with Hegel's usage in *The Philosophy of Right*, trans. T. M. Knox (Oxford: Clarendon Press, 1942). I define them, however, in a very thin way, a way that accords with the "anthropologist's sense" rather than Hegel's, which, admittedly, is problematic. But my own account *is* Hegelian in inspiration — possibly a sparer reading of some of the problems Hegel wished to solve. I suggest that it would be entirely possible to free Hegel's splendid vision from certain vulnerabilities that bedevil the contemporary reception of his texts. Hegel's prose makes it difficult to vouchsafe his intentions at every turn of the page. But I believe we can recover a leaner Hegel that would ensure the full force of his best analysis of culture, history, objectivity, norms and values, and related notions without concessions to Kantian-like transcendentals, strong forms of (Schellingian) Idealism, or teleologisms of any kind. I am concerned, here, to sort out and clarify the conditions of validating and legitimating normative claims from what may be regarded as the "anthropologist's facts," on which the other relies. Hegel's use of *sittlich* both obscures and illuminates these connections. Very few, however, would now endorse Hegel's rather rich conception of the *sittlich*, which seems to permit him to move too easily from first-order to second-order normative truths.

2. "Objectivist" and "objectivism" are terms of fairly wide acceptance in philosophical circles. They convey the sense, both in science and morality, that there are uniquely true answers to questions of what "there is" in the world and of what is right or wrong regarding how we should act in given circumstances — and that such questions refer to independent states of affairs and/or norms that our natural cognitive and/or rational faculties are capable of grasping or determining. If this were so, then truth-claims and their practical analogues in deciding how to act morally would rightly favor an exceptionless bivalent logic (True and False and Right and Wrong). I take objectivism to be impossible to defend as well as overly restrictive in the light of the actual conditions of scientific and moral inquiry. In general, the eclipse of pre-Kantian philosophy by the innovations of the period that spans Kant and Hegel (without being wedded to their particular doctrines) instantly precludes the viability of the objectivist claim. I don't regard this as an argument, of course, but it is an excellent clue to a whole nest of arguments that would be decisive. For a sense of the standard use of these terms, see Richard J. Bernstein, *Beyond Objectivism and Relativism: Science, Hermeneutics, and Praxis* (Philadelphia: University of Pennsylvania Press, 1989), and Hilary Putnam, "Two Philosophical Perspectives," in *Reason, Truth, and History* (Cambridge: Cambridge University Press, 1981).

3. In the *Statesman*, Plato introduces, as he does elsewhere in the collected dialogues, the idea that human beings are governed best by a ruler who possesses the "royal art" — who knows the one true Good suited to the human condition. Even so, no such ruler could possibly sit by every person's side in order to decide every issue correctly. So the generality of the law already introduces a kind of slippage in the "best" form of rule. Plato's spokesman in the *Statesman*, the

Eleatic Stranger, calls the rule of law under this condition "second-best." But, according to my reading of the elenctic dialogues—usually the early ones, in which Socrates inquires about one virtue or another—Plato's intent may well have been subversive. Here, I take him to be exorcising (at a very stately and unhurried pace) the often pernicious influence of Parmenides and the Eleatics. (Some readers may be astonished by the suggestion.)

I believe that Plato means to challenge the very idea that anyone could rightly claim to possess the royal art. Hence, as the rest of the *Statesman* makes clear, the subversive doubt continues to nag even where we realize that we must have some basis for preferring one kind of state over another and for agreeing to live under the rule of law—even if we lack the royal art itself. I read this as Plato's most characteristic philosophical "joke." I thus take the liberty of speaking of a "second-best morality" as ranging over the entire declension of moral/political speculation as it progressively abandons the pretense of ever knowing what *is* "best" for mankind—except in the arch sense that moral theorists are forever claiming that their own principles are surely best. The elenctic dialogues proceed without any such presumption, which suggests (to me) that we have only the resources of our customs and practices, our *Sitten*, and that they are sufficient for the task at hand. I therefore treat the *Statesman* as itself a late elenctic dialogue, which goes contrary to the usual canonical reading. It makes the *Statesman's* argument much more pointed. For a sense of the canonical view, see Gregory Vlastos, "The Socratic Elenchus: Method Is All," in *Socratic Studies*, ed. Myles Burnyeat (Cambridge: Cambridge University Press, 1994). Furthermore, I take the liberty of reading Hegel's dialectical "method" applied to cultural history as a modern analogue of the elenctic "method." In that way, I construe Hegel's interpretation of politics as a reasonable conjecture in normative terms rather than a privileged or uniquely correct account of the meaning of human history.

Chapter 1

1. Sen has mounted a very strong critique of Rawls's theory of justice, and of liberal economic theory in general, in a larger discussion of economic inequality and interpersonal comparisons of utility and value. He demonstrates how formal comparisons fail to come to grips with the actual differences in the lives of would-be consumers of commodities. The argument centers on the paradoxes of the measurement of economic inequality. But the corrections needed would require a thorough knowledge of the actual circumstances in which "consumers" are in a position *to use* their apparent entitlements in ways that actually fulfil them. I find a pertinent analogy here, admittedly lax on formal grounds but entirely apt in terms of political "capacitation," between interpersonal comparisons of utility and international comparisons of justice in world politics. I mention this only as a suggestion for reflecting on the implications of 9/11. See Amartya Sen, *On Economic Inequality*, exp. ed. (Delhi: Oxford University Press, 1997), especially the "annexe" to the expanded edition, "On Economic Inequality After a Quarter Century," by James Foster and Amartya Sen. See also John Rawls, *A Theory of Justice* (Cambridge, Mass.: Harvard University Press, 1971). Sen's emphasis is always on the practical functioning of human beings in the circumstances of their actual lives, bypassing all contextless or merely mathematized measures of interpersonal comparisons. But, of course, his purpose is to correct methodological abuses in a humane way.

2. I take "constructivism" to be distinct from "idealism," although Kant, as opposed to Hegel, is both a constructivist and an idealist. I use the term primarily to signify that a viable realism with respect to scientific knowledge must escape the paradoxes of pre-Kantian philosophy or epistemology, which it accomplishes by affirming that, relative to objective knowledge, there can be no principled disjunction between cognizer and cognized. Pre-Kantian "realism," often called Cartesianism, assumes the opposite. Idealists (Kant, for instance, as a "transcendental idealist")

believe one way or another that we literally construct the world we know from the representational materials of the mind, that is, from the formative powers of the "understanding." Non-idealists (Hegel, for instance, as a new kind of empiricist) hold that what we construct is a picture or conception of the world-presented-in-experience, not the world itself—and certainly not in any of Kant's paradoxical senses. Kant is a unique figure in this regard. He holds, for transcendental reasons, that knowledge entails a grasp of the necessary conceptual and perceptual structures of the world we know—and (in a sense) construct or constitute. Hegel, however, construes the conceptual and perceptual structures we impute to the world as the result of the contingent and evolving work of our reflexive account of the world-as-we-experience-it. (These distinctions are very laxly formulated here.) The advantage of the Hegelian account is that it helps show the sense in which the objectivity of science and morality is seen to depend essentially on the same subjective conditions—in a way that yields maximal flexibility, without paradox, wherever needed. In particular, Hegel's account shows by its own example (apart from Hegel's personal convictions) how objectivity in science and morality can be coherently construed in constructivist terms, can be historicized, and can even adjust the notions of objective validity and legitimation in relativistic ways without yielding to Kantian idealism. The account I offer *is* Hegelian, but only in the broadest and most generous sense. I take Hegel's *Phenomenology* more as a heuristic guide than as an accurate model of how to construct an objective science and morality. The validity of the account I offer does not rely at all on Hegel's specific arguments. I venture to say that a viable philosophy in our time, whether with regard to science or morality, cannot fail to be Hegelian in the heuristic sense I favor. But I don't deny that a good account of science or morality may well favor some later, sparer Hegelian strategy—perhaps a version of pragmatism, for instance, or perhaps an account like the one I offer here. See G. W. F. Hegel, *The Phenomenology of Spirit*, trans. A. V. Miller (Oxford: Clarendon Press, 1957).

3. Here I begin to fill out my general philosophical orientation and my use of Hegelian themes. I give fair warning that I favor a heterodox reading of Hegel. I emphasize, however, certain philosophical issues that may not seem particularly pertinent at first glance—and the contributions spanning Kant and Hegel in particular—in assessing the reasonableness of the moral theory I am advancing. Frankly, I don't believe it is possible to assess the validity of any moral theory entirely apart from the fortunes of certain large philosophical visions. If Aristotle's or Descartes's or Kant's theories of knowledge and reality were true, then moral philosophy would (in my opinion) have to be very different from what I suggest counts as a reasonable theory now!

4. Effectively, I mean to favor by this epithet whatever may be defensibly yielded by confirming my account within the terms of a second-best morality—that is, either by rejecting any "moral realism" that draws objective moral norms from our cognition of independent nature or the independent world (or from revealed sources, for that matter) *or* by affirming a "constructivist realism" based on the initial data of our *Sitten*. On my view, that would preclude realisms of both the natural law sort and the Darwinian sort. See, for example, Edward O. Wilson, *On Human Nature* (Cambridge, Mass.: Harvard University Press, 1978), and Daniel C. Dennett, *Darwin's Dangerous Idea: Evolution and the Meanings of Life* (New York: Simon and Schuster, 1995).

5. In a sense, my entire labor has been centered on the analysis of what it is to be a self or person. In a curious way, that is also the phantom issue that hovers over the work of both Kant and Hume. I'm persuaded that Hegel thought Kant lacked a coherent account of what a specifically human person is (as opposed to Kant's transcendental subject); Thomas Reid found Hume's *Treatise* to be a scandal for the same reason English-language analytic philosophy has proved to be notoriously shy about airing the cultural complexities of human nature. And in continental philosophy—even in the work of figures such as Husserl, Heidegger, Althusser, Lacan, Levinas, and Foucault—specific discussions of the "self" are notoriously unclear and deficient. For a more ramified sense of the principal themes of my own account, I may perhaps suggest my *Historied Thought, Constructed World: A Conceptual Primer for the Turn of the Millennium* (Berke-

ley and Los Angeles: University of California Press, 1995). My intuition here is that it is impossible to give an account of either science or morality without a careful analysis of the "self" (whatever one's objections to treating the self as an "entity" may be). The essential considerations are these: that the analysis of the nature of the human self and the possibility of an objective morality (or science) are not independent inquiries; that philosophical accounts of the self are wildly diverse; and that those facts themselves are largely ignored.

6. I take the Aristotelian and Kantian traditions to be the most influential in Western moral philosophy. Both, I think, are seriously defective. Here, I single out Rawls and Habermas as the most important contemporary "Kantians" on moral/political questions and return very lightly, a number of times, to their particular views. Both, I would say, exhibit the characteristic abstractness and relative indifference to context that mark Kant's own critical emphasis. Rawls, for instance, requires—in A Theory of Justice—the posit of an "initial position" that blocks or disallows an agent's knowledge of his or her own history, knowledge that he insists cannot be called on if we are to construct a "rational" account of justice. (He's got things topsy-turvy, I'm afraid.) Habermas insists on strict universality in formulating the "rational" principles of morality. But then, he finds it impossible to decide whether he is an adherent of the Critical Kant or of a Hegelianized Kant, or of a pragmatized or Marxified or Frankfurt-Critical Kant, which affects the "logic" of universality itself. I regard both Rawls's and Habermas's notions as completely unworkable. See Jürgen Habermas, "Discourse Ethics: Notes on a Program of Philosophical Justification," in Moral Consciousness and Communicative Action, trans. Christian Lenhardt and Shierry Weber Nicholsen (Cambridge, Mass.: MIT Press, 1990).

7. I touch here on an extraordinarily important but difficult metaphysical matter, the full implications of which I only partly understand. But I must venture a clue at least. In holding that selves are "hybrid artifacts," that selves have "Intentional" natures as culturally emergent "entities," or in suggesting that selves have (or are) "histories" rather than that they have "natures" (as Homo sapiens does), I mean to contrast physically formed phenomena and culturally emergent phenomena. I hold that the cultural is indissolubly "incarnate," or "embodied," in the physical. But, in the sense in which physical things are said to possess determinate properties (size and shape and mass, for instance), cultural phenomena are, qua Intentional (that is, culturally significant—interpretable and subject to historical transformation), determinable only. Though the formal distinction is still too crude, I mean by this that the conceptual relationship between the determinate and the determinable is systematically different in the analysis of the physical and that of the cultural. The contrast is particularly helpful in analyzing the description, interpretation, and appraisal of moral deeds, history, artworks, speech, and the like, which I collect as what human selves "utter" (make, say, do, create). I regard it as astonishing that these themes first take form, in the West at least, only after the French Revolution—in Hegel, in their most masterful early form. There's a great deal that needs to be clarified here, without which, I would say, moral theory cannot fail to be unacceptably primitive. The best explorations of these themes that I have been able to pursue are centered in the analysis of the fine arts. For a promising sample, but hardly more, see my Interpretation Radical but Not Unruly: The New Puzzle of the Arts and History (Berkeley and Los Angeles: University of California Press, 1995).

Chapter 2

1. The mature philosophies of classical Greece may be read as a single continuous effort to reconcile the contingency and flux of the natural world with Parmenides' impossibly strict dictum: "What is, is; and what is not, is not." The Eleatic followers of Parmenides himself had already experimented with the problem—the most famous example of which is surely Zeno's account of the paradox of motion. I read Plato's dialogues, therefore, as struggling with the need

to reconcile the claim of a changeless order (the Forms and the Good) and Plato's own seemingly subversive conviction that, conceding the flux of the familiar world (as in the elenctic dialogues), we cannot convincingly pretend to have any reliable knowledge of the changeless order, although, Plato insinuates, we seem to need richer conceptual resources than we actually have. I am persuaded that what the Greeks lacked—Aristotle as much as Plato—is a grasp of the distinction between nature and culture and the resources of historicity. For this reason, I regard Hegel's critique of Kant as, in effect, a recapitulation of the elenctic struggle with Parmenides. In that sense, my own effort to formulate a constructivist account of moral objectivity is, in its way, a slim gloss on the inclusive narrative of Western philosophy itself. The *elenchus* is, it should be noted, a Parmenidean invention, though keyed to the authority of Parmenides' unacceptable dictum. That is precisely why I regard it as a matter of some importance to view Hegel as providing the best heuristic philosophical guidance at the true beginning of the modern age. The point is this: in my opinion, post-Hegelian thought is best placed to exorcise completely the last vestiges of the Parmenidean influence. (I should add, though, that Protagoras had, in the ancient world, already attempted to undermine the doctrine at its root. "Man is the measure" is indeed the decisive turning point.)

2. The crucial question about Hegel's vision of *geistlich* history, or, more provocatively, "the history of *Geist*," asks: Just where does Hegel's insight come from in tracing the dialectical *unfolding* of actual history? Is that not a problem for both an objective history and an objective morality if we form our conjectures about the narrative *unity* of history *from* an ever-contingent present's "new beginning"? This is how Hegel's great achievement became its own deep problem in nineteenth-century European thought. The master challenge may be attributed to Nietzsche, who is at once a "Hegelian" and the doyen of "post-Hegelians," critics of Hegel (together with Søren Kierkegaard), and perhaps of postmodernists as well. The sense of this unavoidable development—which I take to heart—is laid out in a magisterial way in Karl Löwith, *From Hegel to Nietzsche: The Revolution in Nineteenth-Century Thought*, trans. David E. Green (New York: Columbia University Press, 1991).

3. Part of my reflection here, which concerns the recovery of moral and political objectivity (though it extends as well to the question of the objectivity of scientific truth), is pointedly directed against the "postmodernist" views of Richard Rorty, perhaps the most influential American philosopher at the present time. I respect Rorty's attempt to cleanse the stables—though they were surely cleaned out quite a while ago. The rest of what Rorty collects as postmodernism I frankly believe serves no purpose at all. For my own account of Rorty's work, see my *Reinventing Pragmatism: American Philosophy at the End of the Twentieth Century* (Ithaca, N.Y.: Cornell University Press, 2002). The quickest way into Rorty's own doctrine is through his "Solidarity or Objectivity?" in *Philosophical Papers* (Cambridge: Cambridge University Press, 1989), vol. 1. I don't believe that the issue is merely a matter of philosophical gossip. If we must speak of "postmodernism" or "pragmatism" or "post-philosophy," then I suggest we consider the effort to recover an inclusive form of *constructivism under the condition of historicity*—an effort responsive to the main discoveries of the period spanning Kant and Hegel—to be the most promising middle ground between the classic philosophies of cognitive privilege that belong to the history of philosophy up to the middle of the eighteenth century and its continuation into the nineteenth and twentieth centuries, which Rorty in effect dismisses, and the vacant postmodernism Rorty himself recommends. I take Rorty's proposal to signify a massive failure of nerve. I have no doubt that once that is overcome, we must reclassify our options in a more robust way.

4. I refer here to a generous remark Dewey makes, in passing, in the first section of his conclusion to *Human Nature and Conduct*: "The worse or evil is a rejected good." See *John Dewey: The Middle Works* (Carbondale: Southern Illinois University Press, 1985), vol. 14. I read this, actually, as Dewey's gloss on his own appreciation of both Hegel's account of historicity and Nietzsche's emphasis on the philosophical significance of the "new beginning" of every present. In

the same section, Dewey says very plainly, "Unless progress is a present restructuring, it is nothing: if it cannot be told by qualities belonging to the movement of transition it can never be judged." I see in this clear evidence of the "radicalized" Hegelian cast of Dewey's pragmatism. I would not oppose, therefore, anyone's construing my own discussion as an attempt to bring pragmatism back to its strongest Hegelian intuitions, tempered in the way I am suggesting.

5. I say that if we ask the question assuming that it cannot be answered *easily*—that is, by referring to what it "means" *in* the viable life of any known society—then it *cannot* be answered at all. The question makes sense only within the fluency of our *sittlich* world. Nietzsche is the absolute master of all the ways of posing the matter. He sees the ultimate danger, the disease of calling the entire *sittlich* world into question. But philosophers tend to be too serious about the need for a "genuine" answer, supposing that an answer exists—not unlike the sense in which the question "What makes an objective science objective?" has an answer. (That way of asking, of course, is a mistake.) My point is that the "meaning of life" is *whatever* life means, living in accord with the *Sitten* of our own society!

To *refuse* the answer *and* to go on to insist on a philosophically valid answer is to require us to commit to moral cognitivism and more—so that we might imagine we could get the answer *wrong* and be corrected by consulting the world of human values. But that is to fail to see that to get the "wrong" answer (as in misjudging what is right or wrong in the raising of our children) is already to be committed to "life's meaning" as completely as getting the answer right would be! The point to keep in mind is that what makes life "meaningful" for us may not make life meaningful for the Incas, but the explanation in both instances is of exactly the same kind. Our smooth adherence to our first-order *Sitten*—or the cultural processes by which we first become the "second-natured" selves we are—is the same. (Of course, the answer cannot preclude our recommending changes in our *Sitten*.)

The most sustained and influential attempt in the English-language literature to pursue the question in the "cognitivist" way (the one I am opposing) is surely the one offered by David Wiggins in "Truth, Invention, and the Meaning of Life," in *Needs, Values, Truth*, 2nd ed. (Oxford: Basil Blackwell, 1991). But that is a very different matter from the question, also concerned with "the meaning of life," posed by Albert Camus's *Sisyphus*. Wiggins is misled by the aside. There is a discussion of the Sisyphus story in Richard Taylor, *Good and Evil* (New York: Macmillan, 1970), which apparently distracted Wiggins from the obvious answer. I take "my" answer to afford a distinct advantage for the theory I am advancing, because I take Wiggins to be absolutely right that the answer to the question of moral values is inseparable from the answer regarding the meaning of life. I see no other way of answering Wiggins's own question.

6. The tale about Darwinian prospects, that is, the attempt to redirect moral theory in the large along broadly evolutionary lines (hence, reductively), needs very little in the way of supporting a knockdown refutation. The idea is at best conceptually premature and at worst decidedly ill-conceived. Consider, for one thing, that even the best-known and most dogged of neo-Darwinians, Richard Dawkins, pretty well admits that he personally has no idea how to reduce the cultural world to the biological. (Nor does anyone else.) His well-known conjecture about the "meme," for instance—the imagined material particulate that, applied to cultural phenomena, might match the evolutionary role of the gene in physical biology—goes utterly contrary, on his own account, to the selectionist tendencies of genetic processes. This seems to have been almost completely overlooked by Dawkins's champion, Daniel Dennett, among others. (See Dennett, *Darwin's Dangerous Idea*.) Furthermore, the only other strong biologized account of the moral and cultural world, the one developed by the sociobiologists, is hopelessly inept on the essential issues. For a careful reckoning, see Philip Kitcher, *Vaulting Ambition* (Cambridge, Mass.: MIT Press, 1995). There is no use trotting out any Darwinized morality as the would-be paradigm of objectivist accounts if reductionism cannot itself be validated, although that's hardly to

deny that serious moral theories must come to grips with the question of species survival and the general features of human biology.

The principal difficulty the Darwinians have never managed to resolve is this: moral questions are addressed to the concerns of culturally distinct *sub*populations within the species, whereas the Darwinian picture of evolution addresses the fate of the *entire species*. Theodosius Dobzhansky, for instance, has made much the same point implicitly in his studies of the fruit fly. It turns out that the best prospects for the survival of the fruit fly strains Dobzhansky studied depend on the continued viability of a certain weakly, but pure, strain that is needed (in a genetically decisive way) in maintaining the strongest hybrid strains within the species. Is there a fundamental moral lesson there? I doubt it. See Theodosius Dobzhansky, *Mankind Evolving: The Evolution of the Human Species* (New Haven: Yale University Press, 1962).

The survival of the human species is certainly a serious question in our nuclear world. We obviously know very little about our genetic prospects. (Consider the question of global warming.) But none of this gainsays the moral relevance of biological factors: for example, whether some forms of homosexual proclivity are biologically determined, or whether the use of drugs and alcohol by pregnant women may severely damage the life and normal development of the fetus. But such considerations go directly contrary to the reductive reading of moral norms. For a sense of his discussion of the functional nonconvergence of memes and genes, see Richard Dawkins, *The Selfish Gene*, rev. ed. (Oxford: Oxford University Press, 1989), and *The Extended Phenotype: The Long Reach of the Gene*, rev. ed. (Oxford: Oxford University Press, 1999).

7. Both Kant and Levinas—in fact, much of continental European philosophy—are occupied with whether, in linking the analysis of moral norms and values with the analysis of the human condition, we must address the "metaphysics" or "ontology" of the human. I don't mind the idiom, but I use it with a light hand. There is no way to understand either Kant or Levinas without considering how, in their very different ways, they pose the metaphysical question. Both approaches seem utterly indefensible, though both philosophers, having introduced an unbridgeable disjunction, proceed to "bridge" it.

In Kant's *Foundations of the Metaphysics of Morals*, trans. Lewis White Beck (New York: Liberal Arts Press, 1959), we are introduced to a principled disjunction between the regulative idea of an autonomous noumenal "agent" capable of judging (by its own lights) what is conceptually and practically necessary in the way of choice and action on its own part (that is, *as* a pristine rational agent) and the thought and action of actual human agents committed in morally pertinent ways. There is reason to believe that Kant was attracted, particularly after the publication of the first two *Critiques*, to recovering the true "unity" of the two approaches applied to both science and morality. In fact, Kant had been drawn to the idea even before the actual publication of the first *Critique*, at least partly by the important provocation of his former student, Johann Herder, during the 1760s. Herder influenced Hegel along the historicist lines for which Hegel is so admired. But Kant never returned to complete the labor. I believe it would have been an impossible project, unless Kant could have yielded in Hegel's direction (and in Herder's, which he emphatically opposed). A full account of this substantial problem is given in John H. Zammito, *Kant, Herder, and the Birth of Anthropology* (Chicago: University of Chicago Press, 2003). The most sustained effort that I am aware of that attempts to sketch the "unified" theory Kant was drawn to (implicit in his criticism of Herder and in elements of the *Foundations* thought to be, at least in part, responses to Herder's views) appears in Allen W. Wood, *Kant's Ethical Thought* (Cambridge: Cambridge University Press, 1999). The essential—I suppose, the unanswerable—question I would put to any would-be "recovery" is this: What would "reason" mean in such a "unified" account, as opposed to its role in the strictly transcendental (or aprioristic) setting of the first *Critique*? I believe that neither the role of the *a priori* (as opposed to the *a posteriori*) nor the idea of the "universally necessary" (synthetic) affirmations of Reason—which catch up the two distinct aspects of Kant's transcendentalism—can be reconciled in any "unified" account, unless the notion of transcendental reason is itself fundamentally transformed or, better, replaced by a logically (but not otherwise) weaker assumption, say, in Hegel's direction.

Levinas, I would say, is simply incoherent in his classic statement, though I don't deny that he labors to recover the ground lost in advancing his essential thesis. The novelty of Levinas's view rests with construing ethics as "first philosophy" in the strictest sense—meaning by that to prioritize the encounter between a self (a responsible self) and "the other" (*l'Autre*), or, better, "all other selves" (*l'Autrui*), beyond, or prior to, any preoccupation with the problems of "being," whether (as with Heidegger) by deconstructing the canonical view of Western metaphysics and replacing it with another way of understanding Being, or by a complete break between the ethical and all relativized, conjectural, contested, and even anarchic speculations about human nature. Whatever the charm of Levinas's thesis, the fact is that, on the strength of his own characterization, the ethical *entails* an answer to the problem of individuation. But if so, then the ethical cannot conceivably be a "first philosophy" in the sense Levinas requires. Q.E.D.

I have tried this argument out on a number of the best-known discussants of Levinas's thesis, and I have not yet heard a serious reply—except to affirm that Levinas is perfectly aware of the question and has an answer (never supplied) or that the question misrepresents Levinas's true position (also never clarified). I put it to you that to admit the second-natured formation of human selves and the *sittlich* nature of morality under the first condition poses more than a textual difficulty for the Levinasians. I press the point, because there is hardly a contemporary continental figure who is as influential as Levinas is in moral matters. The quickest way into his mature thought proceeds through Levinas's *Otherwise than Being, or Beyond Essence*, trans. Alphonso Lingis (Pittsburgh: Duquesne University Press, 1998). We learn, in reviewing the theories of figures such as Aristotle, Kant, Nietzsche, Heidegger, and Levinas, just how difficult it is to avoid certain powerful constraints on the intelligibility of the moral world (specifically, the constraints of reference and predication).

8. I offer Alasdair MacIntyre, *After Virtue*, 2nd ed. (Notre Dame: University of Notre Dame Press, 1984), and Martha C. Nussbaum, "Flawed Crystals: James's *The Golden Bowl* and Literature in Moral Philosophy," in *Love's Knowledge: Essays on Philosophy and Literature* (New York: Oxford University Press, 1990)—together with Nussbaum's "Non-Relative Virtues: An Aristotelian Approach," in *The Quality of Life*, ed. Martha C. Nussbaum and Amartya Sen (Oxford: Clarendon Press, 1993)—as examples of late efforts to ensure the relevance of Aristotle's moral theory for our time. (This serves as a counterbalance to my choice of Rawls and Habermas as contemporary figures of the Kantian sort.) The discussion of their views is distributed in small bits over several chapters.

My principal objections are given in the text itself. But, for convenience of reference, let me say that both fail to come to grips convincingly with the *sittlich* nature of human life—which is more of a surprise in an Aristotelian than in a Kantian. MacIntyre, as I have remarked, rests his argument (meant to endorse Aquinas's account as much as Aristotle's—perhaps, really, Aquinas's more than Aristotle's) on a supposed *internal* connection between a social "practice" and its intrinsic "virtue." If, however, you treat "practices" in what I've called the anthropologist's sense, then MacIntyre's notion of a "practice" is already too strong, too much identified in second-order terms. It is not *sittlich* in the *prima facie* sense at all, as it should be if the argument is to go through. (I've suggested a similar difficulty in Hegel.) In a word, MacIntyre's doctrine is an *obiter dictum* of a privileged sort, which, as it happens, is cast in terms of what would be required *if* our *prima facie* practices were indeed fully "rational" in MacIntyre's sense! (That is, the argument is question-begging.)

Nussbaum's account is meant to collect the actual *sittlich* data, whether in her travels abroad to distant lands or in reading novels like those of Henry James. In both cases, she does identify what she takes to be moral in the *prima facie* sense—hence, against MacIntyre's sort of reading—

but she does so *through* Aristotle's lens, or what she takes to be his lens: always in search of discrete "virtues" that can be anthropologically confirmed and shown to accord reasonably well
with what she takes Aristotle's model to propose. Nussbaum never considers the full significance
of the historicity, the idiosyncrasy, the contextedness of particular virtues, or the place of any
would-be virtue in a holistic notion of "moral" or *sittlich* life (that is, *prima facie*), which would
at once have called into question her distinctly abstract method of comparison. For example, it's
said that for Australian aborigines, a meaningful life requires remaining attached to "their" land.
When the Australian government moved particular populations away from their ancestral homes,
they could no longer function in the old ways. If that were acknowledged at the *sittlich* level —
paradigmatically — I cannot see how *any* straightforward comparison with, say, societies in India
or elsewhere would either be possible in Nussbaum's way *or* would convincingly yield "non-
relative" virtues that might confirm her version of the Aristotelian thesis. Whatever virtues are,
they presuppose a holistic unity of life that goes against the idea of comparing discrete virtues —
or, of course, "non-relative" virtues in Nussbaum's sense. Cultural life is holistic in the Intentional sense; *a fortiori*, so is the concept of a virtuous life.

It's clear that Nussbaum means to be responsive to "local traditions and practices" as well as
to "features of humanness that lie beneath all local traditions and are there to be seen whether
or not they are in fact recognized in local traditions" ("Non-Relative Virtues," 243). She means,
of course, that there are valid moral commonalities to be found. But if birth and death and growth
and pain and the mastery of language are suitable instances of our standard concerns, then the
argument is still lacking; if the "universals" (or "transcultural" values) are morally valid, then we
still need the confirming argument.

Nussbaum's thesis is meant to count against the "relativists." But either she is unclear about
what the relativists claim regarding "virtue ethics" (for instance, what I have just suggested) or
she has not actually supplied the counterargument. I would be prepared to say, for instance, that
Aristotle's *Nicomachean Ethics* and *Eudemian Ethics* provide no convincing argument against
the relativists. Nor does her discussion of James's *The Golden Bowl* supply what's missing. There
is a deep provisionality and openness in Aristotle's ethical works, scrupulously noted in A. J. P.
Kenny, *The Aristotelian Ethics* (Oxford: Clarendon Press, 1978); see also John M. Cooper, *Reason and Human Good in Aristotle* (Cambridge, Mass.: Harvard University Press, 1975), which I
do not find adequately reflected in either MacIntyre or Nussbaum. Both of the expository accounts just mentioned are, I suggest, easily reconciled with a relativistic reading of the Aristotelian
texts. In fact, it makes a perfectly reasonable argument to hold that Aristotle was himself aware
of the cultural "relativity" of *sittlich* values, which others might have drawn on (in second-order
terms) against his own preferences, though he himself intended to be quite frank about his own
persuasion — which, of course, hardly affects the diminished standing of specifically moral norms
in his own mind, say, with respect to "intellectual" virtues. Aristotle offers a loose model of "virtue
ethics," not a canonically tight analytic "method." And, as I say, he offers next to nothing about
history in the modern sense or about the distinction between biology and culture.

9. I cannot see how Kant's formal position in the *Foundations*, bearing on the Categorical
Imperative, could possibly be recovered from the extraordinarily effective *reductio* that Hegel
produces in a few pages. It exposes the complete artificiality — and arbitrariness — of Kant's most
famous view of the dictates of practical reason. I don't regard Hegel's maneuver as slight in any
way. On the contrary, it must be taken seriously. It exposes at a stroke the entire clockwork nature of Kant's moral speculations. That Kant was one of the greatest of Western philosophers
seems to me to have nothing to do with the matter of assessing his actual doctrine. Furthermore,
Hegel's argument leads us to understand that *any* "recovery" would have to change, in a fundamental way, our approach to moral matters (and more), and that Kant's sort of transcendentalism is just a dreadful mistake. For Hegel's text, see G. W. F. Hegel, *Natural Law*, trans. T. M.
Knox (Philadelphia: University of Pennsylvania Press, 1975), 77–78.

Let me put the point in a slightly different way, which may suggest how Hegel's *reductio* challenges all of Kant's progeny—for instance, the views of Rawls and Habermas. It may save a bit
of time. Kant's argument regarding Reason depends on two considerations. First, we *know* that,
with respect to empirical science, whatever knowledge we may claim depends on certain necessary *a priori* conditions of understanding. Second, we can therefore *think* of ourselves as perfectly rational agents, modeling the "rational" directives we give ourselves by relying on the formal
features of the universal laws of nature. But if Kant's transcendentalism is false or indemonstrable (as I believe it is), and if the "rational" directives Kant would have us follow are completely
vacuous, then it is very hard to see how theorists like Rawls and Habermas could possibly defend
their own moral universalisms. I don't believe they can. I pursue the question in some depth in
a discussion of Habermas's position in "The Vicissitudes of Transcendental Reason," in *Habermas and Pragmatism*, ed. Mitchell Aboulafia, Catherine Kemp, and Myra Bookman (London:
Routledge, 2002).

10. Rawls retreats—but, finally, without yielding a philosophical inch. In *Political Liberalism*, he *seems* to admit the *obiter dictum* that *A Theory of Justice* really amounts to, but a close
reading of the text confirms that he does not really relent. If he had, he would have viewed his
own thesis ("justice as fairness") as the frank expression of a liberal ideology, *not* a Kantian-like
recovery of what a "rational" agent would ineluctably adopt as his timeless moral principle. Rawls's
philosophical strategy would have been completely altered: he would have been caught up in
the flux of history. But that, of course, is precisely what he does not wish to concede. See John
Rawls, *Political Liberalism* (New York: Columbia University Press, 1993). That is also why Rawls's
theory cannot possibly escape being construed as an instrument, however well-intentioned, of
American "colonial" policy, if applied in the international arena.

11. If one looks at his account of moral/political norms and values, without endorsing his
theory of the class struggle, Marx appears to favor a form of "economic" determinism that directly entails a principled respect for the diversity of *sittlich* values in a spirit very close to Hegel's.
At the same time, Marx clearly harbors a conviction about the conditions of well-being appropriate to generic human nature, which many think brings him very close to Aristotle. The idea
of generic humanity, which Marx never really developed, cannot be altogether apt; as one sees
from the *Grundrisse*, Marx construes human nature in distinctly historicized terms. So there is
an unresolved—and double—puzzle bearing on Marx's sense of the objective standing of "bourgeois" and "proletarian" values *and* on the standing of *either* of these class-oriented, implacably
opposed conceptions and the conception Marx begins to sketch for the communist utopia—the
values associated rather vaguely and naively with what Marx calls the *Gattungswesen* (man as
"species-being"). The conceptual link between these two notions is supplied by the idea that the
proletarian revolution, though class-oriented, effectively represents the ultimate liberation of the
entire human race. Hence, the class interests of the proletariat should evolve quite naturally along
the lines of fulfilling the universal concerns of mankind.

Much of this has lost its bloom following the collapse of the Soviet empire and the eclipse of
the Marxist theory of class struggle—except for the important fact, of course, that Marx's doctrine
can now be seen for what it is: a humane critique of capitalist exploitation. Seen in this way, without subscribing to the labor theory of value or the theory that class opposition is the decisive engine of historical change, there is no reason to believe that Marx's critique of capitalism has lost
its relevance. On the comparison between Marx and Aristotle, see Nicholas Lobkowicz, *Theory
and Practice: History of a Concept from Aristotle to Marx* (Notre Dame: University of Notre Dame
Press, 1967), and *Marx and Aristotle: Nineteenth-Century German Social Theory and Classical An-
tiquity*, ed. George E. McCarthy (Savage, Md.: Rowman and Littlefield, 1992). For a sense of Marx's
scruple regarding the moral relevance of differences in class orientation within socialism and between socialist and bourgeois values, see Karl Marx, "Critique of the Gotha Program," in *Selected
Works*, by Karl Marx and Frederick Engels (London: Lawrence and Wishart, 1950), vol. 2.

12. I can think of few analyses of the evolution of the modern state that are as instructive as Oakeshott's *Of Human Conduct* (Oxford: Clarendon Press, 1975). Oakeshott's book compellingly confirms the fact that that history was never "rational" in any deliberate or progressive sense. Yet it does provide, by its own detail, a basis for something very similar to Hegel's *geistlich* constructions of Western political history. In making *that* possible, however, which was hardly its purpose, Oakeshott's book undermines *any* presumption that such a history might claim objectivist standing. On the contrary, it opens the door to the widest sort of diverse speculation about the normative meaning of political history. (If Hegel would demur in the "right-wing" way, then so much the worse for his theory.)

Chapter 3

1. Stevenson's theory is now a museum piece, of course. It was, quite literally, the victim of two philosophical fashions. The first was the irresistible influence of logical positivism's persuasion that moral judgment could not be deemed meaningful on the grounds of its being testable with respect to truth in the way in which scientific or factual statements were said to be (and hence is no more than "emotive" or emotive and imperative at the same time). The second was the massive lack of interest at the time in the moral (as a way of obviating the positivists' own limitations). In its day, Stevenson's account was one of the most celebrated theories of moral discourse in Anglo-American philosophical circles. Stevenson himself became completely fed up with the sort of circus fame he achieved. He once confided to me, in a chance conversation late in his career, that the reception of the emotive theory had had the effect of making his general theory of language—which he took to be more important—almost completely unknown. See C. L. Stevenson, *Ethics and Language* (New Haven: Yale University Press, 1944).

2. The classic discussion of the relationship between morality and the law invokes the opposed, but linked, doctrines of natural law and legal positivism. The first holds that there are determinate normative laws somehow imprinted on human nature—perhaps as a result of God's creation, as Aquinas claims in the *Summa Theologica*—from which positive law must be derived if it is to be valid. (See the *Summa Theologica*, trans. Fathers of the English Dominican Province [New York: Benziger Brothers, 1948], vol. 1, QQ. 90–97.) The second takes a number of different forms involving the debate about whether there is a necessary connection between law and morality—as in Jeremy Bentham, John Austin, and Hans Kelsen, who deny that there is. Positivists divide as to the nature of a "legal system" (for instance, as to whether all valid decisions are deducible from legal rules and whether the system of law rests on rational grounds). For a very short but instructive survey of the classic literature, see H. L. A. Hart, *The Concept of Law* (Oxford: Clarendon Press, 1961), chapter 9 ("Laws and Morals"). I reject both doctrines. The first I take to be incompatible with the constructed nature of human norms, whether moral or legal; the second, in its essential claim, fails to acknowledge the common *sittlich* grounds of both morality and the law. Still, to admit this much is not yet to admit that the validity of legal judgments requires, or derives from, the objective validity of the morality to which it is linked. There's a non sequitur there that has done a good deal of mischief. For a sense of this, see L. J. Devlin, *The Enforcement of Morals* (Oxford: Oxford University Press, 1959).

3. This is one of the most baffling concepts of moral/political life, hemmed in by utterly unrealistic assumptions and beliefs. Given John Rawls's recent essay, *The Law of Peoples; with, "The Idea of Public Reason Revisited"* (Cambridge, Mass.: Harvard University Press, 1999), I make out three very different views of the matter at least. Rawls himself makes it clear at the start of his essay that, in speaking of the "law of peoples," he does not mean to speak of what, in Grotius and similar-minded theorists, is meant by *jus gentium*, "the law of all peoples"—that is, of what is common to them in the way of law, and particularly, law that holds between (all) peoples *qua* peoples.

If this is what *jus gentium* really means, then it is completely utopian, or it depends in a privileged way on some version of the natural law doctrine (that is, to ensure the supposed universality of moral/political norms). I reject the idea, of course. However pretty, it is impossible to confirm—and, in any case, it is simply a way of stonewalling in the face of events like 9/11. I note also that Rawls's book was published in 1999, although Rawls actually considers extending his "law of peoples," which he realizes *cannot* be universalized, to "decent nonliberal peoples" (he has the Muslim world in mind). Needless to say, Rawls's notion of a "realistic utopia"— roughly, international law based on an extension of the principles of "liberal democracy"—is too utopian to be realistic and too simplistic in its American manifestation to be trusted in a dangerous world.

4. The analogy is not entirely frivolous, though I invoke it here in the lightest possible way. What I mean is that legal practices favor an explicitly rationalized system, though it must remain open to enlargement and revision in accord with *sittlich* changes; it succeeds best, in this regard, if the *sittlich* is itself distinctly regular and predictable ("normal," as Kuhn might say). Of course, Kuhn uses his own distinction to great effect in setting the stage for his enormously important contribution regarding what he calls a "paradigm shift" in the provision of explanatory theories within the natural sciences. The Priestley/Lavoisier controversy involving the explanation of combustion is one of Kuhn's principal examples. The fundamental conceptual change that the quarrel produced signified a "revolutionary" change in chemical explanation. I press the lesson of Kuhn's account in a more pointed way later, in examining the relativistic and incommensurabilist aspects of moral disputes—and, in general, in disputes involving the description, interpretation, and evaluation of *sittlich* phenomena. Here, I am merely laying a foundation, so to speak.

I believe that Kuhn made a contribution of the first rank, one that bears on the whole of human inquiry, even admitting the obvious differences between descriptive and explanatory language applied to physical nature and human culture. Kuhn himself was rather dismayed by the full implications of his own theory and retreated, in his later years, from defending the full force of his original discovery. As it happens, the philosophical academy was delighted with his retreat—promptly drumming him out of professional discussions regarding the logic and methodology of scientific explanation. In a modest way, then, and with due care, I return later to the application of Kuhn's account of conceptual incommensurability, a distinction that, I venture to say, is as valid and as substantial as anything English-language philosophy has produced in the same half-century in which Kuhn's work has played its important role. See Thomas S. Kuhn, *The Structure of Scientific Revolutions*, 2nd ed. (Chicago: University of Chicago Press, 1970). Relativism and incommensurabilism cannot be ignored in moral theory. (They cannot be ignored in the analysis of the natural sciences, either. But they are.) I construe the entire issue as profoundly dependent on Hegelian and post-Hegelian innovations (also normally ignored). Kuhn is obviously influenced—though by the most indirect of means—by Hegel's historicism.

5. Here we touch on the "scientistic" analysis of practical reason. Scientism I take to fail in general, even with respect to the sciences. But its application to moral and other practical problems flies in the face of, say, the historical contingencies of "reason" that events like 9/11 present. For a fashionable, informed account of the scientistic sort, see Robert Nozick, *The Nature of Rationality* (Princeton: Princeton University Press, 1993). On the general problem of scientism, see my *Unraveling of Scientism: American Philosophy at the End of the Twentieth Century* (Ithaca, N.Y.: Cornell University Press, 2003).

6. There is no algorithmic solution to the problem of predicative generality in natural-language discourse. I venture to say that the only "solution," philosophically, is *sittlich*! If so, then theoretical reason is itself a form of practical thinking, to be construed, perhaps, in a post-Hegelian spirit, in a sense in which Marx and Dewey and Wittgenstein (the Wittgenstein of the *Philosophical Investigations*) might be said to agree. I take this to be a judgment of the greatest strategic importance philosophically. In Wittgenstein's case, the irony is that, in surpassing the bril-

liant success of the failed *Tractatus*, Wittgenstein—who had very little in the way of a formal mastery of the classics of the history of philosophy—turned intuitively and probably unwittingly back to Hegel's themes, against Bertrand Russell's deliberate campaign at the start of the twentieth century to stamp out "Hegelian" philosophy within the British academy. Wittgenstein's insight, however, was itself too easily misunderstood, as may be seen from one of the most consulted discussions of his remarks about "family resemblances." The point is that the problem of predicative generality infects the distinction of family resemblances in the same way that it affects all standard cases. See, for the unintended evidence, Renford Bambrough, "Universals and Family Resemblances," *Proceedings of the Aristotelian Society* 60 (1960–61). Most discussants, including Bambrough, fail to distinguish carefully between the problem of the logic of general predicates, complicated by admitting the historicized nature of predication itself, and the formulation of general concepts for classificatory and explanatory purposes.

7. Michel Foucault is a terribly problematic figure in the analysis of moral/political issues. The best clue I can offer as to how to understand him is perhaps this: he is not a Nietzschean at all! (He was, of course, profoundly influenced by Nietzsche, though.) This can be readily seen by reading Foucault's "Nietzsche, Genealogy, History," in *Language, Counter-Memory, Practice: Selected Essays and Interviews*, ed. Donald F. Bouchard, trans. Donald F. Bouchard and Sherry Simon (Ithaca, N.Y.: Cornell University Press, 1977). In the final analysis, though he obviously grasps the historicized nature of the *sittlich* order of cultural life, moving from age to age, Foucault almost never treats any such order in specifically historicized terms. On the contrary, he reads every historical age (what he calls an *episteme*) very nearly in the structuralist manner—that is, as a synchronic system—though he opposes structuralism. See, for instance, his *Discipline and Punish: The Birth of the Prison*, trans. Alan Sheridan (New York: Vintage Books, 1977), and *The History of Sexuality*, trans. Robert Hurley, 3 vols. (New York: Pantheon, 1978, 1985, 1986). Here, two inescapable bits of evidence present themselves. First, Foucault does not discuss the historicized transition from any one *episteme* to another; instead, he maps the resultant differences discontinuously. Second, he lacks a developed account of human persons as actual historically effective agents. It's for these reasons that, although his attraction to radical causes exerts a definite charm, his own "theory" (there is really no theory) offers no practical instruction as such. There seems to be no point, in Foucault, to moral/political commitment. In this regard, he suffers by comparison with Sartre, whom he opposes in a very telling way. This also helps explain the profound difference between Foucault and Nietzsche. For a sample of Foucault's late views, see his interview, "The Ethics of Care for the Self as a Practice of Freedom," trans. J. G. Gautier, S. J., in *The Final Foucault*, ed. James Bernauer and David Rasmussen (Cambridge, Mass.: MIT Press, 1988).

8. In repudiating the "just war" concept, I do not mean to deny that wars may be just. I mean only that, as with the concept of international law (with which it is inextricably linked), the just war notion is, in actual practice, an instrument of political hegemony. It was outmoded at once during the period of the French Revolution by the mere institution of a citizen army and was completely bankrupted by the new technology (and social implications) of high-altitude bombing and the like. Add to this the fact that the newer forms of war in our time are hardly legible in terms of grievances between well-formed states—and that what are traditionally viewed as forms of peaceful economic penetration and expansion begin to loom, in our globalized world, as potentially new forms of warfare! The unresolved instabilities threatened by North Korea's attempt to improve its standing in the world market by producing and selling nuclear technologies afford a telling confirmation, regardless of one's sympathies on "either side." See Michael Walzer, *Just and Unjust Wars: A Moral Argument with Historical Illustrations* (New York: Basic Books, 1977). For a sense of some exploratory attempts to come to terms with the concept of terrorism, see *Philosophy in a Time of Terror: Dialogues with Jürgen Habermas and Jacques Derrida*, ed. Giovanna Borradoni (Chicago: University of Chicago Press, 2003). Perhaps the single most im-

portant consequence of the eclipse of the just war concept in the context of the technologies of modern warfare and capitalist forms of penetrating foreign economies centers on the diminishing relevance of the category of "innocent" populations (in war) in the extended conceptual space that assimilates terrorism, forms of manufacture that *might* have a military use, ethnic sympathies, and the like to war itself. By such measures, the market and all the forms of (peaceful) cultural life might be made to seem instruments of war!

Chapter 4

1. A terminological caution is needed here. Philosophers as diverse as Heidegger, Levinas, Wittgenstein, Dewey, Rudolf Carnap, and Rorty—and, of course, Nietzsche—have favored "dismissing" metaphysics altogether, or emphasizing its limitations and distorting tendencies, or recommending a radical change in conception that might no longer be usefully called "metaphysics." Here, I use the term laxly, in speaking of certain very general analyses of what "is" or "exists." For instance, regarding distinctions between such referents as stones and selves (to bring the issue back to an earlier topic), I see no harm in calling *that* metaphysics. I also mean to emphasize that the very idea of an ethical or moral point of view makes no sense unless it addresses interpersonal relations in some suitably pointed way. But that, I argue, presupposes the individuation of selves, and *that* sets an insuperable constraint on what a metaphysics must include and on whether metaphysics can be completely overcome (Heidegger) or ethical questions effectively raised without implicating metaphysical provisions (Levinas). It may be that both Levinas and Heidegger introduce deeper puzzles than those raised by metaphysics and morality. (I won't dispute the possibility.) But if they do, and if what they wish to discuss entails *reference or individuation or predication of any kind*, then I argue that they cannot possibly succeed.

Let me draw your attention to what may be the best and most sustained recent attempt to recover the specific "metaphysical" tradition that Heidegger means to supersede: the one offered in Stanley Rosen, *The Question of Being: A Reversal of Heidegger* (South Bend: St. Augustine's Press, 2002). Rosen is well placed to appraise Heidegger's reading of the "Platonic" tradition of metaphysics. He characterizes his own account, which bears on the Socratic analysis of goodness and has little to do with the "metaphysics" of Platonic Ideas, as "a commonsensical reflection on the nature of ordinary experience" (xi). I should like to think that my own argument converges with this much of Rosen's serious effort at a recovery, regardless of whether, beyond that, we agree at all. Heidegger's challenge goes deeper than the defense of any one or another metaphysics would allow. But unless one insists that there is some uniquely correct account of the nature of the human self or subject (the human *Dasein*, in Heidegger's idiom), there cannot be any uniquely correct account of what to regard as an objective morality—a finding confirmed by 9/11 without the metaphysical labor.

2. My sense of Heidegger's intention in *Being and Time* goes this way: *Dasein* is not actually defined as human—or as restricted to the human—but the human is, or instantiates, *Dasein*. *Dasein* signifies what *exists* in the sense of manifesting a run of unique powers that, as we understand matters, only humans exhibit, relating to language, history, the sense of the past, agency, future undertakings, intentions, living among (and with) other humans, care, meaningful events, and a concern for Being, among other typically human concerns. (Physical objects do not exist, in Heidegger's sense.) I grant all this. But even this cannot be affirmed without acknowledging that the "human" *Dasein* must be individuated, must be subject to reference and self-reference and predication, and must be able to speak from the first-person vantage that other persons may similarly occupy. It is worth noting that, in his dictionary, Michael Inwood actually cites a passage from Heidegger's 1928–29 lectures that effectively treats *Dasein* as plural, that is, as individuated. See Michael Inwood, *A Heidegger Dictionary* (Oxford: Blackwell, 1999), 32.

See also, for an extremely temperate account of Heidegger's moral vision, Lawrence J. Hatab, *Ethics and Finitude: Heidegger's Contribution to Moral Philosophy* (Lanham, Md.: Rowman and Littlefield, 2000). I find myself in considerable agreement with Heidegger's sense of what is problematic in ethics—as Hatab explains Heidegger's concern—though I confess I fail to see that what must be admitted here requires an eclipse of the "subject/object" distinction. It requires, rather, a grasp of the "constructive" or "constructivist" nature of that very distinction—which effectively favors Hegel, say, over Descartes. But Hatab is quite right (apart from reporting Heidegger's view) to criticize those "modern moral theories [that] repeat the problematic disengagement from finite being-in-the-world critiqued by Heidegger" (3). I agree entirely with this much of Hatab—and Heidegger. See Martin Heidegger, *Being and Time*, trans. John Macquarrie and Edward Robinson (New York: Harper and Row, 1962).

3. As far as I know, the distinction was first regularized by Ferdinand Tönnies, *Community and Civil Society*, trans. Jose Harris and Margaret Hollis (Cambridge: Cambridge University Press, 2001). I regard the two notions as functionally inseparable predicative distinctions ranging over the whole of cultural life—*not* separable, as Tönnies's own usage allows. *Gemeinschaft* does not designate any actual "collective mind" or "agent" in any sense akin to Durkheim's claims, and *Gesellschaft*, which ranges over cooperative processes of every kind, cannot by itself account for the emergence of collective practices—as when an aggregate of apt speakers shares a common language. I take this to be the essential point of Rousseau's important joke about the origin of political states: they cannot be the result of some initial contract, for the capabilities that bring the state into existence must already have been present in initiating and holding to such a contract. The matter bears strategically on my account of the role of the *sittlich* in moral theory. It is worth remarking how easily philosophers reduce the *gemeinschaftlich* to the *gesellschaftlich*. See, for instance, John R. Searle, *The Construction of Social Reality* (New York: Free Press, 1995). I take all such conceptual maneuvers to be fatal to both science and morality. The attraction of the reductive strategy, among analytic philosophers at least, lies with the vain hope of escaping what has come to be known as "the hermeneutic circle," that is, the irreducible and ineliminable part/whole relationship that characterizes linguistic meaning paradigmatically and, by analogy, the meanings of cultural phenomena in general. See, for the most influential contemporary version of the hermeneutic position, Hans-Georg Gadamer, *Truth and Method*, trans. Joel Weinsheimer and D. G. Marshall (New York: Seabury Press, 1989). The validity of the hermeneutic thesis both undermines the claims of reductive materialism and conveys the sense in which the *gemeinschaftlich cannot* be reduced to the *gesellschaftlich*. The most sustained account in defense of the reductive thesis appears in Margaret Gilbert, *Of Social Facts* (Princeton: Princeton University Press, 1989). The conviction is widely shared in analytic philosophy (for instance, by David Lewis). But it makes an appearance in Max Weber as well.

4. I capitalize Intentional to signify my own coinage. The "intentional," of course, has an important history in phenomenology both in the empirical work of Franz Brentano and in the work of Husserl (early and late). But neither Brentano nor Husserl ever offered an account that could have sustained the primacy of the theorem "the Intentional = the cultural," which centers on the essential distinction between physical nature and human culture and the intrinsically historicized and collectively significant nature of the Intentional. It is extraordinary how little attention has been paid to the Intentional (or cultural) in Husserl, for instance. I pursue the theme in some depth in my *Historied Thought, Constructed World*, and, of course, I take it to color the prospects of objective morality in a decisive way.

5. I am pleased to pay homage in this way to the stunning work of the early Buddhist philosopher Nāgārjuna, who signifies, by the phrase, that there are no first principles and that there is no hierarchical priority of concepts—that they all "arise together," "arise dependently," or are "dependently arisen" (*pratī byasamutpanna*), that they implicate one another in our discourse and exist as fluxive—and that *that* is not itself a first principle of any sort! I am nearly illiterate

in Asian philosophy. But I cannot see how an adequate account of the self and what may count as an objective morality could possibly fail to require an exchange with the whole of the Asian world. I mean my own remark as no more than an acknowledgment. See Nāgārjuna, *Mūla-madhyamakākarikā: The Middle Way*, trans. David J. Kalapahana (New York: SUNY Press, 1986).

6. You cannot fail to see that if moral reflection, like human life itself, is inherently histori-cized, then there cannot but be a deep and insuperable informality, interpretive diversity, and public tolerance regarding what to count as objective (in the constructivist sense). Yet we suc-ceed in science, and I say we succeed in morality as well. The idea goes completely against canon-ical views of the nature of objective history and may even be viewed as entailing an intolerable paradox, which would amount to a serious misconception. But the thesis requires that we dis-tinguish between physical time and historical (or Intentional) time. Otherwise, we could never rightly account for the complexity of the objectivity of human history. In the same sense in which we grasp the "meaning" of our childhood in the progressive evolution of our mature lives, we grasp the meaning of the historical past retrospectively *in a historicized, temporally evolving way*. Moral appraisal must come to terms with that extraordinary fact. I take this to be a gloss on Hegel's dialectical account of the meaning of history. For a well-known example of the opposite reading of history (by a theorist also attracted to Hegel), see Arthur C. Danto, *Narrative and Knowledge* (New York: Columbia University Press, 1985). An important application of the complex lesson of historicism concerns what may be fairly called "moral anachronism." For example, the moral criticism of slavery in the ancient world—as if its condemnation rested on timeless moral prin-ciples that could be invoked "at any time" in history—is plainly unconvincing. And yet there are almost always developing *sittlich* sensibilities that either already address the defensibility or inde-fensibility of such important practices (witness serfdom and slavery in eighteenth- and nineteenth-century Russia and America) or could support pertinent enlargements of existing *sittlich* themes at any given time. (Think of John Brown's abolitionists, for instance.) For similar reasons, I would hesitate to condemn ill-informed or superstitious societies, Western or not, that segre-gated men and women and that shunned a woman during her menstrual period out of fear of contamination. But that could hardly be expected to justify, within informed societies today, any strenuous differentiation between men and women politically, educationally, economically, or in related ways.

7. I regard the thesis as, at best, an extraordinary piece of self-deception and, at worst, a pro-fessional game whose rules are either deliberately mystified and misrepresented or are whatever they may happen to be—given the American Supreme Court's actual decisions and legitimating rationales, developed in the detailed manner demanded, all the while construed as remain-ing changeless in meaning and/or intent, according to the so-called strict constructionist reading. Two claims will give a sense of the unacceptable simplicity of the usual requirements: first, that the original meaning "of the Constitution" is so straightforward that interpretation is normally not required (Antonin Scalia); another, that the "original intent" of the drafters of the Constitu-tion is so straightforward that there is really only one valid interpretation that defines the right application of the Constitution to the legislation it reviews (Robert Bork). Both fly in the face of the well-known difficulties of written documents of nearly every kind. Indeed, pertinent discus-sions among theorists of American constitutional law are embarrassingly ill-informed about the entire hermeneutic literature. For instance, there is almost no discussion to be found regarding the problems of historicity or the nature of the competence of interpreters. See, for a sample of some well-known views among those most closely associated with the current work of the Supreme Court, Antonin Scalia, "Common-Law Courts in a Civil-Law System: The Role of United States Federal Courts in Interpreting the Constitution and Laws," in *A Matter of Interpretation: Fed-eral Courts and the Law*, ed. Amy Gutmann (Princeton: Princeton University Press, 1997), and Robert H. Bork, *The Tempting of America: The Political Seduction of the Court* (New York: Si-mon and Schuster, 1990).

8. In analytic philosophy, "naturalizing" is a code term for "scientism": the analysis of knowledge and reality in terms restricted to materialist categories employed in strictly extensionalist terms. The term makes its most important and influential appearance in W. V. Quine, "Epistemology Naturalized," in *Ontological Relativity and Other Essays* (New York: Columbia University Press, 1969). But it also appears, in variant form, in the views of Davidson and Rorty. In a very real sense, its governing idea has dominated English-language analytic philosophy, affecting the analysis of morality, throughout the twentieth century in a way tethered to the theories of the positivists and "the unity of science program." I believe that it has never succeeded—and very probably cannot. I examine the entire movement of scientism in the second half of the twentieth century in *The Unraveling of Scientism*. Needless to say, the account I give of a second-best morality is opposed to the scientistic thesis. Sellars, whom I mention in a few pages, is actually drawn to a version of scientism and, in exploring the idea, has addressed the question of the analysis of the self vis-à-vis moral matters. (His doctrines have been problematically, but pointedly, revived by Rorty.) See Wilfrid Sellars, "Philosophy and the Scientific Image of Man" and "The Language of Theories," in *Science, Perception, and Reality* (London: Routledge and Kegan Paul, 1963).

Chapter 5

1. Perhaps the best-known contemporary study favoring something very close to the idea of a cultural or religious war is Samuel P. Huntington, *The Clash of Civilizations and the Remaking of World Order* (New York: Simon and Schuster, 1996). The supporting argument is actually rather shadowy, however. Edward Said apparently opposed the idea, but I've not seen his argument.

2. I am very much drawn to Kuhn's seminal work on incommensurabilism and paradigm shifts in the context of the history of the physical sciences, though I acknowledge that Kuhn was not able to defend his thesis effectively. As noted earlier, he was dismayed by the outcome of his own research and retreated from his findings. The important point to bear in mind, however, is that most of the usual attacks on Kuhn's thesis claim that the thesis is incoherent or paradoxical in the extreme—which is simply false. My own opinion is that Kuhn's philosophical critics never made a compelling case and may even at times have falsified the actual text of Kuhn's original argument. His idea is both coherent and sensible—and, as my argument holds, if it is also viable, it is well worth enlisting in the analysis of moral judgment and commitment. I have discussed the incommensurabilism issue in my *Unraveling of Scientism*, chapter 2. For Kuhn's original view, see his *Structure of Scientific Revolutions*, 2nd ed. For a sense of the contrived reception of Kuhn's thesis in English-language analytic philosophy, see Donald Davidson, "On the Very Idea of a Conceptual Science," in *Inquiries into Truth and Interpretation* (Oxford: Clarendon Press, 1984).

3. The classic accounts of relativism appear in Aristotle's *Metaphysics*, Book Gamma, and in Plato's *Theaetetus*. What is most remarkable about the general philosophical treatment of relativism, however, is how really careless it has been. For a sample of the unsatisfactory treatment of the question in our own day, see, in particular, Hilary Putnam, *Renewing Philosophy* (Cambridge, Mass.: Harvard University Press, 1992); Myles Burnyeat, "Protagoras and Self-Refutation in Plato's *Theaetetus*," *Philosophical Review* 85 (1976); and Richard Rorty, "Hilary Putnam and the Relativist Menace," in Rorty's *Philosophical Papers*, vol. 3.

Index

abortion, 7–8, 20, 56–58
adaequatio (commensuration), 70–71, 72
agency (human), 93–97
    Lacan and, 94
    Sellars on, 94
    theory of, and larger issues, 96–98
Alexander, 28, 29, 38
Antigone (Sophocles), 4, 45, 60, 69, 112, 124
Aristotle (Aristotelian thought), 5, 21, 28,
    38–39, 43–44
    and Kant, 5, 12, 14, 38–39, 40–44, 69,
      97, 98, 114
    and Marx, 138 n. 11
    on "the mean," 42–43
    Nicomachean Ethics, 28, 38, 43–44, 97
    See also virtues

bivalent logic, 23, 61–63, 102, 123
Bodin, Jean, 111

"capacitation" (Sen), 1
Categorical Imperative (Kant)
    Hegel on, 38, 137–38 n. 9
    Kant on, 40–42
Churchland, Paul, 94
"collective"
    defined, 82–83
    link between selves and morality, 81–82
    as predicable, 93
constructivism (constructive realism), 6–7,
    10, 98, 130–31 n. 2
cultural realism, defined, 37
cultural world, 13
    determinable meaning of, 90
    emergence of, 33

Darwinian thought (neo-Darwinian thought),
    11, 31–32, 45, 134–35 n. 6

Dasein (Heidegger), 80–82, 84, 94–95,
    142–43 nn. 1–2
Descartes, René (Cartesian model), 8, 10–
    11, 13–14, 30, 78
determinable/determinate, 90
Dewey, John, 32, 45, 133–34 n. 4
Durkheim, Emile, 93

Eleatic mode of reasoning, 29
elenchus, 133 n. 1
elenctic dialogues (Plato), 29–30, 34–35
equality, 75
Erscheinungen (Hegel), 8
"ethnocentric solidarity" (Rorty), 31

"family resemblances" (Wittgenstein), 59
faute de mieux, 6, 24
feminism, 99
first-order/second-order, 36–37
Foucault, Michel, 10, 11, 67–68, 78,
    89–90, 93
    and agency, 89–90
    and Nietzsche, 141 n. 7

Geist (geistlich)
    Hegel on, 39–40, 85
    heuristic for culturally collective, 85
Gesellschaft/Gemeinschaft, 83–84,
    143 n. 3

Habermas, Jürgen, 14, 29, 42, 64, 132 n. 1
Hegel, G. W. F., 6, 8–11, 12–13, 18, 30,
    39–40, 46, 48, 84–85, 88, 89,
    102–4, 107–8, 127
    and Cartesian model, 8
    and Kant, 8–9, 11, 13, 30, 38, 65,
      137–38 n. 9
    and *Sitten (sittlich)*, 8

historicity, 87, 89
history, meaning of, 87–89, 90
Hobbes, Thomas, 7, 11, 43
human beings
    Heidegger on, 79–82, 94
    as inherently moral agents, 79–80
    Levinas on, 79–82, 94
    as second-natured, 78–79
human rights, 72–73
    legal or moral, 73
    universal, 73–75
humanitas, 75, 113–15, 120, 127
    defined, 113
    as doctrinally empty, 127
Hume, David, 42, 78

ideology, defined, 33
incommensurabilism
    and incommensurability, 120–22
    and relativism, 123–24
    See also *Sitten, sittlich*
Intentional = cultural, 86, 143 n. 4
international law, 52, 91–92

James, Henry, 38
Jaspers, Karl, 81
jus (legal sense of justice), 17
"just war," xv, 71, 112–13, 141–42 n. 8
    and differences between moral and legal
        matters, 91–92
    and disjunction between war and peace,
        112–13
justitia (moral sense of justice), 16–17
    contrasted with *jus*, 17
    determinate/determinable, 17
    See also *modus vivendi*

Kant, Immanuel, 5, 8, 10–14, 30, 37–39,
        40–42, 70, 94, 96, 97, 135–36 n. 7
    and Aristotle, 5, 12, 14, 38–39, 40–44,
        69, 97, 98, 114
    as Cartesian, 10
    and Categorical Imperative, 38–39, 69,
        137–38 n. 9
    *Foundations of the Metaphysics of
        Morals*, 38–39
    and Hegel, 8–9, 11, 13, 30, 137–38 n. 9
    and Levinas, 37–38
knowledge, human, 86–88
Kuhn, T. S., 54, 89, 121, 140 n. 5, 145 n. 2

Lacan, Jacques, 93, 94
"law of peoples" (Rawls), 139–40 n. 3
legal change, 52
legal positivism, 53
legal propositions, contrasted with moral
        commitments, 17–19, 49–50
legitimation, xiii–xiv, 33–34, 35, 77–78
    dialectical powers of, 77–78, 101–3
    in historicized conditions, 103
    inseparable from *Sitten*, xiii–xiv
    "rational" vs. "revealed," 105–7
    no ultimate grounds of, xiii
    See also "second-best" morality
Levinas, Emmanuel, 37–38, 79–82, 84–85,
        89, 93, 94, 135–36 n. 6
liberalism, 74, 116, 118
liberalitas (moral generosity), 22–23, 55
Locke, John, 43, 71

MacIntyre, Alasdair, 5, 38–39, 44–45,
        138–39 n. 8
Marx, Karl (Marxist thought), 43, 60, 73, 83,
        99, 102–4, 107–8
    and *adaequatio*, 42
    and Aristotle, 138 n. 11
meaning of life, the, 32, 134 n. 5
    and the nature of selves, 32–33
    and the *sittlich*, 32
minimum bonum, 68–69
modus vivendi, determinable only, 17
moral agents, 79, 86, 92, 98–100
    and collective sensibility, 64
    as ideologues, 98
    theory of, *contra* Levinas and Heidegger,
        79–82
moral and political, continuity of, 87
"moral law," 50, 53–54
moral progress, 61
"morality," meaning of, 79
moral/political issues
    conditions of resolving, defined, 23
    as constructivist, 11
    contrasted with legal issues, 1–2, 18–19
    as determinable, 17–18
    between ideologues, 4–5
    as improvisational, 24
    and power, 19–21
    as practical, not theoretical, xvi
    radical discontinuity between, and legal
        issues, 54–55

and utopian thinking, 19, 81
See also "second-best" morality

"naturalizing," 93–94, 145 n. 8
Nietzsche, Friedrich, 31–32, 33–34, 68,
    89–92, 93
9/11
    as a new paradigm, xv, 34
    opposed convictions about, 2–3
    philosophical challenge of, xiii, 3, 30–31
nominalism and conceptualism, 58
normative predicates (predication), 58–59
norms, not apart from second-natured world,
    34
nullum malum
    defined, 22–24
    and liberalitas, 22
Nussbaum, Martha, 38–39, 45, 138–39 n. 8

Oakeshott, Michael, 45, 139 n. 12
objectivism (objectivist thought), 13, 35,
    129 n. 2
objectivity, moral
    as construction faute de mieux, 6, 10, 23,
        34–35, 37
    contra objectivism and naturalism, 13, 35
    defined, xvi, 35
    grounded in the sittlich, 38
    limited scope of, 62–63
    as logically weak, 67
    and modus vivendi, 61–63
    not centered in propositions, 67
    and reason, 8–9
    as "second-best," 35, 77
Other, the (Levinas), 79–80
"ought"/"is," 40

"paradigm shift" (Kuhn), 239 n. 1
Parmenides (Parmenidean thought), 29,
    132–33 n. 1
Plato
    elenctic dialogues of, xviii, 4, 6, 8, 25,
        29–30, 93, 94, 125
    and Parmenides, 132–33 n. 1
    Republic, xvii, 6, 18, 25, 29, 35
    Statesman, 4, 9, 25, 29–30, 34, 129–30
        n. 3
    Theaetetus, 125
    See also "second-best" morality;
        Socrates

postmodernism (Rorty), 30–31
practical reason
    contrasted with theoretical, 17–18
    and determinable modus vivendi, 8, 15
    moral/political issues within, 8
    norms of, not legitimated on theoretical
        grounds, 8, 13–14
pragmatism (pragmatist thought), 18, 32
predicative generality, 140–41 n. 6
prima facie, defined, 9. See also Sitten,
    sittlich
Protagoras, 124–25
providentiae (partisan goods), 15, 29
prudentiae (practical interests) as prima facie
    norms, 14–15
Putnam, Hilary, 120

rationaliter (reasonably)
    defined, 7–8
    among reasonable ideologues, 5–6
    and unreasonable dispute, 6
    See also practical reason; prudentiae;
        "second-best" morality
Rawls, John, 5, 14, 20, 39, 92, 106, 132 n. 5,
    138 n. 10, 139–40 n. 3
reason (reasonable). See rationaliter
relativism
    advantage of, among "second-best"
        moralities, 24–25
    and cultural relativity, 123
    and "incongruent" claims, 126
    indefensible versions of, 125–26
    logic of, 123–24, 125–26
    Putnam on, 125
    and "second-best" morality, 46
    See also incommensurabilism
"right" and "true," 13, 79
rights. See human rights
Rorty, Richard, 30–31, 33, 133 n. 3
Rousseau, Jean-Jacques, 83, 84

"second-best" morality, xvii, 4, 9, 101–2
    as in acting rationaliter, 7
    contrasted with the "best," 24–25,
        29–32, 35, 77, 110
    and diversity of sittlich norms, 31–32
    as faute de mieux, 4
    general assumptions of, 3, 5–6
    as Hegelian, 8
    as methodological constraint, 8

"second-best" morality *(continued)*
    and second-natured selves, 7–8
    in *Statesman* (Plato), 130 n. 3
    See also Plato: *Statesman*
Sellars, Wilfrid, 31, 97
selves (human persons)
    and agency, 93–96
    collective aptitudes of, 89
    defined, 12, 86
    embodied in *Homo sapiens*, 11–12,
        83–84
    historicized, 89, 144 n. 6
    as hybrid artifacts, 132 n. 7
    as moral agents, 12, 78–79
    not natural-kind entities, 11–13
    as second-natured, 13–14, 32–33, 78, 84
    See also "second-best" morality
Sen, Amartya, 1–2, 113
    on capacitation, 1
    on Rawls, 1, 130 n. 1
Sitten, sittlich (customs and practices), xvi
    in anthropologist's sense, 9, 40
    conflicts involving, 8
    first-order normative form of, 101–2
    Hegel on, 9, 39
    and Hobbes's usage, 7
    moral reasoning and, 24
    and *prudentiae*, 15
    as term of art slimmer than Hegel's use,
        7, 9, 129 n. 1

    no ultimate legitimation of, 33
    See also Hegel, G. W. F.
Socrates, 8, 18, 25, 29, 33
Sophists, 93
Stevenson, C. L., 51–52
Stoics, 12
suicide, 21–22
summum malum, 20–21, 65–66
    bearing witness to, 20, 66
    defined, 65
    as obligatory, 65–66

theory and practice, 78
Thrasymachus, 18–19, 63–64, 91
Thucydides, 89
Tocqueville, Alexis de, 19
Tönnies, Ferdinand, 83, 143 n. 3
"true" and "right," as constructions, 13, 79

UN Universal Declaration of Human Rights, 5
universalism, xiv, 42
"utterance" and human agency, 86–87, 95

virtues
    Aristotle on, 24, 38–39, 42–44, 45
    MacIntyre on, 44
    Nussbaum on, 45

warfare, technology of, 110–11, 129–30
Wittgenstein, Ludwig, 59